ST. FRANCIS
of Dogtown

ALSO BY WM STAGE

Ghost Signs: Brick Wall Signs In America

Mound City Chronicles

*Litchfield: A Strange and Twisted Saga of Murder
in the Midwest*

*Have A Weird Day: Reflections & Ruminations on
the St. Louis Experience*

Pictures Of People Portraits 1982 – 1993

The Practical Guide To Process Serving

Fool For Life – A Memoir

*The Painted Ad: A Postcard Book of
Vintage Brick Wall Signs* with Margaret Stage

Not Waving, Drowning [Stories]

The Fading Ads of St. Louis

Creatures On Display – A Novel

No Big Thing – A Novel

ST. FRANCIS
of **Dogtown**

Wm. Stage

Floppinfish Publishing Company Ltd.

St. Louis, Missouri

Stage, William – Wm. [1951 –]
— fiction, contemporary
1. United States—the Midwest—Irish-American neighborhoods
2. St. Louis, MO—murder / criminal investigation—vigilantism—tavern culture
ISBN 978-0-578-52462-7

Cover Photo: Wm. Stage, 1995
Cover and Interior Design:
Michael Kilfoy www.studiox.us
www.wmstage.com

Printed in the United States of America
Set in Adobe Jenson Pro

floppinfish

Human brutes, like other beasts, find snares and poison in the provision of life, and are allured by their appetites to their destruction.

— Jonathan Swift

If it was raining soup, the Irish would go out with forks.

— Brendan Behan

For Dennis Black, Brother at Arms,
who would have enjoyed this book were it
not for that awful mishap. Charlie didn't get
you, a patch of ice did. Tough break, pal.

ACKNOWLEDGEMENTS

CERTAIN DESCRIPTIONS of and comments about Kerry Patch and Dogtown at the beginning of Chapter 14 are attributed to John "Jack" Brod Peters, writing decades ago in the long-defunct *St. Louis Globe Democrat*. Thanks to St. Louis attorney Victor Strauss for providing the detailed and colorful legalese in the personal injury lawsuit mentioned in Chapter 18. Heartfelt thanks to Patty Rush, Charlie Allen, Michael Kilfoy, and my wife, Mary Stage, whose thoughtful reading of this story and subsequent suggestions made it just that much better.

Brief passages were taken from the following musical compositions: "The Minstrel Boy," lyrics Thomas Moore, Irish, 1779 – 1852; "Raglan Road" lyrics Patrick Kavanagh, Irish, 1904 – 1967: the piece was originally a poem titled "On Raglan Road," by Kavanagh which first appeared in 1946; "Copperhead Road," lyrics Steve Earle, American, 1955 –

CITY OF ST. LOUIS
AUGUST 1989

"SEEMS LIKE HALF THE STREET SIGNS in North St. Louis are either missing or turned ninety degrees, so you think you're on Kossuth when in fact it's Red Bud. Get you lost real nice if you don't look sharp. Could be a random thing, the signs. They get old and fall down or some drunk on the way home aims his car at one. Or it could be deliberate. A concerted prank by the crafty folks of these run-down neighborhoods to confuse outsiders, trip them up so they'll have to stop and ask directions. Then the fun begins. It doesn't much matter these days since I know these streets so well I can listen to the radio, eat a burrito, drink my coffee or beer, depending on the time of day, *and* drive, all at the same time, and still find my destination. With any luck, and luck is at least half of it, find the party at home. If so, make my delivery—a summons, a subpoena, an order of protection—and I'm out of there before the person just served has time to think about it and decide to lash out at the messenger ..."

He turned on to Vandeventer and saw some corner boys clocking him, urban princes looking for sport on a weekday afternoon. He smiled, gave a friendly wave, his arm already out the window; they stared back, sullen and suspicious. He went back to rehearsing the talk he was to give to the students in Shirley Yount's Legal Systems in American Society class at the community college. The assignment asked of him: To convey a typical day in the life of a process server, and "don't sugar-coat it, okay." He brought the compact SONY recorder back up to the steering wheel, holding it with his driving hand.

"Thirty-five bucks a serve. Some say I earn my living the hard way, as a private process server in St. Louis, a metro area of two-and-a-half million, and one that only a few years ago edged out Detroit for the claim to City with the Most Violent Crime Per Capita in America. Just yesterday two cops were shot up on North Taylor, one of them, twenty-four years old, killed. It takes brass balls to shoot cops in the afternoon. If they'll shoot a cop, it stands to logic they wouldn't think twice about doing the process server. Maybe I'm lucky. I'm regularly in those neighborhoods where it all goes down, knocking on doors, going into bars, shine parlors, backyards, asking questions, hoping to hand off some papers and be on my way. I keep a look out. I don't chit-chat with random people unrelated to my mission. I carry a Louisville Slugger in the backseat of my Escort. I also have a squirt gun filled with ammonia in my glove compartment, and that is meant for dogs that like to hide under porches and sneak up behind you. I believe I fear dogs more than I do people. Rabies is no joke.

"I don't carry a handgun, although I am permitted one. Which is sort of ironic, I suppose, since lots of guys and some gals go through the three-evening process server class with the City Sheriff Department just to be able to get a gun permit. When they get their license they don't even go to work serving papers, they're just content to buy that nine millimeter and ride around with it in their glove compartment. Makes them feel safer, they say. Not me. I think that if I carried a handgun, someone would take it from me and shoot me with it. I'm not some cynical hard-boiled private eye who talks out the side of his mouth and sneers at danger, I'm a keep-it-simple process server, almost a glorified courier. Carry a piece? Think about it. Most people are not going to try to kill you for merely knocking on their door. And if they are paranoid enough to open fire, what are the chances that you, the intrepid process server, can get the drop on them? Besides, it's hard to conceal a handgun beneath shorts and T-shirt, which is what I wear eight months out of the year."

In fact, he was dressed for comfort right now, wearing khaki shorts and a plain black T with a splotch of taco sauce down the front. Today was another scorcher, the day starting out at 76 Fahrenheit, and climbing to 93 by noon. And muggy, jeez, your clothes sticking to you, heat rash on your armpits. But you got used to it, this St. Louis steambath, what other choice did you have?

"They call us Specials," he went on, "short for Special Process Server. The court provides that a Special may be hired to serve process instead of going through the Sheriff. In fact, we get a lot of the papers that the sheriff deputy failed to serve. I always think that it's too bad the plaintiff or his lawyer didn't come to us first. The job likely would've been accomplished straightaway, first time around. After all, the sheriff deputy has one hundred fifty papers to work while the Special has only a small fraction of that. The sheriff deputy will work the papers basically from nine-to-five on the weekdays. The Special works *every* day of the week—at least this one does—and whatever oddball time that's required. Stakeout at midnight. Fine, you just charge accordingly. Whatever it takes to get the job done, that's our creed."

He swerved to avoid a tramp in the street, standing there in rags, wide-eyed, haranguing thin air.

He lit a smoke and continued his spiel into the recorder. "I say that I've been lucky because in the six years I've been at this, I've been assaulted only once. Yelled at, threatened, doors slammed in my face, you bet—but physically assaulted, just once by an irate citizen. And I understand why he was enraged, although that sure as hell doesn't justify the action. It was because he was standing inside his front door and when he realized who I was and what I wanted, he went to shut the door. More like slam it. I reacted and with sudden movement reached inside the closing door and tagged him on the arm with the summons and petition. That's good service, service by touch. To him, it was an act of aggression. I had violated him in his castle. The papers fell to the floor inside the door; he kicked them outside to the porch where I stood. I told him he'd been served and turned to leave. He came after me. I scrambled down the steps and across the lawn to my idling car in the street. The man was short and stocky, built like a frickin' bulldozer. He owned a construction company and was being sued for performing shoddy work.

Now he was about to do a job on me.

"In crossing the lawn—hastily, I might add—I could feel him right behind, lunging for me. It was like some recurring dream where the lumbering monster is gaining ground, so close on your heels you can smell his nasty breath. Well, he caught me on the sidewalk, swung me around and took a poke. His clumsy roundhouse punch flew past my Irish mug without connecting, but in trying to avoid the blow I tripped and fell off a high curb onto the street. I lay there as he stood over me, fixing to kick the stuffing out of me. I curled up, waiting for the boot. But what do you know. He took one good kick at my ribs and that was enough. Get a real job! he yelled, and stormed back to his castle. I got up, shook myself off, waved to the neighbors standing on their porches, watching the show ..."

He stopped suddenly for a kid crossing St. Louis Avenue against the light and the tape recorder fell to the floor. He pulled over, picked it up and hit PAUSE. He took this intermission to consult the *Wunnenberg's Street Guide* to see where his next turn would be. Street guides were a necessity; he didn't have the entire metro street grid committed to memory. He turned the SONY to RECORD and again held the device up to the steering wheel, blabbing as he drove.

"So I got roughed up a bit. I knew that this was going to happen sooner or later, some altercation, and now that it did happen it wasn't so horrible. But I did fall on my bad shoulder, the one with bursitis and an old rotor cuff tear. I didn't sleep that night for the pain and the next morning I went to Dr. Emanuel and got a three-week supply of Naproxen. That stuff works pretty well.

"These incidents have their purpose. A close call has the effect of making you even more careful than normal. It reinforces the pledge you once made to always be circumspect. Vigilant. Street smart.

"While the job has the potential to be perilous on any given day, it is by and large a pleasant undertaking that consists of driving far and wide, knocking on doors, asking for certain individuals or, in the case of a business, asking who's in charge, then handing off papers to people who do not want them. You learn to think on your feet. You learn to assert authority when encountering resistance. You understand and appreciate that you are a nuisance to those persons on the receiving end of things. I think it's funny that I am paid to be a nuisance. My mother, God rest her soul, would say it is the perfect job for her 'little troublemaker.'

"Even though my appearance could easily be mistaken for that of a tradesman, I'm a professional. An officer of the court, same as a lawyer or a bailiff. I am bound by a personal code of honor to do my best to effect service. I go the extra mile for my lawyers. Some of these defendants thinking they may be able to avoid service, they don't know what they're up against with this dogged Mick holding their lawsuit in my satchel. When they hire me, they hire a human bloodhound. My success rate in getting the job done hovers around ninety-four percent ..."

Too boastful? Well, it's true, so why not broadcast it. He went on.

"As I say, the job is not normally one perilous situation after another but it does have a component that is not at all pleasing. That component is frustration. Frustration is part and parcel of the job. People not coming to the door or lying to your face. Driving fifty miles to find no one home, driving to another town to find that the address they gave you is non-existent. You have to be super-persistent to overcome the frustrations encountered in this job. Today is no exception."

The street suddenly dead-ended with an unexpected feature placed there by the Street Department, three giant concrete flower pots, flush with green, leafy sweet potato vine and marigolds. Probably a ton each and spaced so a car couldn't get through. This was the city's most recent solution to crime, corral the bad guys trying to make a clean getaway while adding a little cheer to the neighborhood. It's the thought that counts. He did a U-turn and went out the way he'd come in.

"Where was I?" he asked the SONY. "Frustration, right. So, it started with a trip to an apartment complex on the Northside. The building buttoned up tight—secured entry, passcode required to enter. It was morning, a little after eight. I waited until some resident left and then entered, ignoring his shrill protest that I cannot 'just go in,' that I have to be buzzed in by the tenant. I got to the apartment, a scarred and marked up door in a series of such doors, and knocked. Finally the door cracks open. A pair of yellowed eyes blink. The door opens a little more. Some bewildered-looking black dude in his skivvies that I must've woken up. I ask for Curtis Lee Jackson. This begins a brief Q and A in which I have to give certain information in order to get certain information. The guy looks at my logbook which partially conceals the summons tucked inside. What you want with him? he asks. I have a delivery for him, I say. Which is not a lie. Sometimes that line is enough, but now the guy wants to know what kind of delivery. Time to pull the cat out of the bag. It's a summons, I say, I'm a process server. And I show him my process server ID on a lanyard. He studies it. Just a minute, he says, and walks off like he's going to get Curtis Lee. Maybe he is Curtis Lee. Ten minutes later I'm still standing there. Oh, I get it … the joke's on me.

"From there I went to West County to serve a couple business subpoenas. This is where the glorified courier reference comes in. These depo subpoenas are usually generated in a divorce and they go to the spouse's employer, to the school in which their kids attend, to the hospital where someone had gone to the emergency room, to the the police department which responded to calls for domestic disturbance, and so on. Records, they want records to mount their attack on the other party, show what a negligent, malicious, uncaring jerk they have become in the course of this troubled marriage. Nothing could be easier, just walk in, find the right person—the school secretary, the assistant manager at the bank, the desk sergeant at the patrol station, whatever—and hand them the subpoena. They're used to it, it's not uncommon for a business to get served with a subpoena for records. Then get their name and title, write that in my logbook along with time of day and any special notes. It's the easy ones like these that balance out the difficult ones."

He got to a red light and fired up another Marlboro, scratched himself, and watched an argument between a man and a woman waiting at a bus stop. She was giving him hell for something. The light went green and he started out, but not before looking both ways.

"I had an ambush scheduled for twelve-thirty," he continued. "A couple was to meet in the parking lot of a supermarket in Florissant to exchange their five-year-old. The plan, devised by the ex and reluctantly approved by her lawyer, was to serve the dad after he handed off the kid and was walking back to his car. It was the only course of action since he was self-employed and the mom did not know where he lived. I got there early, my habit, had a smoke and waited for the mom to arrive. Some process servers love this cloak and dagger stuff; I hate it. Because it is essentially an aggressive act on the part of the process server and because there's a child present, so much can go wrong. She pulls up, flashes her lights. I get out and speak with her for a minute, assure her that I won't make a move until the kid is with her. I go back to my Escort, papers at the ready. Right on time he drives up in a shiny red Saab. He parks two parking spaces over from her. Damn. Such a short distance means very little time to intercept.

"Then it unfolds. He exits, I open my door, one foot on the pavement, summons in hand. He unbuckles the kid, brings her over to mom, doesn't linger to give a report on the kid. Then he's walking toward me, a yuppie with a thirty dollar haircut, and I am walking toward him. He sees the situation immediately and makes a dash to the Saab. I am two steps behind him. He swings open the door, jumps in, locks the door, and starts the engine. I stand there, pressing the face of the summons against the window, telling him he's been served. He shows me the middle finger. As he hits the pedal I slap the summons beneath his windshield wiper. He peels out, switches on his wipers and the papers go flying everywhere. A blizzard in August. Crazy.

"The mom, the client, drives over, her window rolled down. Worried look on her face. Is he served? she wonders. I mean, does that work? I had to laugh, imagining the guy telling the judge what happened here. As far as I'm concerned it works, I told her. Let him try to prove he's not served.

"But he won't have the papers, she says—look, they're all over the place. Yeah, I tell her, but that's on him.

"She shakes her head in disgust. He's such an asshole, she says, and drives off. That's how it goes, I might've told her, the modern cycle of life. Marriages end, cars collide, contracts are broken, all so lawyers and process servers can make a living." He put the Sony down.

Finally, he reached the destination. It had taken so long because he'd come from South County, some twenty miles away, a Show Cause Order successfully served. Here, it was a pawn shop on Natural Bridge just west of Newstead. He had a subpoena for records directed to "Person In Charge." Something about the sale of a 12-gauge Winchester last year, a weapon likely used in the commission of a crime. He walked up to the door, tried it and it was locked. He peered inside and saw no activity, the place dark. He looked at the hours posted on the door. Plain as can be, the sign read Closed Wednesday. Ridiculous, of all the days to be closed.

The rest of the day was spent going to law offices, picking up papers and dropping off returns of papers already served. There was a lot of clerical work involved in this job. For each paper served one must create an Affidavit Of Service to be filed in court. Just the basic information: who, where, when, and manner of service. The fleeing guy in the supermarket parking lot would be Service By Refusal, and he would notate a brief account of what transpired. It took about five minutes for each affidavit, and that, along with his invoice, would be submitted to the various lawyers he worked for.

Francis liked going to law offices. Certain lawyers were friendly and sometimes they'd chat. The lawyer might bring up some promising case he'd just landed and hoped to clean up on. Daydreaming about a trip to Aruba on the client's dime. In turn, Francis regaled them with harrowing escapades on the mean streets of St. Louis. They'd shake their heads in amazement and say something like, "You be careful out there. I don't want to have to get another process server."

If the lawyer was out or busy, sometimes he'd flirt with the secretaries. Stuck in the office most of the day, bored with filings and petitions, and looking for distraction. Francis could tell they liked him, saw him as a free spirit, an intrepid figure who's out there in the thick of the action. He once got a date with one of these secretaries and it went well, though the rest of the staff had their little fun with her. Frances, how's Francis? they'd say. Has he offered to take you to France? Ha ha. It was a funny coincidence, that's for sure, her being Frances and him being Francis.

— 2 —

FRANCIS X. LENIHAN WALKED IN MURPHY'S sometime past three and Tommy the barkeep had a freshly-poured pint of Busch ready to go. The man was an encyclopedia of everyone's preferences. The place was buzzing. There were the regulars like Jason Moon the plumber, Ed Gannon the head of Local 68 the Pipefitter's Union, Cookie Halloran the house painter, Big Mike Shotwell a part-timer at the zoo, Mary Ann Cronin who just got off work at the Dogtown Bakery down the street. Over there George Finney, sitting with an inflatable cushion between his hemorrhoids and the barstool, and Mickey Queenan the retired high school teacher with his coffee and Bailey's Cream. Mickey was also known as Mickey One as there were three drunks named Mick or Mickey in Dogtown. Some of the hard drinkers had already gone home to sleep it off, having opened the bar at nine this morning. Absent was Red Rush, high school graduate, leg-breaker for the Teamsters Union, member in good standing with the esteemed fraternal organization The Sons of Erin, and black sheep of a family that had produced two priests and three nuns, his siblings.

Murphy's was the legacy of Bowden Murphy, beloved Democratic Alderman of the Twenty-Fourth Ward who served Dogtown for thirty-one years and took his Guinness with "a bump of Jamie." When Bowden died about ten years ago the entire population of Dogtown turned out for the wake held in this very establishment. There was Bowden propped up in his casket, cantilevered at one end of the bar, clad in a crisp blue suit, tasteful tie with green shamrocks, eyes closed in peaceful repose, and mouth shut—definitely untypical of the living Bowden. The cops said it violated health codes, and called in the health inspector who threw a fit—until they all were given their daily dose and then all was peachy.

Folks filed past, weeping, shaking their heads in dismay, offering toasts. Many of them put some trinket or memento in the casket with him. By the end of the wake he looked like a mannequin festooned with ornaments, including half a dozen rosaries, the beads wound between his bony fingers. So crowded was it that the mourners spilled out into the street and Bowden's sons had to set up a makeshift bar with two full kegs lugged up from the basement.

Francis had heard of waking the dead in their favorite tavern, but this was the first he'd seen of it. It was fitting that the affable old politician would be the life of the party even in death.

Murphy's was his home away from home, and he lived just a few blocks over. He loved the beer-soaked atmosphere, the smell of a million smoked cigs and cigars, the ancient pressed tin ceiling, the pocks in the walls where someone had thrown an object in anger, the graffiti in the john: Cross Your Fingers, Not Your Eyes, and more. Loved the people on both sides of the bar, their proclamations, their arguments, their witticisms, their whines. There was no kitchen but little bags of chips and pork rinds and peanuts were for purchase behind the bar. No TV but one hell of a jukebox with some kickass songs by the likes of The Chieftains and The Pogues and Sinead O'Connor and U2 and his favorite, the Boomtown Rats. Four selections for buck. No pool table, space being limited, but there were a couple dartboards on the far wall beneath the portrait of Pope John Paul II. Regulation dartboards, not the electronic kind.

Dead center behind the bar was a framed portrait of a young handsome fellow in a dark suit and tie, seated, arms folded across his chest, a serious almost defiant look on his face. Until his assassination in 1922, Michael Collins was one of the leaders of the fledgling Irish Republican Army, and he was included in many of their toasts.

At the end of the bar there was a collection jar for "the Irish Immigrants," whoever they were. A glass gallon jar that once held mayonnaise and a screw-on lid with a slot for coins and bills. It was out in the open, up for grabs, but no one in their right mind would try to make off with it. The lone exception being Seamus Morrison who, three sheets to the wind one night, tucked it under his overcoat and out the door he went. Seamus brought it back the next day, no explanation, no apology, but the jar definitely held more cash than before.

The place was a social club for fools and misfits and nutjobs and blowhards and he was proud to be a part of it.

Francis sat there on a stool, occasionally stealing a look at himself in the big, smudged whiskey mirror situated behind the bar, content to drink and smoke and think about nothing. For sure, he knew how to drink. He drank daily to his fill and rarely got sick. Hungover, yes, but not *sick* sick. A few fellas came over and asked him about his day, knowing he usually had some amusing anecdote. He recounted the fiasco of the child exchange gone awry and they offered stale wisecracks like "Here's to the one that got away," and "Maybe if you'd said 'pretty please' he'd a taken it."

He sat there and let the alcohol do its work. At length he found himself having a pithy rumination which went something like this: I am a dedicated beer drinker. Beer is my reward for having put in a full day's work. I don't care that I wear a noticeable gut, I enjoy the taste of beer and the buzz it gives me. I love the way it looks in a glass just after being poured. Then, ah yes, the bar itself—the dispenser of my addiction. I will always head to a bar sometime after three no matter where I am. I view the bar as a haven from the oppressive world outside with its traffic jams and snot-nosed panhandlers and garish signs saying do this or buy that. At first the beer has a calming effect, inviting introspection, and seems to help put things in perspective. Many a problem has been solved with a glass of suds in front of me. But after a time the beer makes me gregarious and that is amplified when in the presence of other gregarious persons ...

And so it was a fortuitous moment when Aidan and Patrick, two brick masons of his acquaintance, walked over with a gorgeous pint of Guinness and set it in front of him. It was a proper pint—twenty imperial fluid ounces, about nineteen US fluid ounces—in a proper pint glass with a relief of a harp on the outside.

"Nice collar," Francis remarked. "A perfect pour it looks to be."

"He poured it just for you," the one said, motioning to Tommy. "The man's an artist."

Francis leaned forward, caught sight of Tommy, his tattooed arms resting on the bar, looking back at him. Francis toasted him in gratitude.

"Would you mind singing it?" ask the other, "'Twould be much appreciated."

Francis took the pint and chugged heartily. When he set it back down a third was gone, and he wore a thick foam mustache. He knew exactly what they were asking. He got asked almost every time he came here.

"Sure thing," he told them. "Why not?"

Aidan called out for everyone to shut their traps. "Francis here's gonna sing for us."

Francis stood, took another hit of stout, and let loose. Guinness was the exact right thing for singing an Irish ballad, giving his voice a rich and vibrant tenor. Lending the performance a certain verve, and imparting a significance to every word in the song. He sang it the way he was taught, so long ago, in the kitchen with his mother and father and brother. "The Minstrel Boy" was a timeworn ballad about a young man who is a minstrel and a warrior. He is slain on the field of battle, probably with the hated English, and just before he dies, rather than allow the enemy to take his beloved harp he "tore its chords asunder."

A short song and a sad one, and that's why it was a big hit here. It took only a few minutes of their time and it struck a powerful chord among the maudlin and sentimental Irish, leaving half the listeners crying in their beer.

He was wrapping up now, belting out the song with great passion and fervor.

" ... and said No chains shall sully thee,
thou soul of love and bray-ay-ay-vry!
Thy songs were made for the pure and free,
they shall never sound in slavery!"

He finished, took a modest bow, and held his pint up high. Hoots and hollers, hearty applause.

"Thank you for the clap," he said, and they groaned and guffawed and there were calls for another round. He took his seat again, made a quick study of all that surrounded him. Murphy's Bar, he mused, my people, my haunt, my life.

ANTONIA, MISSOURI
AUGUST 1989

THE OLDER MAN NUDGED THE YOUNGER ONE beside him in the cluttered cab of the F-150. "This is it."

The other one looked in the distance, squinting in the early morning glare. "Showtime," he said.

They were parked in the lot of a State Farm office which didn't open for another hour and a half. Down the road about a tenth of a mile, a black Town Car backed out of a driveway and headed their way. They ducked down as the car passed and turned onto the primary road. Deke started the engine and they drove to the spot where the Town Car had been.

Deke had been scoping out the sprawling ranch-style house on Coady Road for two weeks now, the home of a bank president. Deke had read about the man in the paper, always attending some fundraiser or social function. The banker fit the profile they desired, a professional person with regular hours and living some distance from his neighbors. Deke didn't know that the mark lived alone until he began surveilling the premises. He was cheered by that knowledge and he was equally heartened by no sign of a dog.

They were quite capable at breaking in homes. Capable, but not much finesse. No lock-picking for these guys. Deke carried a short-handled rubber mallet with a chamois cloth wrapped around the head. He poised the tool inches from a glass pane that framed the door at the rear of the residence. "Here goes," he said, and tapped the glass hard. It broke easily with only the slightest of sound. There was a sigh of relief when no alarm sounded. There had been a sticker on the front door that the home was protected by some security company, and both Deke and Stoney thought it was a bluff. They were right, but, still, it was a gamble. Had an alarm sounded, they would've tore out of there like nobody's business, cursing the day alarm systems were invented.

Deke reached inside the broken window, unlocked the knob, and turned the deadbolt. They were in. Deke looked to Stoney, fingering his mustache like some baboon, a camo-style Stihl cap with a stylish curve to the bill pulled down over his brow. "You take the upstairs. I'll be down here. Twenty minutes tops, okay?"

"You know I ain't got no watch."

Deke gave him a look. "I'll let you know, man."

Both carried gym bags, large black plastic trash bags, and a couple bed sheets for wrapping and padding the more fragile items. They wore thin spandex gloves. They were schooled in the places where people kept their valuables. Twenty minutes. Get in get out. The expected haul? Securities, coin and stamp collections, antiquities, sterling silver. Jewelry, you would think was at the top of their list, but much of it was so customized that it would be readily identified if it came to down to a bust. It was a potential liability. Still, they took it anyway. Power tools and nice cameras were always welcome. Anything their fence would deem buyable. What they couldn't fence they took to the bigger flea markets held somewhere far from Podunk, Missouri here. Twice a year, maybe, off to Eureka Springs or Branson or as far away as Tulsa. Make a weekend of it. All day Saturday and sometimes over into Sunday hawking their stolen goods, every sale one hundred percent profit. In the evening do the tourist thing, see the sights, hit the clubs.

Stoney came down and found Deke in the dining room cleaning out the drawers in the big hutch, the silver utensils making a clatter as they fell together. With a grunt, Stoney lifted his gym bag and Deke could see it had heft. One trash bag bulged as well. Deke nodded approval. They never spoke at the scene about what they'd found; that would come later at the place.

"I'm not taking the china," said Deke, "even though it's worth a bit. We'd have to wrap it all piece by piece or it'll break."

"Yeah, nothin' worse than busted china." Stoney lit a smoke and watched Deke do his thing. "Where'd you say this guy works?"

"Charter Bank over in Festus. Why?"

Stoney chortled, said, "Might as well be Third National Bank of Fuck Me! He's due for one hell of a surprise when he gets home."

"You got that right." Deke looked at his watch. "Close to done here. You wanna check the living room once more? And put that goddamn fag cigarette out, will ya? Pocket the butt, too. Rule number one, no evidence left behind."

"I don't insult your brand, why you gotta insult mine?"

"Because men don't smoke those fucking things. How many drags you get from one? Five? And don't give me that shit, it ain't the quantity, it's the quality."

"Yeah, yeah." Stoney took a moment to survey the room. He heard tick tock, tick tock, conspicuous like. Why hadn't he heard that before? It was coming from a beautiful and imposing timepiece over near the staircase. He went over for a better look. "Well, hello grandfather."

Deke looked up from his business. "Yeah, I thought about that. It's tempting, but the problem is it's so dang big I doubt it'll even fit lengthwise into the truck."

Stoney peered into the glass door that showed the clockwork, parts moving in there. "She's a real beaut," he declared, "probably worth at least a grand. We gotta take her."

"Too risky," replied Deke with finality.

Stoney ignored that and began handling the big clock, testing it, putting pressure here and there. He tilted it, set it on the carpet. It stopped ticking. He hunkered down, jiggered it a bit, and pulled at the base. It came free. "Check this out," he said, holding the wooden piece up like a prize. "It's got sections. Now it's two foot shorter."

"Damn your ass, I told you leave it be." Deke stood up, went over.

He walked around the downed clock. "Seth Thomas," he read the name on the face. "I heard a that." Deke scratched the stubble on his face in thought. Stoney could see them carrying it out. Deke looked to Stoney. "Well, what the hell. You got your heart set on it, we'll take 'er."

"You won't regret it."

"Don't count on that. I got enough regrets to fill a rain barrel."

The pickup was already backed up to the front door. They peered out the window, waited until they saw no traffic whatsoever, then they exited. Walking briskly to the rear of the truck, they unlatched the camper shell, set it on the ground. They arranged the goods in the bed, the Seth Thomas laying face up on the bedliner. They covered the goods with full-sized blankets, then replaced the camper shell and drove off.

Deke checked his watch again. "Twenty-four minutes," he said.

Stoney couldn't tell if Deke thought that was good or bad. "Pretty fucking good, you ask me."

"I don't like running late," he grumped. "Deadlines are meant to be kept."

They rode Old Highway M on up to M and into a burg called Otto. It was here that they had made their rendezvous. At the spot, Stoney jumped out and made for his Challenger. "Don't dilly dally, no side trips," Deke called after him.

"I'll be there before you!" Stoney called back without looking.

They drove northwest from there, side roads leading into territory more and more remote until there was nary a residence to be seen. Stoney up front and Deke staying well behind so as not to catch the dust. Finally, where two gravel roads came to a T, they came to a sign that said BERGDORF WASTE HAULING. They followed another gravel drive, tall weeds on both sides, into the premises and at length came to a turn-off. They followed that for a quarter mile or so, shocks getting a real workout from the ruts, and came to a fairly large Quonset hut, brambles all around it. Deke backed the F-150 up to the door. He got out and put a key to the padlock on the door. They went in together.

It looked like the back room of a pawn shop. Shelves of merchandise, boxes overflowing with small appliances and cookware. TV sets, a high-end dining room set, tool boxes full of tools, lawn mowers, a motor scooter, a shiny Evinrude 250 HP outboard motor. Leather jackets, fur coats, men's suits hung on racks. There was a concrete Sasquatch, caught in mid-stride, a lawn ornament pilfered as an afterthought. Weapons. Christ, there were shotguns and deer rifles and a crossbow. Ornate urns and vases, Oriental carpets, brass instruments including an oboe and a tuba. Everything crowding something else. So chockablock with purloined items was this stash house that there was barely room for the stuff they had just taken.

"We are definitely due for a flea market run," said Deke, shaking his head.

"We need to get that old bugger out here soon," said Stoney.

"He had some medical problem, he's out for several weeks."

"We could photograph the stuff and send the pictures to him."

"He's old school like me," said Deke. "Has to see the heifer, pull its teats, before he buys it."

"Aw, fuck it then."

They unloaded and found places for all the stuff. The grandfather clock was back on its base, but try as they might they couldn't get it to tick tock again. "I'll fool with it when I have time," said Deke. He let out an exasperated sigh, looked Stoney straight in the eye. "Hey, look, I'm sorry I barked at you back there. I get a little tense on the job, you know."

"No worries," said Stoney.

"I think of myself as the guy calling the shots," he continued. "I mean, I got more experience and I like to believe I got the common sense to go with it. But then I realize, too, that you're in it with me. We're partners, thick and thin, I've got to give you some credit—"

"Mighty white of you."

"—even though your ideas more often than not are half-baked, bordering on idiotic!" Punching him playfully on the arm.

Stoney chuckled. "You are somethin' else, man. You know that?"

Deke said, "Tell you what. Let's celebrate. You come over to my place. I've got some beer and some smoke. There's barbecue in the fridge. Horseshoes, you like to play horseshoes?"

"Never played."

"I got a regulation horseshoe pit in my backyard. It's a game of skill with a bit of luck thrown in."

Stoney shrugged. "Sure, sounds like a plan. I got nothin' else goin'."

— 4 —

STONEY FOLLOWED THE F-150 OUT to Deke's place. It was all two-lane winding roads, nice drive on a Tuesday morning, very little traffic. Stoney had known Deke about three years now and had been to his place only once before, to drop off some venison as a Christmas present. He remembered it being in a subdivision of sorts, except there weren't a lot of homes and they were spread far enough apart that privacy was guaranteed. The mailing address was Cedar Hill, he knew, but the actual location was maybe twelve miles outside the small town of Cedar Hill. There were many such developments in Jefferson County, islands of human habitation in a pastoral setting, many of them having a man-made lake in the middle, stocked with bluegill and crappie. Nothing else around, five miles easy to the nearest gas station or market. Stoney was like Deke in that respect, he liked his isolation, although Deke had it much better than him.

Deke made a left onto a road, the entrance to the settlement. A classy sign, all-weather vinyl made to look like weathered wood, proclaimed AVONHURST ESTATES. "Well, la-de-da," muttered Stoney to himself. The main road snaked up a modest incline with nice houses popping up here and there. Some were set back and partially visible through a cover of trees and some closer to the road with a verdant expanse of lawn to accent it. There weren't a lot of vehicles to be seen, some of the residents probably still doing the nine-to-five. He drove up on one place and saw a woman out in the yard, gardening, tending to a flower bed about halfway between the house and the road. He slowed down. She was in jeans and yellow T-shirt, bent over but facing the road, jabbing at the dirt with a trowel or something. Brown hair pulled back in a ponytail and a straw sun hat. Just as he passed she straightened up and took a look who was going by. He waved and she waved back. Friendly, looking his side of forty. Nice body too, medium build yet stacked. Hmm. Even as he drove on he kept her in the rear view.

Deke wasn't kidding about being stocked with provisions. First thing he did was to heat up the barbecue, a batch of pulled pork he'd gotten at some fair. They put it between slices of white bread, some pickles and onion for garnish, and they chowed down. By now it was past noon and thirst was upon them so they went for a cold one. Or two or six, who was counting? It felt good to just kick back and bullshit with a partner, another successful heist behind them.

Stoney was looking at a picture of Deke and two kids stuck to the fridge with a magnet. His partner with a perplexing smile on his face, one arm around a boy and a girl, younger. "You still in touch with them?" he asked. "Hope so."

Deke smiled and crinkles appeared around his blue eyes. "In touch? Hell, they both live here. When they're not tomcattin' around, staying out 'til all hours, getting into god knows what." He paused, wiped an imaginary tear from his eye. "Kinda makes me all misty just thinkin' about them days."

"Yeah, you told me what happened, your wife left them with you just as soon's you got outta the joint. But that was a while ago and I thought, uh, maybe they'd gone off on their own by now."

Deke took a big swig from a bottle of Miller High Life. Stoney could hear it going down: glug, glug, glug. "That bitch had it all planned out," Deke explained. "She was just waitin' for me to get out so she could split with that photographer, move to Nevada or wherever the hell they went to. Four years in prison and finally free and looking forward to a little recreating and then she lays it on me the minute I walk in the door—didn't even pick me up, by the way, I had to take a fucking bus here. She lays it on me, matter of fact, and there's no arguing with her. 'I been caring for these brats by myself, four long years,' she says, 'and now it's your turn. Goodbye and good luck.' And out the door she went."

"That's cold as hell," said Stoney. "And women 'sposed to be the nurturers."

"Derrick was sixteen and Eve was nine. I had to take a crash course in single parenting. Lucky for me there was lots of other single parents around. Mostly women, and that turned out okay. Know what I mean?" He gave a sly wink.

They got another beer and Deke brought out a bottle of Jack and two shot glasses. They downed one and then another. "Hits the spot," said Stoney, feeling the burn in his innards.

Deke lifted his shirt to reveal a dark, furry mat on a pale field of flesh.

"You flashin' me?"

"Puts hair on your chest. That's what my daddy used to say, and by god it's true!" He gave a good laugh.

"What's the boy do for a living?" Stoney asked out of the blue.

"Derrick? You know what he does. I done told you. He works for that waste hauler where we keep the stuff. He drives a truck, goes all around Jefferson and St. Francois and Washington Counties. Hauling waste, just like the sign says. Derrick's who arranged for the use of that building, asked the owner if he could use it for storage. The owner says sure, go ahead, I ain't need it. How about twenty bucks a month so it's official? That's how we got us a nice secluded hidey hole for all our precious things."

"Oh yeah, that's right. I musta forgot." Stoney poured another shot, held it up, swirled it around and then down the hatch. "So he knows what we're up to then?"

"Hell, yeah, he knows, and he'll be going with us on the next market expedition."

"Oh, I see. He gets a cut, too?"

"You don't worry about that," said Deke emphatically. "You'll get the same. His share'll come outta mine. I just want to get him more involved in the business."

"To the business," said Stoney, holding out his bottle.

"To the business," said Deke, returning the toast. "Long may it prosper."

"Ah," said Stoney, contentedly, wiping his mouth on his sleeve. "You know, I been wanting to talk to you about the direction of the, uh, business. Okay we talk shop for a minute?"

"You got the floor."

He had to be careful in his words, he knew Deke had a temper. "Well," he began, "seems to me this home break-in routine is kinda penny ante. I mean, stealing household items and then having to fence the stuff only to get a fraction of its worth. And then what's left, bring it to flea markets and hawk it to any slob that happens by, like, 'Please buy my shit.' Flea markets. Really? Like we're some bumpkins with a junkyard." He looked at Deke, listening intently. It was all so reasonable to him, it should be the same to Deke. "So, what I'm proposin' is bring it up a notch. I'm talkin' stores, shops, businesses that are gonna have more on hand, more lucrative offerings, even cash. Commercial break-ins, but no banks or credit unions, nothin' like that. We can still do the homes, but we go after a vulnerable business every so often, too. Whad'ya say?"

"I hear ya cluckin', Big Chicken, but consider this. You know those stickers on the doors of the homes we enter? This Property Protected By Bumblefuck Security." He gave a derisive snort. "Well, that won't be no bluff with those businesses. You haven't done time, and you are very lucky in that. I know I ain't goin' back because I'm careful." He paused, took a hit of Jack. "No way in hell am I goin' back," he added emphatically. "Anyway, you ought to be content with the operation as it exists now. Just be happy with what you got."

"Well, it's just that—"

"Hold that thought," said Deke. "Be right back."

Deke came back with a small pewter tray that held two fat lines of coke. He set it down on the coffee table where they sat. "You like to get your head up?" he asked.

"Does a bear shit in the woods?" replied Stoney.

Deke handed him a tightly-rolled bill. "You first then."

Stoney hunkered over the tray, forefinger sealing off one nostril, tracing the line of white powder with the the other, making it disappear. He came up for air. "Oh mama, that is just what the doctor ordered!"

They made short work of the coke and then had a few more beers with a few shots of Jack Daniels thrown in for good measure At length, Deke said, "Well, you ready for some horseshoes?"

Stoney looked at the clock in the kitchen which seemed to slide down the wall as he tried to make out the time. Head swimming in a sea of delirium, he said, "Ah, no thanks, pal. I'm a little too fucked up for that."

"Pussyin' out on me, huh? So be it, but you at least got to see my horse. I think you can handle that. Come on, let's go to the barn."

It was just before four when he left. When Deke asked him if he was okay to drive, Stoney waved him off and slurred that if he could find the road then he could sure as hell make it home. Deke shrugged and gave him a brew. "One for the ditch," he said.

On the way out Stoney slowed by the house where he'd seen the woman gardening. He thought about how nice she seemed, how he'd really like to get to know her. About thirty yards past the home, he swung around and went back. He parked in her driveway. He walked up to her door, gardening gloves and a watering can on the porch. He knocked. She appeared, quite surprised, and he gave her the warmest smile he could muster.

To her it looked like a leer.

Earlier, her hair had been in a ponytail, but now it was loose and draped casually over one shoulder. She had the nicest blue eyes. She wore the same clothes as she had on earlier. He saw she wore no bra beneath that T-shirt. "Afternoon, ma'am," he said, doffing his cap, "may I trouble you for a glass of water?"

FRANCIS CHECKED HIS CHEERIOS to make sure there were no silverfish in there. He had seen them before, floating in milk, and carefully removed them. "Down South they got weevils," he told Petey, "up here we got silverfish. Don't know which one's more nutritious." He looked to the green and yellow parakeet perched atop a chair beside him. "I know what you're thinking. If it isn't one thing it's another. All you can do is try to deal with it, no sense in complaining. Right?" The bird cocked its head. He pointed to the bowl before him. "You want some? Or would you rather have a Nutribar? You like those." He patted his shoulder. "C'mon, climb aboard. We'll see what's around." He stood up, Petey on his shoulder, and they went searching for treats.

He had arisen around 5:30, all hungover from the previous evening's tippling at Murphy's. He'd stumbled into the bathroom, splashed cold water on his face and almost avoided looking in the mirror, knowing the wretch that waited there. And sure enough, there he was, framed in his woeful condition, looking like shit, eyes bagged, bloodshot, hair sticking up in a wedge. He greeted the wretch with a two-fingered salute. "Party on, soldier."

He left the apartment at quarter to seven, Petey back in his cage. The hangover put aside for another day. Outside it was already muggy, the start of another blast furnace day in St. Louis. Heat and humidity, the bane of the outdoor worker. He would sweat through his clothes a half-dozen times today. His car had crappy air conditioning but he didn't use it anyway; he liked the window open as he drove, the breeze on his cheek, the sounds of life happening.

He heard the clank of tools at work and he followed the sound to the alley behind his building. There, in a one stall garage, his downstairs neighbor and landlord, Phelim Burke, lay beneath a jacked-up two door sedan, legs sticking out, pounding away at some mechanical aberration. "Hey, old man," said Francis. The pounding stopped and Phelim slid out on a wooden platform with rollers.

"There he is, the process server in all his glory." Phelim stood up.

He was in his mid-fifties, about five-eight, compact build, with a shock of wavy white hair and the world-weary face of a hard laborer. He wiped his mitts on a red shop rag, took a pack of Pall Malls from the pocket of his overalls and tapped one out. He offered Francis one.

"Not my brand."

"Well, ain't we picky?"

"Those things are wicked. All the lifers in the army used to smoke Pall Malls. You must really hate your lungs to smoke 'em."

"Ah, you gotta die from something. So, you heading out to serve a few derelicts, eh? You're the cat and they're the mice, that how you see it?" Phelim grinning broadly. "You gonna wait for the right moment and pounce on them. Wham bam, you're served. On to the next one."

Francis chuckled. "Nah, it's not like that. Mostly just knocking on doors and hoping somebody will answer and that they'll be straight with you. And for the most part, they're not derelicts or perverts or criminals. They're just people like you and me who're going through a divorce or behind on their child support or who've been in a car accident."

Phelim sucked on his cig, thoughtful-like, Francis waiting for some profound comment. "I ever tell you that I got served once? Some guy claimed I overcharged him for ruining his engine." He spat on the floor. "Hell, I went to court on the appointed day, had three character witnesses to vouch for how honest I am, how fair my prices are, and you know what? That son of a bitch never even showed up. Case dismissed."

"That's insane you'd get sued for something like that. Everyone knows you're the best and least expensive mechanic around. Even Laird Conner's going around telling everyone that he brought his old Chevy to you with some ping in the engine and how you did some adjustment and charged him just a buck."

Phelim puffed smoke in Francis' direction. "I got low overhead and pass the savings on to the customer." This was true. The garage was his free and clear, and the city didn't know the one-car-at-a-time repair shop existed—there wasn't even a sign—and so Phelim paid no taxes on the business.

"There's a bunch of us don't know what we'd do without you," said Francis. "I mean it, you're the bomb."

Phelim almost blushed. "Thanks, boy. I give it my best, you know that."

"Yeah, and speaking of which, I'm having a problem with my second gear. It doesn't want the shifter, makes a grating sound and pushes it out. I have to go from first to third."

"How many miles you got on that beater?"

"Hundred and seventy-two thousand."

"Your clutch is probably wore out. Tomorrow, I'll give it a look-see."

"But I need it every day."

"Can't help you there."

He started walking down Tamm toward St. James. It was early enough, he could make the 7:30 mass. He wasn't a regular, but attended when the mood struck him. For the most part he found the service reassuring and nostalgic; he had gone to eight years of grade school there. Kneeling in a pew alongside others faithful to the teachings of the church, listening to the priest drone, hearing the rote responses, it dredged up all sorts of memories relating to childhood and a happy one at that. Sometimes the homily, if he paid attention and chewed on it a bit, left him feeling inspired to become a better person. Nothing wrong with that.

So he strolled down the sidewalk of a fresh new day, and he saw the neighborhood waking up. People coming out their doors, heading off to work, the bakery opening its doors, the lumberyard already a bustle of activity. In another week, children would be starting school. He waved to Mrs. Keaton walking her terrier, Bingo, a baggie of dog poop in one hand and a rosary in the other. Near the church, on the lower branch of a maple, a squirrel spoke to him in some rodent language, chattering emphatically, its fulminating diatribe directed at Francis, no mistaking it.

"Hey, take it easy," he told it, "I'm just passing through. There's room for all of us."

He was a few minutes late, the mass already underway. People were standing, reciting prayers, their voices in unison reverberating throughout. He took a seat in the back; a multi-hued shaft of light shone on him from the prism of stained glass above. Gazing around, he took in the flock. Middle-aged to elderly residents of Dogtown. Keepers of the Faith, the young people having no time or inclination for such foolery. Except for the altar boys, he was one of the youngest there.

Fr. Eagan saw the mass through without a problem, not like the last time when he couldn't find the chalice to hold up, signifying the Blood of Christ. If the mass has a climax, the Body and Blood symbolic enactment—the Transubstantiation—is it. Finally, an altar boy located it at the old priest's feet, shoved back a ways under the marble altar. At the Eucharist, Francis lined up with everyone else and made the slow procession to the front where Father and a Eucharistic minister handed out communion wafers.

"Body of Christ," intoned Father, looking him over, proffering the host.

"Amen," said Francis, sticking out his tongue. He knew that the new trend was to take the host in one's hand and then pop it in one's mouth, but old habits died hard. And besides, he had once been taught that it was disrespectful for a lay person to touch the host; it was a most sacred thing.

He went over to a grim-faced man who held a large brass goblet of communion wine. The general consensus: it was Boone's Farm, sweet as it was. Old Man Tierney was ahead of him and he heard the intonation, Blood of Christ, heard Old Man Tierney say amen, and then saw Old Man Tierney forcibly tilt the goblet and start to drain the contents. They both held the vessel, the Eucharistic minister by the stem and Old Man Tierney with a firm grip on the bowl. There ensued a mild tug-of-war with the communal beverage sloshing over the rim and resulting in Old Man Tierney finishing off the wine before letting go. Old Man Tierney turned to Francis and anyone else nearby, gave a wink, wiped his mouth with the back of his hand, and returned to his seat.

After mass he was hailed walking down the steps to head back home. Francis waited as Joe Lennon caught up and they walked together. Funny how in Dogtown, even today, you were almost as likely to run into a chum at mass as you would be in a bar or at a party. Joe was a friend from the neighborhood, a security guard over at the community college where Francis once worked as a grounds-keeper. Joe was in his late-twenties, a big galoot with wavy red hair and a trusting, earnest face.

"How'd you like that sermon?" he asked. "Foot washing in the olden times. Sounds like something we should bring back, you think?"

"That what you got out of it?" asked Francis, amused. "Some novel approach to a fuller social life?"

"Well, it would be something different, another way of meeting girls. 'Hey, those feet look pretty dirty. How'd you like a nice foot wash, over at my place, uh?'"

Francis chuckled at the idea. "I don't think that's what Father had in mind, talking about Jesus doing it. The well-off folks back then, they had their servants wash the feet of their guests 'cause it was beneath the station of the rich guy to do that. But Jesus went ahead and did it anyway, just to show humility."

"Or he had one of them foot fetishes. I'd do it, too, some pretty girl. Start with the feet, work on up to the calves, the thighs, keep on going if she'd let me."

Francis lit a smoke as they walked. "You crack me up, Joe. The stuff you come up with."

"How's business?" asked Joe. "When you gonna give that talk to Shirley's class? I wanna be there when you do."

"I'm working on it," he told him, "made some live recordings the other day, driving around the city. First-hand accounts peppered with wisdom and insight, all caught on tape as it's actually happening. I'll play back the recordings and take what I need for my talk."

"That's a good approach, sort of like Charles Kuralt Live in the Ghetto. Speaking of which, when you gonna take me out with you? A ride along, that's all I'm asking. You said you'd think about it."

"I'm still thinking on it," said Francis. "It's difficult enough at times with just me trying to get it done. Another person, I don't know, that might throw me off my game. You understand."

Joe wagged his skull in the negative. "Look, man, I want to get out of the security business. It's too easy, just making rounds hoping some student will get out of line. Or better yet, some outside agitator comes on campus to make trouble and I get to use the stun gun. But that never happens. I need more of a challenge. Private investigation is what's in my sights, and what you do is at least close to that. So come on, let me tag along. Show me the ropes."

"Maybe."

Joe sped up, got in front of Francis, pivoted, and began walking backwards so that he faced him. "Maybe is not a good answer. Maybe means no. Okay, I wasn't going to bring this up, but you have to do it. Why? Because we're related. Lennon. Lenihan. Same basic name, same people. Probably came over on the same boat. We're like brothers. Brothers are loyal, they don't deny each other." He gave a big grin. "So whad'ya say now?"

Francis took a final drag on his Marlboro and flicked the butt into the street. "I say you know how to wear a guy down. If I agree to let you ride along, will you shut up about it?"

"Yeah, of course."

"Then take a day off and let me know a day in advance. Some days I start pretty early."

"Do I pack a lunch or do we grab some fast food along the way?"

"Whatever you like, but we will be done in time for happy hour."

Francis got to the law office at the same time the new phone book arrived. The delivery guy going along, thick glossy phone books piled on a hand truck. "Here you go," he said to Francis. "Two of them for upstairs, you don't mind."

"How'd you know I'm going upstairs?" Francis asked.

"I'm clairvoyant," the guy answered.

"And I'm gullible," said Francis, "nice to meet you."

At street level was a music store that had been there forever. There were no records or tapes for sale, but you could get your instruments tuned or repaired or buy any kind of sheet music. The owner, Vic Kilgoar, now in his 70s, had played tenor sax in a popular Big Band ensemble, Moonlight Serenade, back in the day. Francis sometimes heard strains from within, tentative notes from aspiring musicians who paid the modest fee for lessons from Vic. Francis walked up the steps of the old building looking at the front and back covers of the newly-minted directory. The front had a picture of the statue of St. Louis on horseback, sword raised, upheld, like he's about to do some damage. The facade of the Art Museum in the background, because that's where the statue sits, in Forest Park. The back cover showed a geeky looking guy, bespectacled, balding, with a concerned look on his face. An ad, and one that cost a fortune.

He got to the upper floor and placed one phone book at a door with a sign that read DOGTOWN REALTY. Paula Hite, the owner, would be in later. He took a few paces and came to a door with gold leaf lettering on the glass pane. BARRY CONDON - ATTORNEY AT LAW. Barry was at his desk, shuffling paper, drinking coffee, a small transistor radio dialed in to KMOX, the morning talk show.

"Morning," said Barry without looking up.

"And a good one it is," countered Francis, "brimming with promise." He took a few steps, set a box of TastyKake cinnamon buns on Barry's desk, then set the phone book where Barry could see it, back cover up. "Get a load of this," he said, tapping the geek on the snout.

Barry leaned forward, studied the ad, huffed scornfully. "Miles Levinson, attorney extraordinaire. Already has the lion's share of P.I. work, and he's hungry for more. Lots more. Screw him."

"But look," said Francis, "next to his name. J.D. and M.D. The guy's a doctor *and* a lawyer."

"Yeah, isn't that sick?"

"Does that mean he can sue himself for medical malpractice?"

"If only."

Francis sat halfway on a corner of the desk, glancing at the sheafs of legal documents that were Barry's life. "I got your message, and here I am, ready for action."

Barry began to search through several stacks, mumbling something about the need for a secretary. Francis watched with amusement. Barry looked up, said, "I could find it faster if you'd wipe that jam off your kisser, thank you."

"Ah, here it is," he said. "*Schurzinger v Schurzinger*, Affidavit For Termination of Child Support. My client, Tom Schurzinger, is about to come to the end of years of payments to his ex to the tune of three hundred eighty bucks a month. You see there where I've checked off the reason. The child, their daughter, has attained the age of twenty-one—and then some—and is not enrolled in any educational program. She is emancipated. As soon as you serve the ex, one Elizabeth Schurzinger, his long-standing burden will be lifted."

Francis took the papers, thumbed through the entire document, went back to the first page, the most important to a process server, the page with the name and address. "Cedar Hill, that's Jefferson County."

Barry studied him a moment. Was that a balk? He knew him well enough to know Francis was game for just about anything. "Yeah, so?"

"So all right, I'm good to go. This afternoon, probably."

"Good. It'll be a nice drive, and you're getting paid for it. Enjoy yourself."

Francis moved on to his "office" within the law office. It had no door, just a desk and two chairs, a standing metal file cabinet, an IBM Selectric II typewriter, and a telephone all situated in a corner by a window that overlooked Tamm Avenue. A coat rack held a rain parka and a 35 mm. Pentax dangling on a strap. The sole decoration was a large colorful calendar on the wall, compliments of the Tom Boy Market; each month featured a different Norman Rockwell painting illustrating the more sentimental moments of Americans at work and at play.

A few years back Barry had offered Francis this arrangement, seeing that he needed a boost in his fledgling practice. No charge, he'd told him, just bring me some work and buy some donuts once in a while. Barry specialized in domestic law—divorce and paternity and child custody; he even did some adoptions. Francis didn't move in that world so he couldn't bring Barry any new clients, but he did buy the donuts and the best ground coffee available at the Tom Boy Market. The arrangement was a very good one, for Barry gave Francis a fair amount of work and Francis did his best to see that everything got served and the cases were able to move forward. Francis saw Barry, twelve years his senior, as a diligent and somewhat disheveled lawyer, a sort of father figure in his crazy life. Barry saw Francis as an affable goof, a trusted confidant, and a definite asset to his practice. When it came to serving process, Francis was like a dog with a soup bone. Once he's on it, he can't let go—he'd gnaw on that thing until it's finished, ground down to the nub.

This morning would be a piece of cake—knock on wood. At a law firm in Clayton he picked up four depo subpoenas for records going to four concerns: a medical clinic, a school, a plumbing company, and a therapist. Pretty easy stuff, the only glitch being that they were spread out all over the metro area. He knocked out the clinic and the school right away. The plumbing place, the employer of the client's soon-to-be-ex, was a bit dicey in that the receptionist wouldn't take the paper and said that the only person who would was the owner and he was currently unavailable. For how long? asked Francis. I don't know, said the receptionist airily.

"*About* how long?" from Francis.

She gave him a don't-fuck-with-me look, said, "Again, I don't know. It's a conference call, could be five minutes, could be an hour. Have a seat if you like." She went back to her romance novel.

He went out to his car and got a copy of *National Geographic*, keeping several issues on hand for just such an occasion. He went back to the drab reception area, took a seat, crossed one leg over the other, and opened the magazine to a story about an island in the

Chukchi Sea, in the Russian Arctic, a place the American naturalist John Muir once visited, calling it "the topmost, frost-killed end of creation." This island was a refuge for all sorts of interesting animals and there were great photos of musk oxen, walrus, polar bears. Here was a fantastic close up of an arctic fox with a big white egg in its mouth. The caption said that these foxes steal as many as forty snow goose eggs a day and ...

"Can I help you?"

Francis looked up and saw a burly fellow with a sparse com-bover and a barrel chest stuffed into a crisp white shirt with a repp tie—the big cheese, and he seemed annoyed. Francis put down the magazine and stood up. He introduced himself and explained his purpose. The fellow accepted the tendered subpoena and studied it. "I'm sorry," he said, "this man doesn't work for us anymore and we don't have his records." He went to hand the papers back, but Francis wasn't accepting.

"I can't take that back," firmly yet politely, "it's already served."

"Bullshit!" he said, his face turning a deeper shade of red, "you can't just come in here and—"

"Look, if you can't comply with it then call the attorney and take it up with him. My job is simply to pass it off to the proper person, which I just did. Now, do you want to tell me your name or do I get it from the BBB?"

"Don't you get surly with me."

"Surly to bed, surly to rise," said Francis.

"Get the hell out of here—now!" Steam coming out his ears.

"I'm already gone," said Francis. "Have a good one." A half minute later he walked back in and the boss was giving the receptionist an earful. He broke off and glared as Francis went over to where he'd been sitting. "Jesus H. Christ, I told you—"

"Forgot my magazine," he said, apologetically, and walked out a second time. So much for easy service.

The final stop, the therapist, proved no less troublesome. The subpoena was made out to Madeleine Goehner MSW, LCSW, her practice located in an office building in Creve Coeur. This meant it had to be served only to her, not a receptionist or a fellow therapist in the same suite. He knew from experience that it was verboten, once the session had begun, to barge in and interrupt the intimate discourse at play between therapist and client. There was no way of knowing when the session begins. If you missed it when the therapist came out into the waiting area to collect the next appointment then you were expected to wait the fifty-five minutes until the next break. Therapists, it seemed, were more important than other professionals whom it was customary to interrupt or call away for a brief spell to come get their papers. That didn't sit right with Francis.

The waiting room was empty and dimly lit. There were a couple sofas and new age music softly playing from some hidden speaker. Some sort of fragrance filled the room. Lavender? It was all very calming. No one to speak with, just a sign on the wall: PLEASE HAVE A SEAT AND SOMEONE WILL BE WITH YOU. Right. He tried the only door leading to suites within. It opened, and he entered their sanctum sanctorum. Still no sign of activity, although some of the suites in here were open. He walked the carpeted hall and heard conversation. He came to a door with Madeleine's name and honorifics set in flowery cursive. He listened: two voices, animated, one plaintive. I am a spy, he thought, as he knocked gently twice and the cracked the door.

"Hello, sorry to bother you, but I'm a process server with a subpoena for Madeleine Goehner." He saw two women sitting on patchwork floor cushions, one blubbering, mascara running down her cheeks, a total wreck; the other with mouth agape, an amazed look on her face. "I take it that's you," addressing the woman in the pantsuit.

She stayed where she was. She gathered all her indignation, sputtered, "Here now, you can't just —I mean, it's an ethical violation to come in here uninvited, interrupt this session. I'll have you reported. Who do you work for? Do you have a license? Let me see your license."

Francis saw this wasn't going well. "First things first," he said, handing her the subpoena. She glanced at it for a second and tore it in two.

"That's what I think of your subpoena!" she uttered through grit-ted teeth, shaking the split paper in each fist. "Out! Out with you!"

He wagged his head in disapproval. "That's a bit dramatic, don't you think? You might want to read that part where it says 'the State of Missouri Commands You.'"

Francis about-faced and shut the door softly behind him, not wanting to disturb them any more than he already had.

— 6 —

He took lunch at Riordan's, a bar over in Kirkwood that did a brisk noon trade, having a Reuben with slaw and a couple Buds. He'd brought the Jefferson County street guide in with him and had it laid out on the table. This address looked to be some distance from the actual town of Cedar Hill, a subdivision it looked like, several streets spoking off an elliptical primary. Most of it a straight shot down Highway 30, then a bunch of turns. Forty-five minutes he estimated. He paid with a ten and keep the change. A blanket of muggy heat covered him as he left the AC and walked to his car.

Gravois Road started near downtown and traveled diagonally through the urban environment in a southwesterly direction for a long, long ways. When it crossed over the I-270 loop it became Highway 30 and continued on another fifty miles to St. Clair. Francis caught it at Lindbergh and headed out into the hinterland. Neighboring Jefferson County. The boonies to a city-bred man like Francis.

He stopped at a filling station with a convenience store and bought a six pack and a bag of peanuts. That's when he realized he'd left the street guide back at Riordan's. Here, they had a Jeff County street guide, but instead of spending eight bucks he simply copied the directions into his log book. He gassed up the Escort and got back underway, feeling pretty damn good about this assignment—driving along this gray asphalt ribbon, arm out the window, heading into terra incognito. To enhance the experience, he had a fresh pack of 'boros, a cold Bud between his legs, and Van Morrison on the 8-Track. Rock on.

He got to Cedar Hill and kept on going, the turn-off still up a ways. About six miles further he saw Highway B and took it to the south. Two more beers and he began seeing signs for towns he'd never heard of. He checked his scribbled directions again and it appeared that he should have turned on Highway BB back in Cedar Hill. Just like these yokels, he thought, name roads after letters in the alphabet, inviting confusion, when with just a little more effort they could be giving them proper country road names like Cloverdale or Haybale or whatever might strike the fancy of Bubba the County Planner. He turned around and headed back the way he came.

At a Cedar Hill convenience mart he discarded his empties and bought a couple 40-ouncers. He found the *Wunnenberg's* on a rack in the back and once again checked to be sure of his destination. He glanced at his watch: 3:35. He'd taken nearly two hours for a forty-five minute trip. Tooling down BB there were limestone bluffs on one side and cornfields on the other. He saw a pair of turkey vultures pecking at some grisly thing in the road, not even flying off as he passed, just eyeballing him with malevolent stares. Then he found himself behind some great huge farm vehicle, a combine or harvester or whatever you call it. The thing was going twenty miles an hour and there was no room to pass. If this was country living, you could have it.

He stopped to piss and a passing car with teenagers honked enthusiastically at him. He quickly zipped up and waved back. His watch said 4:05, the place wasn't very far now. It was on the right, he knew, the street going into the subdivision. And there it was, Stratford Drive. A manicured median with a rustic wood paneled sign surrounded by tall ornamental grasses announced the entrance to Avonhurst Estates. The road wound up a middling incline with residences spaced about a city block apart. Turn-offs here and there with names like Falstaff and Hamlet and Touchstone, characters or places from Shakespeare. He was looking for Portia. It was getting more and more countrified. Some of the homes had fenced-in areas, modest in size, with a few cattle or horses out grazing, although it wasn't a farming community. The livestock probably more of a—what would you call it? A gentleman's hobby.

* * *

Stoney staggered out of the home, trying not to trip as he negotiated the ten yards of driveway to his parked car. If anything, he was more tanked than when he went in, for, after he had done that lady, he found a bottle of Lambrusco on the kitchen counter. Now he was burping it up; kind of sweet, it didn't sit well on top of all that whiskey and beer. He felt his face burning where she'd scratched him. Bitch. Why couldn't she just go along, it could've been so good for both of them. He knocked at her door only wanting some company, maybe get it on, too, but she had to go and ruin it and, well ... he had his way anyhow, didn't he? Best to lay low for a while. Should he worry about what next? Probably, but for now the booze was shooing away thoughts of deputies on the lookout and him getting caught. He thought of Deke just down the road. Deke would find out, but he would understand. Deke was all right ... and he has a horse. Through a haze, Stoney remembered going to the barn and Deke showing him a horse, big brown animal with a black mane and a patch of white on its nose. He went to pet it and the thing tried to bite him on the forearm. Fucking horse, can't accept an act of kindness.

He got to his car, tried three times to get the keys into the ignition. He talked to his car, as he often did, asked it to just get him home so he could sleep it off and then figure what to do. He fired her up and put the shifter into reverse and backed her out. Just then he saw a mid-size black station wagon coming over the crest about fifty yards distant. An arm out the window. *Well, fuck me.*

* * *

Francis turned into Portia Way, no homes in sight. He puttered along looking for an address, sycamores and oaks measuring his progress. There, a mailbox—408. He was seeking 566. He got ready the four things he needed: the papers to be served, his city courts-issued process server ID, his log book and a pen. It would be on the left up here just a ways now, over that crest. On the other side of the crest, he saw a nice lawn and a mailbox. There was a thick row of six-foot tall canna lilies lining the property at one side of the lawn, red blooms at their tops. There was a car coming toward him, and it looked as if it was just leaving the place.

The car slowed as it got closer and the driver held up his palm: Hold up, there. Francis stopped, and the blue Dodge Challenger with no front plate pulled up alongside so they were door-to-door, only feet apart. Just them, no one else around. The driver fortyish, unshaven, wavy brown hair beneath a camouflage-style cap, some-thing written on it. Stoner grin, snaggletoothed, with a porno mus-tache—Francis was unimpressed. He took a few seconds to look Francis over, and Francis saw that he was having trouble focusing. The driver held a thin cigarette in his left hand which rested on the window frame. He put it to his lips, took a few quick hits. Nervous? Seconds went by. He seemed to be working up some comment. Francis waited.

"Hey ya doon?" Francis processed this drawled salutation: What're you doing here?

"Got some business up the way," he replied, then turned his head to give a hearty beer belch.

"What kinda business?" The guy pretty much out of it, trouble getting his words out.

"Confidential business," answered Francis, also inebriated but nowhere near as much as this joker.

"Confidential, huh? Thas' a good one," he smirked.

"If you're security, just say so."

He nodded—or was it a tremor? "Nah, I ain't no security, more like a caretaker. An' thas' why I'm askin'."

Francis motioned to the home in plain view now. "I need to knock on that door, and deliver something."

"I kin take it," the guy shot back.

"No you can't," corrected Francis.

"Won't do you a bit a good to knock on that door," he pressed, playing with his mustache, "that lady's not there. She went on vacation, back next month."

"Thanks for the heads up" he said, about done with this nonsense, "but I've come this far and I'll just give it a try."

"You ain't listen to me." The tone just short of menacing.

"I guess we're done here," said Francis, seeing for the first time that the guy wore angry scratch marks on his cheek, plain as day. Like he'd gotten into it with a tomcat, raked him good.

"Suit yerself. You wanna waste your time, be my, uh, my … hell, go for it." He took a drag on his slender cig, shook his head like he was disgusted with the general state of things. He gave Francis a goodbye nod, took his foot off the brake, and pulled away slowly, the engine making a rumbling sound. Francis turned in his seat to watch. The Challenger was in cherry condition, the envy of any gearhead. On the rear of the receding car Francis caught sight of a bumper sticker FOLLOW ME TO MERAMEC CAVERNS and a vanity plate N-AGADA, smiling at the reference.

Francis put the engine in neutral, pulled up the emergency brake, left the car running in the street. He'd leave it running when this far from home. It was an old car, what if it wouldn't start again? He knocked at the front door of the charming domicile on Portia Way. For a minute he became distracted watching a ruby-throated hummingbird scouting the pale blue blooms of a Rose of Sharon bush. He knocked some more, quite emphatically. No answer, but there was a dog barking inside. Proof that shitfaced-on-something yahoo was lying about Elizabeth being on vacation. But why? He peeked in windows, saw nothing but furniture, a nicely kept house. Finally, and somewhat reluctantly—loathe to tip his hand, but maybe she'd cooperate—he left his card on her door, asking that she call him.

—7—

"No mister, she don't stay here. She just comes by to visit."

Francis met the gaze of this pudgy, middle-aged woman, searching her pale blue eyes for signs of false witness. "But isn't that her name on the mailbox, Sahe Covic—did I pronounce that right?"

"Sha-ha," corrected the woman.

"Right, okay, her name is on the mailbox and you are her mother, correct?"

"Yes, but I don't know when I see her. She sometime come by on Sunday, but not for sure."

"Okay, look. You say Sahe doesn't live here, but you can't or won't tell me where she does live. She's your daughter, you know how to get in touch with her. I'm going to leave this summons with you and you can call her and say come pick this up."

"I guess I could do that," she sighed. Francis got her full name and handed over the alias summons with petition which demanded a jury trial and up to $25,000 damages for an auto accident that happened three years ago.

"What is this?" asked the mother.

"I've explained it twice already," he replied, patiently. "It's a summons, a legal document. Your daughter is being sued."

"No, this," she said, pointing to a conspicuous red blotch the size of a dime on the face of the clean white summons.

He leaned over to scrutinize it. "Uh, not sure. It could be ketchup. I had a burger earlier."

"It looks like blood," said the mother, dubious. "Let me see your hands." Reluctantly, he complied, but covered up his thumbs. "Not to hide anything," she said. "All of the hands, please." He uncovered his thumbs, poor ravaged thumbs. "There, look! It *is* blood. You give me legal document stained with blood? This is how you do things in America?"

Sheepishly, "Well, I'm sorry I got blood on your summons, but it's served all the same."

"You must stop the biting right now," she exhorted, caressing his hands a mite too sensually. "Is not right for a handsome man like you."

"I can't stop!" he told her. "It's a nervous habit I've had all my life. It could be worse. I mean, some people pick their nose."

"They have at the Walgreen's some bitter potion you can put on your fingers that will stop the biting and chewing."

"I know," he said. "I tried that a few years ago, but the stuff tasted so bad I threw it away."

He drove off feeling good. He had just served a Bosnian in the Bevo Mill neighborhood, and before that a Latino, Rodrigo Dominguez, and before that a Vietnamese guy, Thanh Nguyen. It was International Day in the field. Now he was headed for North St. Louis to get service on one Reginald Duckworth. Once there, on East Prairie Avenue, it took a while to find Reginald's abode. Every fourth house was boarded up and half of them lacked addresses. And boy, was it hot, over 100 for the fifth day now. As he liked to say, if it weren't for the heat and crime, St. Louis would be the ideal place to live.

He began walking the block, studying the address sequence. The numbers appeared to increase by four and based on that he extrapolated the likely residence of Mr. Duckworth. Actually, residence was a compliment to this rude dwelling which could have been a crash pad of the homeless. The front door was open, but, common to many Northside homes, there was an outer full-length padlocked gate preventing entry.

"Mister Duckworth?" he called several times. A bird flew out the door. Within he could see clothes and various belongings strewn about. There was a motorcycle over in one corner that was being worked on, several parts on the floor oozing oil. The grungy gray wall directly in front of him was charred from fire and this wall, along with the others, was decorated with all kinds of concert fliers and public notices that had been removed from telephone poles and buildings. Girlie pin-ups, too.

Again he called the name. This time a voice answered, but it came from behind. He was three doors down, shuffling in Francis' direction, a guy about thirty, brown as mahogany, shoulder-length dreadlocks, martini glass in his hand. When he got close Francis asked him if he lived here.

"Proud to say I do," he beamed.

"Then you must be Reginald Duckworth."

"Who wants to know?"

"I'm a process server. You know what that is?"

He thought for a second. "You serve process?"

"Right, and I've got one for you."

"Let me see," and he took it and spent a minute reading it. Francis took the opportunity to study his cocktail, which was gorgeous in every way down to the green olive skewered on a tiny red plastic spear. Even the glass had been chilled. The guy lived in a hovel, but he had a perfect cocktail on a sweltering afternoon.

Reginald finished reading and his reaction was fiery. "This some bullshit, man! It say I'm being evicted for non-payment of rent. It say I owe eight hundred dollars. Look at this dump! You think I should have to pay even fifty bucks to live here? Ain't no running water, ceiling's falling down and it smells like a rat died in the floor. Maybe something bigger, dead possum."

"Yeah, I hear you," Francis said, sincerely. "Maybe this is a blessing then. Time to move on, new digs."

Reginald sipped at his cocktail and reflected. "You know, brother, you right. You right as can be. Thanks for the papers. Now it's official, I'm bookin'. Sayonara, baby ... say, you got any change?"

It was still early. Francis decided to see Phelim about the transmission problem. He could leave the Escort there and walk to Murphy's. He pulled up to his place on West Park and there were two guys on the porch. Slacks, short sleeve dress shirts, loosely-knotted ties, down-to-business haircuts. Mormons again? They stood there as he walked up, satchel in hand. One of them called his name.

"That's me. What's up gentlemen?"

The dark-complected one pulled out a side-opening badge case and flashed him with it. Francis saw a shiny gold star. "Detective Bernard LaRocca, Jefferson County Sheriff," he said, giving him the severe once-over. "Homicide," he added.

The other one looked familiar. Francis had seen him around the neighborhood, some connection with the Hibernians. "Detective Sergeant Brian Scanlan," he offered. "Metro Police."

By the looks of them, they could have been from Central Casting. The Mutt and Jeff contrast in build and stature. The demeanor, too. If not good cop/bad cop, then at least stern cop and almost friendly cop. Just now both of them were eyes on Francis, sizing him up.

"What can I do for you?"

"You were in Cedar Hill the day before yesterday," said LaRocca evenly. "You paid a visit to a home on Portia Way. That right?"

"Yeah, I was there to serve a paper."

"We found your card on the door, that's why we're here."

"She made a complaint? Wait, no—you're homicide."

"You always leave your card at murder scenes?" from Scanlan, his idea of sarcasm.

"Let's have a talk," said LaRocca. "You want to invite us in?"

Francis pondered this. "I thought you always go to the station for interrogations."

"Not an interrogation," said Scanlan, "you're not a suspect. Yet. And your place will do just fine."

* * *

The call came in at 7:35, a 911 to the dispatch in Hillsboro. A very distraught woman claiming that her friend had been brutally slain and possibly raped. She had found the body of Elizabeth Schurzinger in her bedroom, marks around her neck and nude from the waist down. Between sobs and gasps, the woman explained that she and Elizabeth go for a walk each morning and today when Elizabeth didn't show, well, the door was unlocked. She went in to see what was wrong and ...

Squad cars and EMS vehicles, sirens wailing, descended on the home at 566 Portia Way. Crime scene tape was quickly put up. Neighbors in the general vicinity heard the commotion and walked over to watch, Deke among them. The solemn gathering witnessed a figure sheathed in a black body bag being rolled out on a gurney and loaded into a Jefferson County EMS unit. An older woman stood near the front door, cradling a dog, tears running down her cheeks. With red rack lights on cruisers pulsing, a couple of detectives on the scene took the opportunity to interview some of the neighbors standing around. Did you see her yesterday? What time? Did you notice any visitors, any unfamiliar vehicles? Delivery trucks, utility vehicles maybe? Taking names and addresses. Deke turned and walked off before they got to him.

* * *

They went up the stairs to Francis' flat, the three of them, silent. Francis was about about to say excuse the mess, but they were imposing on him so why should he make apologies?

"You'll have to excuse the mess," he told them as they entered, "the cleaning lady's on strike. Let me clear off this table. Would either of you care for a drink? I've got water and OJ."

"No, thanks," said Detective LaRocca, looking around with cop eyes.

Francis quickly positioned three chairs around the small round dining table. He brought out three glasses of tap water anyway, set them down. The two officers took their seats, LaRocca with a small notebook in front of him. Francis went to the wire cage that hung from a cable on a stand. He made little avian sounds for Petey. "Hey, buddy, how's it going? We got company. I'll be with you in a bit." He left the cage door open.

LaRocca explained that the case was still very hot, and that all available manpower was working every possible lead and, with any luck and even more diligence, heading toward an arrest. He, Francis, was a person of interest because of the calling card he'd left. Scanlan had been borrowed from City Homicide as a co-investigator because he, Francis, needed to be spoken to and he, Francis, was out of LaRocca's jurisdiction. "Otherwise," he said, "we'd have to take you into custody and taxi your butt to the Sheriff Department in Hillsboro where the décor isn't quite as nice."

Francis nodded that he understood. He heard a dialect in LaRocca's speech, what some called outstate, definitely rural.

They walked him through the preliminaries. His name, occupation, how long had he been at this work? What all had he done the day in question? Who had given him the papers to serve? What sort of papers were they?

While Francis went through his satchel, actually a durable Book Of The Month Club tote compliments of the city library, LaRocca studied him. "That your uniform, what you wear to work in?"

Francis looked at his attire, cargo shorts, T-shirt that said Big Muddy Music Festival, and Converse All Stars with thick gray socks turned down at the ankles. "Yeah," he answered, "most of the time. When it gets cold I have a long-sleeve navy blue pullover, says Toledo Mudhens."

LaRocca rolled his eyes. "Must be nice, dress for work like you're going fishing. Hell, why bother with clothes at all? Pajamas will do. Maybe we're in the wrong profession, you think?" looking to Scanlan now. "I wouldn't mind coming to work in my pajamas."

Mocking he could take. "I'm an officer of the court," said Francis, "I have to dress appropriately." Francis continued riffling through a series of full-size manila envelopes until he came to the one marked SHURZINGER. Along with his process server ID, he laid it on the table. LaRocca took it, studied it, wrote down the relevant information.

"Why did you choose that day and time to go out there?" LaRocca tapping his pen on the table, thinking he might be on to something. "I mean, did you know anything about her before you left? It's a long drive, she may have a day job. Why not go in the evening when you know she'll probably be home."

Francis thought about this. "I think of myself as an eccentric person often driven by whim." There, that explained it.

"In other words," pursued LaRocca, "one time is as good as another."

"And you say there was no answer?" asked Scanlan.

"That's right," he confirmed, "I knocked and knocked, rang the bell, called out loudly in case she was in the basement or something. Only sign of life was a dog barking from somewhere inside. I even walked around the entire house, thinking she might be in the backyard. Nothing."

"How long were you there?"

"A good twenty minutes, I mean I'd driven forty miles to get there, I wasn't just going to knock a few times and say, Oh well, I'm done here—even though some jackass tried to tell me she'd left town."

Their ears pricked up at this revelation, the two passing significant looks back and forth. "Tell us about this individual," said Scanlan.

"Everything," put in LaRocca, pen poised over his notebook, "start from the initial encounter."

Francis was happy to tell them all that he knew, especially if it meant they would leave soon and he could get over to Murphy's Bar. He told about seeing the Challenger pull away from the house, gave them a detailed description of the driver, what he could see of him, from the torso on up. The camo cap with some brand name on it, the mustache, the welts on his cheek. He repeated verbatim what was said between them, emphasizing that the guy was blasted—conveniently leaving out his own bibulous condition.

"Four o' clock in the afternoon, he was pickled. Blotto. Booze for sure, but maybe drugs, too."

"Why do you say that?" wondered LaRocca.

"I could smell the booze on him, we were that close. But his pupils were dilated, and just drinking doesn't normally do that, right?"

LaRocca was about to answer when Petey landed on his shoulder. The parakeet began picking at some minute loose thread on his shirt. "Hey," he exclaimed, "get this thing thing offa me." He brushed at it with the back of his hand, "Shoo!" Scanlan didn't even try to stifle his mirth.

Petey made a loop and landed on Francis' outheld forearm. "Come on, Petey, back in your prison. The detective doesn't like our feathered friends." He threw a grin at LaRocca.

LaRocca stood up, all five-foot-five of him, said, "Listen, Frank, uh, I gotta use the can. Where is it?"

"Francis."

"What?"

"I prefer Francis. Frank is a hot dog."

"Okay, *Francis*, please point me to the can."

After LaRocca was out of earshot, Scanlan said, "I've seen you around, some of the bars and restaurants, the parade for sure." He was talking about the Hibernian Parade, held every March 17 in Dogtown whether that sacred date fell on a weekday or a weekend. "And I knew your dad—long ago, of course. The Hibernians *and* the Knights of Columbus. He was embedded in those fine organizations, and I was just coming up."

"Yeah," nodded Francis, "I wish I'd gotten to know him better."

"He died too soon," said Scanlan. "Food poisoning, was it?"

"That's what they say, but there was always some question about that."

"Oh … I didn't know. Well, anyway, he was a good man, always reaching out to someone, looking to help out in some way—or looking to spread the word on Hibernian culture. I looked up to him."

Across the table Francis saw a fair-complected fellow, early-to-mid fifties, tall, about six foot, his own height, with square shoulders and a sincere expression. "Thanks, man."

"Brian."

LaRocca came back and joined them. "Okay," he said, "back to this person on the road. He was alone?"

"Yes."

"You've already described him, but there's more. How did he

speak?"

"Country accent or dialect, whatever you call it. Kind of a twang."

LaRocca tapped the butt end of his ballpoint on the table. Francis chewed on his thumb.

"What about the vehicle? You said it was a blue Dodge Challenger, late model. Muscle car, huh? What else did you notice?"

"It was mint condition and ..." Francis shut his eyes, trying to recall. " ... there was a white racing stripe down the middle of the hood. Um, and there was no front plate, which I noticed right off the bat, but as he drove off I turned around and got a look at the rear."

"And?"

"A bumper sticker, Meet Me At The Cave. Something like that."

"Caverns!" injected LaRocca.

"That's it," said Francis. "Meet Me At The Caverns." He looked away a second. "Meramec Caverns!"

"Great," said LaRocca. "That narrows it down to, oh, ten thousand."

"Did you happen to see the plate?" asked Scanlan.

"Yeah, it wasn't a regular plate, it was one of those specialty jobs." The officers were on the edges of their chairs, waiting for the specifics that would lead to this mystery man, but try as he might, Francis couldn't crack the code. "It was some sort of phrase or part of a phrase, kind of like an inside joke maybe." Francis put his head down, fingertips spanning his face, concentrating. He looked up. "Um, it started with a G or has a G in it."

The two men looked at one another. "Well, hell," said LaRocca.

"Come on," said Scanlan. "Try harder. What else?"

Francis shook his head no.

LaRocca said, "We're going to get you with a sketch artist, probably tomorrow, and he'll do his thing and create a picture of this guy based on what you tell him. I don't want you to leave until you're certain that this picture is as dead on as it can possibly be. Understood?"

"Okay," said Scanlan, "thanks for your time." He motioned to the business cards that they'd both left on the table. "You think of anything else, you call us, okay?"

The detectives were partway down the steps when Francis stepped out and called down, "He smoked Virginia Slims."

They stood out on the curb next to Scanlan's standard issue, budget-conscious Chevy Caprice. "What did you think?" asked Scanlan.

"The guy's living like he's camping out."

""Acknowledged," said Scanlan. "Other than that?"

"Nervous," added LaRocca. "You see him chewing his fingers? What's he got to be nervous about?"

Scanlan gave a wan smile. "Being questioned by two cops about a murder? That'd make most people nervous."

"Something about that guy doesn't sit right."

"That guy doesn't have an evil bone in him," said Scanlan.

"Maybe he had some evil son of a bitch in the passenger seat."

"He said he was alone." He regarded his fellow detective, saw that he was agitated. "Look, Bernie, he gave us a line on a likely suspect. We're going to have to do some digging, sure, but can't you at least be happy with that?"

HILLSBORO, MISSOURI
SEAT OF JEFFERSON COUNTY

"There's enough evidence that we should have made an arrest by now. *Should*. One of the saddest words in the English language. Whitey Herzog *should have* replaced Jose DeLeon with Chris Carpenter in the third inning. But he didn't and they lost the game. We *should have* had this case wrapped up with the perp cooling his heels in our well-appointed jail. But we don't. And why not? Diligence and doggedness, a decided lack thereof." Sounds of disgruntlement from the small band of cops gathered in the briefing room.

"That's it," said Jefferson County Chief of Detectives Vincent Stockman, "go ahead and moan for all the good it will do. All right, all right, I'll give you some credit. I know you've been out there asking questions and I know you haven't had much to go on. But you haven't turned up anything either, have you? Then, finally, yesterday afternoon, Bernie here turns up something concrete, which we will get to in a minute after I summarize what's unfolded thus far into this very troubling homicide."

Five detectives including Bernie LaRocca shifted in their folding chairs and most of them took this brief pause to sip at their coffee or soda and give each other knowing looks. It was 8:15 on a Friday morning, the long Labor Day weekend looming before them. Elizabeth Schurzinger's murder was foremost on their minds, and two of them even knew her in passing as a volunteer who tended the splendid flower beds in Metropole Park on the outskirts of town. A pretty woman with a floppy sun hat and a ready smile. It galled them to be accused by Stockman of not trying hard enough.

"Okay then, what have we so far? What tantalizing nuggets of information have come our way?" A large man in a khaki colored sport jacket and maroon polo shirt, Vincent Stockman gazed upon the faces of his detectives.

"I thought you were going to summarize," said Andy Pilchow, the rookie of the group with two years on the squad. "You want us to lay it out?"

"That would be just peachy," said Stockman.

"All right," said Detective Pilchow, rising from his chair to stand and face Stockman. "Late afternoon, Tuesday last—the time of the attack is estimated between two and six, broad daylight, someone enters the home of the victim who was alone except for her dog. No forced entry, but did she know the attacker or did she just have her door unlocked? It's not exactly a high crime area and it's a good bet that there are many unlocked doors out there. Complacency, trust in neighbors, whatever. Anyway, the assailant gets in and an altercation ensues, the victim fighting for her life, chairs knocked over, furniture moved, a vase and a battery-operated clock broken, probably thrown at the attacker. They both end up in her bedroom, my guess is he overpowered her and dragged her there—her sneaker marks on the walls where she was kicking." Pilchow pivoted away from Stockman to address the others. "And then … then he rapes her and strangles her with his hands and leaves her lying dead in her own bedroom with her jeans and panties and brassiere on the floor and her T-shirt up around her neck. Takes her life from her, and discards her like some dime store trinket. Her last moments on earth filled with terror and shame."

"Waxing poetic, are we?" scowled Stockman. "Save that shit for the ladies' auxiliary. Back to tangibles. Was this perp careful during his little playdate? Did he attempt to cover up evidence, clean up afterward?"

"Not one bit," offered Detective Anna Riggs, always eager to contribute. "There are fingerprints galore, but AFIS is turning up nothing. A shame. I mean, you would think—well, our perp apparently has no criminal record. Never been fingerprinted. Then, semen from the body, and flesh from under the fingernails. Let's hope she scratched him good. So we have his DNA, but unfortunately the means to connect this DNA to its owner is not there, the technology years away."

"That'll be one hell of a boon when it does get here," commented Detective Pete Kostedt. "It will do for criminal investigation what the computer is doing for clerical work."

"Yeah, quite the asset," sniffed Detective Mark Berlinger. "Like to put us out of a job."

"You'd rather let some asswipe walk free than make use of new technology?" countered Kostedt. "That's a Luddite for you."

"You'd better be careful tossing around the insults," Berlinger rumbled.

"All right, enough," from Stockman. "Get back on track."

Supposing he was done, Detective Pilchow sat back down. Detective Riggs continued, "Evidence technicians also found some muddy tracks on the carpeting, took measurements and whatnot, hoping for a print and they say it looks like a Western boot, possibly size twelve. They bagged the dirt as evidence, and turns out there's horse manure in it. So," she concluded, "we have at least two things in the For Sure column. Our perp has scratch marks on his body, most likely the face, and he had recently been to a stable."

"Witnesses?" asked Stockman.

"Nothing of any value," offered Berlinger, "but we only canvassed those neighbors in the immediate vicinity of the crime scene and some of them were not home."

"All right, the picture's coming into focus. And now when you go back out there, you have something else to work with. Yesterday LaRocca, along with a member of St. Louis City homicide, paid a visit to the process server who'd left his card on the victim's door. Turns out this server, Francis Lenihan, encountered a man leaving the scene and had words with him. Both of them in the street near the house, side by side in their cars, like patrol officers gabbing. According to Lenihan, the driver was intoxicated and called himself a caretaker. Said that he knew the woman was not home and that Lenihan needn't even try the door. This was around four. This Lenihan went ahead and tried to serve his paper on Schurzinger, an affidavit to terminate the child support she'd been getting. When there was no answer he left his card on her door and departed."

Stockman looked them over, one by one, waiting for something. Finally, Anna Riggs said, "And?"

His only female detective, Stockman assessed her for the zillionth time. It was just a bit off-putting, her thyroid condition, apparently difficult to treat, that made her eyes bulge and look as though she was glaring at you. He pointed a finger at her like she'd won a prize. "And … the guy was driving a blue Challenger, mint condition. Best guess: early to mid-seventies. White racing stripe down the length of the hood. No front plate but the rear, as Lenihan observed, had a sticker, Follow Me To Meramec Caverns, and a vanity plate that said, well, we don't know what it said. Lenihan said it was some kind of phrase or slogan, coded maybe, had the letter 'G' in it. Told Bernie he'd try to remember."

"That's nice of him," from Kostedt.

"Guy's a flake," put in Bernie LaRocca.

"Meanwhile," said Stockman, "I've got the DMV working on indexing Dodge Challengers with Missouri vanity plates. We should have something by early next week. And here is a sketch of our possible suspect compliments of our brethren at the Saint Louis Police Department." He held up the black and white portrait on an eight and a half by eleven sheet, a rangy-looking guy with a ball cap, for all to see.

"The cap had some brand name on it, but Lenihan can't remember that either," said Stockman.

"Burt Reynolds," said Anna Riggs. The others looked at her. "More *Deliverance* than *Smokey And The Bandit*," she clarified.

"Nah, it's Dale Earnhart," from Mark Berlinger, a NASCAR fan.

"All right, people" shouted Stockman, command voice, "I've done *my* homework on this so listen up. There are eighteen homes covering a hundred thirty-two acres in this subdivision. I want you to go back out there this morning and ask about this car and driver. To help you in this task, I have gone to the County Assessor and gotten the names of every resident, or, more specifically, every property owner. Because the records show only the names of the property owners but that doesn't mean those owners live there, the place might be rented out or some other family member living there. It's a start, just do what you can. And don't forget to inquire about security cams on the house, on the neighbor's houses."

"How about we run criminal checks on these property owners?" put in Pilchow. "See what shakes out."

"That is an excellent suggestion," said Stockman, "and one that I've already started. But since it involves research and multiple jurisdictions, state and local, it's going to take time. I promise you, Andy, you'll be the first to hear the results." Then he handed out copies of the sketch as well as the sheets of names and addresses culled from the assessor's office, exhorting them, the cadre, "You're detectives, get out and detect."

* * *

They fanned out, Riggs and Kostedt taking the roads to the right of the main trunk, Stratford Drive, Berlinger and LaRocca taking those roads forking to the left, which included Portia Way. Pilchow took the homes on Stratford itself. Pilchow chose to walk from home to home, but the others drove from one to the next in the air conditioning of their cars. The day was already hot; they weren't interested in getting exercise or sweating up their clothing. They were able to speak to someone in most of the homes they tried. If it wasn't the primary bread winner, it was his or her spouse or offspring or parents. They brought up the murder in this otherwise peaceful locale and asked each one, Have you seen any suspicious activity of late? Were you home on the day of the crime, that is, three days ago? Did you happen to see any vehicles that are unfamiliar to you? Okay, how about a blue Dodge Challenger? Maybe with vanity plates?

"What time a day would I have seen it?" wondered a woman in a frowzy housedress, curlers in her hair.

"Sometime in the afternoon of that Tuesday," Berlinger told her, notebook in hand.

"Sorry," she said, "I have bridge club all afternoon on Tuesdays. It goes from lunch to cocktail hour, if you know what I mean."

They showed her the sketch and she commented that the fellow looked like half the guys down at Wild Oats Tavern on a Friday afternoon.

They approached the Schurzinger residence, looking forlorn with a few strips of yellow-and-black crime scene tape laying on the lawn. A Toyota Corolla sat in the driveway, trunk open. Garage open, too. A young woman came out the front door carrying a cardboard box, which she placed in the trunk. LaRocca and Berlinger pulled in behind her. She turned, put her hands on hips, waited for them to get out before resuming her labor.

"What have we here?" asked LaRocca, without accusation, walking up on her. Large stature, early twenties, fair-complected, long honey-colored hair with a tie-dye sweatband across her brow. She wore sandals and a colorful Mountain Girl dress that swept the concrete. Around her waist was a sort of utility belt, leather with various objects attached including a raccoon tail and a leather pouch. Probably something she keeps her stash in, thought LaRocca, who took her for some kind of hippie.

"I'm Elizabeth's daughter, Rose," she announced in a husky voice. "I've come to get some of her stuff. Some of mine as well. And you are?"

LaRocca introduced himself and his partner. "I knew you were cops the second I saw you," she told them.

"That obvious, huh?"

"'fraid so."

"I'm sorry for your loss," said LaRocca, Berlinger nodding his condolence as well. "I was aware that your mother had a daughter somewhere in the area, but we couldn't locate you to tell you what happened. We had to call your aunt to identify the body."

"That's all right, I didn't need to see her chilling in some meat locker. I prefer to remember her in sunlight, animated and intelligent. Mom-like." She paused a beat. "So you're here looking for clues or someone who saw something, I guess."

"That's right," said Berlinger, "we are very much on this case. High priority."

LaRocca cleared his throat. "Listen, I'd like to speak with you, but not right now. Would you mind coming to the station in Hillsboro sometime this afternoon, say, around two?"

"Yeah, that'd be fine. I'll hang out here for a while, soak up the vibes. Hey, do you guys know what happened to Blackie? Mom's dog."

"I think a neighbor has it, your mother's friend who she goes walking with ... I mean, *used to* go walking."

"Oh, I think I know the one. Thanks, see you later, then."

They split, each going their own direction, and then Rose turned and called, "Peace Haven Farm."

"What's that?" LaRocca wondered.

She stood there awash in sunlight, answered, "A commune out on Boyd Branch Road near Valles Mines. That's where you find me."

They drove on, Berlinger and LaRocca, soliciting residents along the way. Eventually, on a street named Bolingbroke, they came to a ranch house, stucco walls, no gables, no cupolas, just a flat roof with a brick chimney. Day lillies lined the walk leading to the porch and front door. They rang. Deke, at the kitchen table, heard the bell. He left his jigsaw puzzle and went to the door. He wished he hadn't when he saw what was out there. Still, he kept his cool.

"No sir, I ain't never seen no blue Challenger on this road," he told them, certain that his tone was convincingly earnest. "Ol' Rodney down the road there, he's got a black Mustang, could be mistaken for blue."

They regarded this fellow, mid-fifties, blue eyes, about five-nine, medium build, thinning on the crown with brown wavy hair on the sides, wide mouth, and in need of a shave. LaRocca saw a resemblance to Gene Hackman as the FBI investigator in *Mississippi Burning*, a movie which had just come out. It was 10:30 on a Friday, shouldn't this guy be at work?

LaRocca was doing the talking; Berlinger beside him, arms folded.

"And what do you do for a living?"

"Oh, a little of this and a little of that," Deke shrugging resignedly. "Work's scarce right now. I aim to apply for a position at the Rural King over in Cedar Hill. I can direct customers to widgets on aisle thirty-four as well as anyone." He chuckled at this, hoping they would, too. They asked if anyone else was present.

"Nope, just me right now. Got a son who works regular hours, and a daughter who's off running with her friends."

"Would either of them have been home on the day in question?"

"Can't say," said Deke. "The son definitely not, the girl maybe."

"But you were here," said LaRocca.

"I was here," stated Deke, "and I wasn't. I ran some errands around mid-afternoon, probably between two and four."

"Take a look at this" said Berlinger, "it's a person of interest. Have you seen this person around anywhere?"

Deke took the sheet and held it arm's length for better inspection. "I don't have my cheaters on, but I'd say no, never seen him and don't want to."

"Why do you say that?" asked LaRocca.

"Because he looks shady," said Deke, "shady and dastardly." He handed the sheet back. "So how did you come up with that sketch?" he asked. "Somebody must've seen this guy for you to be able to make a drawing of him."

The two detectives looked at each other. "We won't answer that right now," said Berlinger, flatly. "Not with the investigation ongoing."

"It will all shake loose before long," added LaRocca. "Thank you for your time, Mr. Johnson."

Deke went back to his puzzle, a picture of a pair of cute kittens playing with a ball of yarn. He had worked on it for an hour and a half, and was nearly finished with it. Now he'd lost interest. He sat there brooding for five minutes and then he got up. He went to the kitchen window, looked out, and saw a squirrel upside-down on the bird feeder, pigging out on the black oil sunflower seed he'd just bought. He'd have liked to shoot it in the butt with his pellet gun, but there were more important things on hand. He turned to the wall phone, he dialed. He stood there holding the receiver, muttering, "Pick up, pick up." Stoney answered on the fourteenth ring. He sounded out of breath.

"Hey, man, what's doing?"

"Same ol' same ol'. I was out back digging a pit for a privy I plan to put in. So what you got?"

"Something good, something you'll like. Can you meet me at the quarry later on?"

"Yeah, I reckon. What time?"

"Around ten. We gotta talk."

"About what?" Stoney's voice just a shade suspicious.

"I've got a line on a new job for us, one of those places you spoke of the other day."

"Hot damn, partner! Hell yes, I'll be there."

— 9 —

THE QUARRY WAS THE OLD PENDERGAST NO. 2, a private mining concern that had been extracting limestone from the earth for over fifty years. During its heyday, from about 1948 to 1965, it had employed some thirty people, mostly heavy equipment operators, as well as a small army of dump truck drivers, subcontractors who came and went all the livelong day. One day in 1980 the men and machines came no more. All that remained was the hole and it was vast, vast and inviting, for, over time, the void had filled with water and its latter-day incarnation was that of a party venue for local youth. In fact, the very spot on which Deke and Stoney now stood, a graveled promontory, was *the* choice location for daredevil teens to launch themselves off the bluff and into the drink some forty feet below. Earlier that day, many had done so, and their cries of *Geronimo!* or whichever mid-air holler they may have uttered could still be heard as a whisper.

Deke had gotten there first, ascending the modest incline for several minutes before coming to the clearing with no fence and no sign to warn of a serious drop-off here. It was full dark, no moon and no stars. He took a can of Miller High Life from the cooler he'd brought, popped it, and waited. Stoney pulled up before he was finished. Deke watched him park close to his pickup; there wasn't a lot of room to maneuver. Stoney killed the engine and his headlights went, leaving them in utter darkness.

Deke grabbed two more beers from the cooler and moved over to the Challenger. Stoney, lifting himself out of the bucket seat, took one, said, "Hey."

First thing Deke noticed, he wore a large Band-Aid on his left cheek.

"Back atcha," said Deke. They leaned on the trunk of the Challenger. The evening was warm and muggy, and they drank thirstily. At least a minute passed before either said anything. Finally, Deke said, "You wanna tell me what happened the other day?"

"Which day would that be?"

"Cut the shit," said Deke. "You know damn well what day. The day she scratched you up, the day the fucking reaper came to town."

Stoney stepped back, the better to gauge Deke's ire. The man's jaw had tightened. His eyes had hardened, were glaring at him. Stoney gulped. "I won't lie to you, man. No sir, I won't. See, I went to visit your neighbor after I left. Kind of a spontaneous thing, you know? I seen her out there, stopped to talk, she invites me in. One thing led to another and we're ripping off our clothes, can't wait to get to the nasty—you know? Then all of a sudden she freaks out, starts attacking me. I put my hand over her mouth, shut her up, you know? I must've left it there too long, my hand, 'cause she didn't wake up after that. Goddamn shame, too. She was a good lookin' woman."

Stoney shrugged and shook his head resignedly. He guzzled what was left of his beer, said, "There you have it."

"There you have it," parroted Deke. "There you have it? You stupid, *stupid* motherfucker!" Deke punched him hard on the bicep, middle knuckle crooked and protruding, the better to gouge with.

"Ow!"

"How could you shit in my backyard? Shit in your own goddamn yard!"

Stoney pulled at his mustache, took in the demeanor of his partner; he saw wrath on his face. Walking on eggshells here. "Don't blame you for being royally pissed. All I ask is that you think back to the stupidest thing you've ever done and then use that when judging me. All I can say—I mean, there is no excuse—but all I can offer is that it was an act of impulse. I wasn't thinkin' right. I shouldn't a got so wasted that day. My brain was all fucked up—"

"You got that right!"

"Look, it was something that just happened, and it won't happen again."

Deke couldn't help laughing, the ludicrous idea that it *could* happen again. This had the effect of telling Stoney that things were going to be all right between them. "It was unfortunate," he reflected, "that's for sure, but the cops have zip to go on."

Deke threw him a look, said, "I wouldn't be so sure of that, and now they're all over the scene like flies on shit. They talked to me earlier, two detectives. More of 'em in other parts of the subdivision, asking lots of questions, those suspicious cop eyes boring in to you." Just thinking about it caused the bile to rise anew in his throat. "So goddamn your ass, man, goddamn you for putting me in this position. I don't need this shit, not at all."

"It'll pass and things'll get back to normal." ventured Stoney halfheartedly.

"Did anyone see you on the way out?" asked Deke.

"Hell, no."

"You sure?"

"Yeah, I'm sure."

Deke turned on Stoney like a prosecutor questioning a hostile witness. "That so? Then why are the cops asking about a blue Challenger being seen on the day of? Somebody saw you, but you were probably too fucked up to know it."

Stoney winced at this news. "Uh-oh," he said.

"Uh-oh is right. It's only a matter of time."

Stoney stroked the contours of his beloved ride. "I'll get rid of her," he offered, "hide it for a couple years. It'll be all right, you'll see." Deke had no response to this except to stare daggers at Stoney.

One of them desperately wanted to change the subject. "Now can we talk about this job you got in mind?"

Deke was about done talking. Now he just wanted to get this thing over with. "We could," he answered, "but you know what?"

"What?"

"I think I need a new partner."

"Go on."

"No, really," said Deke, darkly. "I can't trust you no more, can't rely on you not to do something stupid that's gonna bring down our whole operation, put me back in prison."

"Aw jeez, it ain't like—"

Deke held up a finger. "You hear me talkin'? I ain't done yet. I was gonna say it's a shame but nonetheless fitting that this pretty car is gonna be your coffin."

Stoney's eyes grew large. "What!"

Deke had been holding a straight razor at his side, folded, concealed in his right hand. In a flash, he flicked it open, brought it up and sliced Stoney's throat with a mighty sweep of the arm. Stoney's jugular opened and he began to bleed out all over his Wrangler denim shirt with the snap front. His eyes were bugging out, aghast, one hand on his throat, pinching the flesh there in a ludicrous attempt to somehow plug the leak. He went to grab Deke by the shirt, but Deke stepped back and Stoney fell to the dirt flailing and gasping. Deke went over. Stoney's eyes open in dumb shock, chest heaving, horrible rasping sounds coming out of him. Deke hunkered down, and the last words Stoney ever heard were, "It had to be done, it had to be done."

Deke had come prepared. He popped the trunk of the Challenger, and with difficulty lifted Stoney and dropped him in. He took off his own clothes and put them in with the body along with the murder weapon. He changed into fresh clothes that he'd brought. It was tempting to just push the Challenger off the bluff and into the waters of the quarry below, but quarries can dry up or get a leak through some underground fissure, so he had a better plan. Down the road about a mile and off on some rutted track that was no better than a logging trail sat a sizable sinkhole. Those things could swallow a school bus, he'd seen it. He'd been there earlier today, made sure it was still there and nothing blocking its gaping cavity. It was there all right, only a handmade sign stuck in the ground to mark the spot. DANGER it said in bold crimson lettering. He'd left a few things there, things he'd need right about now.

He started the Challenger, nosed it down the hill and found the track. He took it slow the hundred yards or so to get to the sinkhole; to bottom out on the ruts would be the end of him. The headlights identified the cavity, a natural clearing around it, and Deke drove to the very rim. He left it in neutral, running, tried pushing it but no good. Next, he found a stick, revved the engine in neutral, slammed the shifter into drive, pressed the accelerator with the stick, and jumped out of the way. The Challenger fairly leapt into the mouth of the hole, and with a crunching and crackling settled in, nose down, engine still running. Deke uprooted the Danger sign and tossed it in after the Challenger. Then, he got the camo netting and pine boughs that he'd left earlier, and covered the car, situated well below the rim, headlights shining down into the great cavity.

He had never before taken a life and he didn't feel great about it, but as he told that shit-for-brains it had to be done. And done it was, damn the consequences.

Then he mounted the bicycle leaning up against a big pine, a Schwinn once used by his daughter Eve. He walked it out of there. Once on the road, him out of shape, huffing and puffing, he rode when he could but had to walk it part way up the hill, back to his pickup. Along the way many thoughts bubbled up, one of which had to do with how silly he might look to a random passerby, a grown man pedaling along on a girl's bicycle. Lucky for him there were no random passersby.

— 10 —

THE BIRDS LAY IN THE GANGWAY, the life gone out of them, their tiny red eyes staring into nothingness. It was obscene, this mass murder—there must have been twenty of them—and Francis had a pretty good guess as to the identity of the culprit. A despicable act, and already a lump began to form in his throat. He got down and examined one. Its coloring, a rich sheen of green and purple from the neck down, had already started to lose luster. "Oh, no!" he pronounced in an emotional whisper, "no, no, no," and a single tear fell on the creature.

He found Phelim in his shop smoking a cigarette and reading a manual on timing belts for GM models. Francis walked up, said hello. Phelim looked up from his reading. "Morning," he offered, more of a statement than a salutation.

"Not for those pigeons out there it isn't."

Phelim put down his manual. "Oh, that."

"Why? And whatever reason you have, it won't be good enough."

"They were shitting everywhere. I got tired of walking in it."

"You killed them for being pigeons?"

Phelim shrugged. "I poisoned them, they never knew what hit them."

"That's pretty drastic, I'd say. You could've called pest control, they'd have come out and trapped them."

Phelim pursed his lips, said, "Poison's cheaper and, besides, pest control would just take them somewhere else and exterminate them."

Francis wagged his head in amazement. "Jeez, Phelim, this is the city. Pigeons live here the same as us. You kill this flock, another one will come and take its place. You gonna kill them, too?"

"We'll see."

"Agghhh, you're impossible, you old fart. Now, who's going to bury them? You can't just leave them there for the flies."

Phelim took a last drag on his Pall Mall, flicked it to the oil-stained floor, ground it out with his shoe, his idea of building drama. "I'll get to it later," he said, a sly smile on his grizzled mug, "make good fertilizer for the garden."

Satchel in hand, Francis walked down Tamm to his office. It was before nine on a Monday. Labor Day, in fact. All the Teamsters and Union people were downtown at the big parade, some marching, more watching the mighty show of power and influence, each and every one feeling pretty damn good about the state of things under the protective and benevolent wing of this or that Local. He was hoping that Barry Condon would be in his office, for he had the return and the bill for the attempted service on Elizabeth Schurzinger. They had talked about it the day after the cops had come, Francis voicing reluctance to turn in a bill. Just give me ten bucks for gas, he'd said. But Barry would hear none of it.

"I sent you on a job," he imparted in that lawyerly tone. "You couldn't do it, not your fault. I want a proper invoice, mileage and time. Make the return *non est.*" *Non est* was Latin, meaning the service could not be accomplished.

"*Non est* by reason of death."

"It's tragic," said Barry, nudging his glasses to the tip of his nose. "I didn't know the woman, obviously, but any time someone's life is cut short ... just be glad you didn't discover the body, you'd be stuck with that walking nightmare."

"How does your client feel about it, the ex who was paying support?"

"He feels terrible. They weren't on the outs, they were friendly. From a distance. He lives in Kansas City. But he did look at the situation from a practical point of view."

"How's that?"

"He said that whether the paper was served or not, the outcome is still the same. He doesn't have to pay any more child support."

But today the office was empty, so Francis left the paperwork on Barry's desk. He went to his own desk and laid out what papers he had. Logistical planning was key in his line of work. He had two depo subpoenas for places of business, which would have to wait until tomorrow, today being a holiday. He had an Order of Protection for some character out in Berkeley, a suburb in far North County. He had three summonses out toward West County. Domestic stuff, divorce and paternity. One of them very far west, an EMT named Brenda Rogers. He called the fire district to see if she was working, got a recording to leave a message. Then, after a careful search, he found the number for dispatch. The dispatcher told him he could not give out that information, the schedule of a certain employee.

"But I'm injured and need help," he said.

"What's your location?" asked the dispatcher, dubious. "We'll send a unit."

"Will Brenda Rogers be on board?"

"Please don't waste our time." Click.

So he made a day of it, driving far and wide and serving three of the four papers including Brenda Rogers, who turned out to be a real fox. While the average Joe would look at a beautiful woman and wonder why on earth would someone want to divorce her, Francis knew better. The Temptations had it right when they sang "Beauty's Only Skin Deep Yeah Yeah Yeah." The prettiest girl in town is just a royal pain in the ass to her discontented lover. This philosophical nugget was one of many that Francis had developed over time while serving papers. As he had said many times, it is a job where you get to understand the human animal in depth, see it at its best and worst.

He wrapped up around 2:30 and made a beeline for Murphy's. A place that one may go to watch soap operas in the afternoon, quietly nurse a drink, and be left alone, Murphy's was not. When Francis walked in, Mickey Hannegan a.k.a. Mickey Three was in a heated discussion with Carl Boehmer about the old standby "Danny Boy."

"How can you disparage that song?" said Mickey Three, leaning into Carl, frowning, one elbow on the bar, hand cradling his chin. "Hell, it's the most played song in Irish history. You listen to the words, those beautiful words, it's guaranteed to make you weep like a tyke."

Carl spit contemptuously on the concrete floor. "Saccharine bullshit," he countered. "Whoever wrote that song knew exactly what he was doing, causing generations of otherwise hale and noble Irishmen to blubber uncontrollable into their beer. Pityful, just pityful!"

Mickey eyed Carl with suspicion. "What do you mean saccharine? What the hell's that?"

"Saccharine, as in sugary," he answered. "Sickly sweet. Danny Boy is a double chocolate truffle layer cake with gumdrops on top, slathered in syrup."

"Some of us like our confections with all the trimmings," said Mickey Three somewhat defensively.

Red Rush, sitting on his customary stool where the L-shaped bar took a turn, heard all this and called them over. When Red called you over, you went. With trepidation. Red had quite the storied past. Rumor had it that he was once a comer in the Teamsters Union. He had a cushy job as a foreman at the brewery, bossing a dozen geniuses and getting to drink Budweiser while doing it. What happened, one day a new guy comes along and he and Red take an immediate dislike to one another. One of the reasons for the discord is that the new guy doesn't want to work as hard as he should. Only Red can lay back and take it easy. Red starts in on the guy, calling him a layabout and a goldbrick, and the guy finally gets ticked off enough to take a swing at Red. Then, with everyone watching, Red wipes the floor with him and the guy ends up in the infirmary with a broken wrist and his nose out of joint. Later that day, after work, Red and another steward were at the local saloon. "Well, I guess I showed that son of a bitch," he said. "SOB is right," said the other steward, "but not the kind you're thinking of. That guy is the other SOB—son of the boss. You didn't know that?"

These days the union hierarchy had Red on special assignment, giving him occasional scurrilous jobs that were supposed to be clandestine. In fact he had just come from such a job at an art gallery over on Skinker, a freelance deal for the Glazier's Local. It was a high-end gallery and looking in from outside he could see all sorts of art—paintings, sculpture, some of it ugly or garish but no doubt it brought big bucks to the art dealer. And all he did was show it, the weasel. Red stood at the front door, opened a thermos and began to slosh something on the windows which began to smoke and stink. It was a holiday and the place should have been empty, but soon, before he even finished, this prim little man in a pink polo shirt came out and wanted to know what's he doing. I'm pouring acid on your windows, Red told him matter-of-factly. But why? asked the art dealer, wringing his hands in distress, I just put these windows in. So they'll look like shit, that's why, answered Red, stepping back to look at his work. But why *here*, the little man whined, why *my* building? Red sneered at the question. Because you used non-union labor to install them, you cheap prick. Oh, said the gallery owner, and went back inside.

Today, a thug for hire, but you could still see the uncorrupt schoolboy in him, the gleeful, well-adapted youth who only wanted to fit in, especially when his ginger hair tumbled forward onto his forehead.

From his barstool Red regarded the two drudges before him. "Now boys," he began, "I can see you've gotten yourselves at logger-heads over this song, and a beautiful song it is … when sung by the right person." The two men stood before Red, drinks in hand, shuf-fling nervously, wondering which of them was going to be dressed down first. Red took a swig of his Four Roses, the ice tinkling. He continued. "Truth be told, 'Danny Boy' is a song written to an old Irish Air, so no wonder that it's been performed by countless artists from Elvis Presley to Tommy Makem. It's like 'God Bless America,' each performer adds their own unique flair." Carl and Mickey nod-ded agreeably, thinking now that Red was giving them a tutorial of sorts and not intending to hurt them.

Red peered at them through bloodshot eyes, he'd been at it since morning, having been among the throng attending the downtown Labor Day hooley. He arched his back, stuck out his forty-four inch chest like a rooster preening. "So you see it's a song with immense variety. If you don't like one version because it's too sugary—as you rightly say, Carl—then there's another that you likely will take a shine to. The Eric Clapton acoustic version is quite nice, and so is the rendition by The Irish Tenors."

"I've always liked the Bing Crosby version," put in Mickey Three.

Red frowned at this, and Mickey wished he'd kept his mouth shut. "Schmaltzy, but beautifully enunciated," he opined. Mickey let out a sigh of relief.

"Yes," rumbled Red, "many fine renditions to choose from and which one is on the jukebox right now? Do you know?"

"Andy Williams?" from Carl.

"No, although that one isn't bad. The one we hear in this joint is by the great Irish tenor Frank Patterson. His is the most passionate and soulful version I've ever heard. And yes, it tends to make me weep—unabashedly. You can hear it sung in *Miller's Crossing*, a fantastic movie by my lofty standards, and you can also hear it here for a measly quarter." Red spread some change on the bar. He took a quarter and held it out. "Carl, would you like to do the honors?"

Carl gave a nervous laugh. He didn't know Red as well as Mickey did, didn't know that Red did not brook any insubordination from his minions. And that's what most of these patrons were to Red, sodden and imperious on his barstool throne.

Red leaned back, ham-sized hands rubbing his ample belly. Absentmindedly, he scratched at the side of his bulb-like nose, host to an intricate map of tiny broken blood vessels. Looking the man up and down, he said, "Carl, you seem like a reasonable fella. Can we agree at least that any performer who attempts 'Danny Boy' will do their very best and show it the respect it deserves?" He waved that question away with his hand. "No need to answer. And may we agree that this tender message of life, love, and death sung by melodious angels with a sweet and rousing delivery is one of the greatest gifts Ireland has given to the free world?"

Carl began to hem and haw, words came out of his mouth but they weren't the right words.

"You fookin' killjoy," snarled Red. "Step forward."

Carl stood his ground. Mickey watched with mouth agape.

"I said step forward, damn you."

Carl took a small step. "Closer," commanded Red.

Carl stepped up and Mickey Three moved aside. "Put your drink down," said Red.

Carl complied, placing his glass on the bar. Drinkers up and down the bar watched with interest. "Mother of God!" cried Carl just as Red chopped him in the throat. Carl staggered backward, making awful retching sounds.

"Now you may buy the next round," said Red, cheerily.

Carl raised his arm signaling Tommy, drinks all around. Then he staggered over to an empty table and sat with his head down in his arms, wishing he'd never brought up that stupid fucking song.

"Thank you, kindly," called Red after him. The bar went back to its usual cacophony.

Francis was on his third Busch when she walked in. All eyes turned to see, for she was young and fetching, imposing in size, and her outlandish garb indicated she was not a Dogtowner. She stood there just inside the entrance and looked around, vision adjusting to the dimness of the place. She made a face and used a hand to fan away the cigarette smoke that was everywhere. She looked around some more, studying this one and that one, and finally she moved toward Francis. Then she stood before him, said, "They told me I'd find you here."

"They were right," he smiled, amused. "And who is they?"

"The old guy in the repair shop behind your house," she said.

"Ah, my keeper. Goes by Phelim, has all the charm of a prison guard. Here, I'll move. Have a seat, will you?"

She wore her size well, decidedly graceful in movement and stature. Her long golden-hued hair, in uneven braids, framed an open face with expressive brows and clear green eyes that looked like they were up for some fun. Early twenties, with an unmistakable vibe of outdoorsiness. Her pulchritude loomed before him and Francis could not help but notice her bosom. From what he could see beneath that cotton print dress—tropical flowers, like an ankle-length Hawaiian shirt—her breasts were huge. He put her at a forty-two double D, but he wasn't all that good with cup sizes.

"I'm Rose," she said, robustly, offering an open palm, "Elizabeth's daughter." This didn't register. "Elizabeth Schurzinger, my mom, the one who was murdered last week."

Francis' eyebrows shot up. "Oh, god, sorry."

"Thank you. I'm still dealing with it, both the loss and the idea that that unholy prick is still out there walking around, enjoying himself."

"Yeah, I hear you," he said, thinking of putting a hand on her shoulder. "Tommy, drinks over here, will ya?" He put his hand on her shoulder. "What'll you have?"

"Vess Cream Soda. But if they don't have that then make it a shot of Cuervo, lime and salt."

They moved to a table, the better to talk. He wondered how she'd found him, not that he was hard to find. She replied that she'd seen his card on the detective's desk.

"He told me how you left it on mom's door. I memorized the name and phone number, and with the phone number I got the address from the *Haines Directory* at the library. I wanted to talk with you."

"Not bad," he said. "Usually I'm the one doing the tracking down. You're the emancipated daughter, the one mentioned in the affidavit I went out to serve."

"That's me, although I was unofficially emancipated long ago."

"Good for you." Francis lit a smoke, offered her one.

"Maybe, if it was a joint, but thanks anyway."

They sat there, taking each other in. "So what can I do for you?"

She leaned in and got close, looked earnestly into his eyes, paused a few beats, stroked her chin like she was debating whether to impart some great revelation. She looked around to see if anyone was within earshot, then conspiratorially, "I want you to find the son of a bitch who did this."

"Oh, is that all?"

"I'm serious, I've decided that you can do it. I want to hire you. I want him brought in. Dead or alive, as the saying goes."

"You know that I'm a process server, not a private investigator."

"Don't you guys all have to do a little detective work from time to time, find people who are hiding or simply move around a lot?"

"Well, yeah, sure."

"Then you can do this for me."

"The cops are on it, let them do their thing."

"The cops haven't done shit! LaRocca called me into his office to give me a rundown of what they've done so far. They don't have suspect one."

"Give them time."

"Time, my ass. My mom's crying out for justice. *I* want justice!"

"I don't know," he said. "I like serving papers, everything's cut and dried. They give you an address, you go there, knock on the door. Every paper has a deadline. I like deadlines. There's no deadline in solving a murder, it could go on for months. Years."

"I'll give you a deadline. It's now Labor Day. How about you have until Halloween? That's doable. And I can pay you. Whether or not you come through, I can pay you well. Mom was worth a quarter million and she had various properties in that area. Once it's all settled in probate those funds will be mine. So, what do you say?"

"Did LaRocca tell you that I saw the guy who probably did it?"

"No, but that's even more encouraging. And that's why you have to give this a shot. If you try, it will happen. I know, because it's in the cards."

"What cards?"

"The Tarot cards."

— 11 —

"You're not serious," said Deke, "please tell me you're kidding."

Forty miles away Deke heard an exasperated sigh. "It's just for a while," he persisted, a slight lisp in his voice, "the foreseeable future, three-four months maybe. You may be hot right now, and I can't take any chances."

Deke pictured Al Byington in his well-furnished office, pretentious art on the walls, speaking on a Princess phone, yellow or some goddamn pastel color a fag would like. Al a.k.a. "Big Al" was a very capable fence with carefully built connections to private collectors, antique dealers, black market entrepreneurs, practically anyone wishing to obtain quality, cut-rate merchandise and not ask a lot of questions. Al had a warehouse in unincorporated St. Louis County, on the flood plain of the Missouri, with at least ten employees who were busy moving stolen goods every day. Deke had been there more than once, and knew that Al's operation made his own look like the

Five & Dime. It was *the* discount mart of purloined goods for the entire Midwest, Chicago excluded.

Deke had phoned to say that he had a nice batch of items and it's waiting for him to take a look. Al was less than enthusiastic. "I read the paper," he'd said. "A woman murdered out your way, a street in a quiet subdivision, a street named Portia Way. And I thought: Wait a minute, Portia, a Shakespearian character. Avonhurst, another Shakespearian reference. I thought, that's the subdivision that Deke lives in."

"Well, yeah," he'd retorted, "a horrible thing. No doubt. But it happening on my street is pure coincidence and definitely no connection to me." Now, Deke was beginning to see that Al thought otherwise.

"Please understand," the lisp really starting to grate on Deke. "I think it's best that we don't associate for a while. I mean, you've got a record, police probably know that by now. So, uh, a murder on your street, a neighbor with a criminal record. Put two and two together, they may be watching you."

"They're not fucking watching me!"

"Yeah? How would you know?"

Deke felt like driving up to St. Louis and throttling the prissy little bastard but Al preempted that, saying he had a doctor appointment and had to quit the conversation.

"Doctor appointment, huh? I hope it's nothing trivial." Deke hung up.

That booger Stoney, he reflected, the guy's rotting in the bowels of the earth and still he's fucking up my operation.

* * *

There were only a few court papers Francis had declined to serve, the reason being that they were directed either to a drinking buddy or, in one instance, to Red Rush himself—a civil suit stemming from an altercation over a Hoagie sandwich. Francis knew that Red would take it personally, being served, and would make it uncomfortable for him in Murphy's, maybe even start some shit, so Francis told the lawyer to get another Special. One with a fat life insurance policy. But Phil Devlin, Dogtown resident and waiter at a famed restaurant in the nearby Italian neighborhood known as The Hill, was fair game. Phil and Francis were mere acquaintances, not pals, although Phil had waited on him and Janie, his sort of girlfriend, while dining at said restaurant on The Hill, where Janie lived. As he recalled, Phil was not overly attentive—they had to find him to have their glasses refilled—and when it came time to pay, Janie urged him to tip the guy more than three dollars. All right, he'd said, but only because the *pasta tutta mare* was so amazingly good. Now he had a Show Cause Order for Phil Devlin, behind in his child support to the tune of seven thousand dollars. It had an upcoming court date and had to be served no later than five days before, which was a couple days from now.

It was another hot one in St. Louis, but then September was not known for granting a respite to the heat. The sun beat down just as unmercifully as it would in August, the humidity dampening your clothes without even any exertion. Devlin lived four blocks over so Francis decided to walk. It was 9:30 and a waiter should be up and running by now. If he worked luncheon he'd be getting dressed for the day; if he worked dinners, he'd be lounging around, watching the tube, whatever.

Francis saw the nightcrawler stretched out on the sidewalk, a big one, barely moving, drying out on the concrete. Ten more minutes it would be a crispy critter. He picked it up, addressed it. "Okay, please tell me, Mr. Earthworm, what you're doing on this sidewalk? What would possess you to leave your nice comfy dirt and venture out into the heat of the day. You know that's not healthy, or are you hoping to commit suicide?" Cupped in his hand, he brought it over to some shrubs, found a place where the soil was at least moist, dug a small hole, placed the creature inside and covered it with leaves and dirt.

He thought of Sr. Thomasina, his third grade teacher over at St. James, and her theory of heavenly access. Sister had made an impression on him in many ways, academically, spiritually, philosophically. Even now, so many years later, he routinely conjured her teachings and musings and one of them was you get into heaven through so many good acts. They don't need to be major good deeds bordering on acts of heroism like rescuing orphans from a fire; small, almost inconsequential ones would do, and the more the better. But saving nightcrawlers from baking on the sidewalk, did that count as a good deed on the heavenly rolls even if the recipient was a primitive annelid? Francis thought so, imagining that Sister would say that we are all creatures of God, no matter how slimy or lowly.

His mother, Bridget, had a similar notion about climbing the ladder to heaven. Her holy cards would get her there.

It was all about purgatory. Francis knew about purgatory, a concept peculiar to Catholicism, because he'd had it drilled into him by the nuns and by Bridget. Purgatory was a state, yes, a state or a condition in the afterlife, neither heaven nor hell but a place of purification, a kind of seedy rooming house, as he envisioned it, where one's spirit awaits entry to heaven. During this wait, which can be a very long time, one reflects on one's sins, committed as a bumbling human on earth. In purgatory the spirit is not wretched, but unrequited, all the while pining to be in heaven experiencing the blissful love of God and Jesus and Mary and all the saints. Almost everyone has to do time in purgatory; with the possible exception of the pope and the martyred John F. Kennedy no one is pious enough to go straight to heaven.

In the evening he'd watch Bridget say her prayers. Kneeling beside the bed she went through a stack of holy cards, each with a short prayer. A recital of each prayer gave one-hundred days' early release from purgatory. Some awarded three hundred days. Bridget was racking up years, decades, centuries of early release, but what, his eleven-year-old mind pondered, is time in the afterlife? Just how long could we expect to stay in this way station, purgatory? Until hell freezes over? Who knew, really, but however long and boring it might be, Bridget was getting out early.

That was long ago, back when he had a mother and a father. Both were gone now, Bridget seven years ago and Martin twenty-five years ago. Way, way, way too soon. The day was etched in his memory like some illuminated page in a book. It was November, 1965, Francis was twelve years old, a seventh grader at St. James. Bridget loved to attend Benediction of the Blessed Sacrament offered at the church on Tuesday evenings. Dad was at work, and he wouldn't go anyway; Sunday morning mass was all he needed, he said. Mother made Francis come along, but Mike, being two years older, got to stay home if he wished.

And Francis grew to love the evening devotion as well. The singing, the prayers, the blessings all directed toward the Blessed Sacrament in its monstrance, up on the altar surrounded by lights. It was a short service, he recalled, twenty minutes tops, and the very best part was near the end when the priest, resplendent in cotta and stole, walked down the center aisle, altar boys on either side, spouting Latin, swinging the ornate incense burner to and fro, pendulum-like, white smoke issuing out, filling the church with a powerful and wonderful fragrance. Made you think you were back in the catacombs or something. The "Tantum Ergo" came in either before or after or during the incense segment, he couldn't remember for sure. But that, too, was a nice touch, everyone singing this catchy tune in the original Latin:

Tantum ergo Sacrementum Veneremur cernui
Et antiquum documentum Novo cedat ritui
Praestet fides supplementum Sensuum defectui
Genitori Genitoque ..."

Something about that hymn, the entire ritual, in fact, made him feel really good inside. But that evening, that fateful evening, that warm feeling was about to turn cold.

They walked home, the night air cool, the skies clear. They talked of an upcoming vacation that dad had planned. Two days in Chicago, one spent at the Shedd Aquarium and the other at the Field Museum of Natural History. That was just like dad, Francis thought, walking along Tamm Avenue on this bright morning, caught up in his reverie, just like dad to plan an outing that mixed fun with education. When they got home a policeman was just inside the door talking to Mike, who was crying. The policeman, a sergeant named Donnelly, had a trace of a tear in his eye as he broke the news that Martin Lenihan had been pronounced dead at the Workhouse infirmary. "We're not sure what happened," he told them, service cap in hand, "except that he was found semi-conscious in Area B, his station, and he was clutching his gut and groaning. He was then rushed to the infirmary, losing consciousness on the way. He was not able to talk, and no one has any idea what happened to him. He'd had dinner maybe an hour earlier, but no one else who sat at the cadre table with him has gotten sick."

As the news sunk in, mother pulled he and Mike close, put her arms around them and they all had a good cry. They were still bawling when Sgt. Donnelly moved toward the door, a prelude to departure. "I can assure you," he said, "that this troubling matter will be looked into and questions will be answered. In the meantime you have the sincere condolences of the Department of Corrections, and should you have any questions about death benefits their number is in the phone book." He put on his cap, and began to walk out but then paused. "I, too, am sorry for your loss. I didn't know your husband and father, but I've heard that he was a good man. It's a shame when we lose good men."

And nothing ever came of their so-called investigation, thought Francis ruefully. To shed light on his demise would have been nice, but it wouldn't bring him back. How do you gauge the loss of a father, the thread having been broken so abruptly? Twenty-five years without him. Decades of additional companionship, guidance, horsing around cut short. He'd been cheated out of those years, and he had to admit that it weighed on him, especially when he passed places in the neighborhood where they would go. The Dogtown Bakery, the Knights of Columbus Hall. He thought of his father, wished that they could have aged together, wished he were more than faded color pictures in an album, wished that he, Francis, could have been on the receiving end of the man's confidences and sage advice and even scoldings. What he wouldn't have given for just one more hug. Instead, Martin Lenihan ceased to exist at perhaps the most influential time of his life. Then he thought of his father in repose in a parlor of the Galvin Funeral Home, mourners all around. Martin Lenihan lay dead in his coffin, his hands looking like wax,

his normally tousled hair combed back, lips stitched closed, the
smile gone forever.

He got to Phil's place, rapped on the front door—shave and a
haircut two bits. Phil came out in his jammies, smoking a cigarette.
"Francis! Hey man, good to see you. What brings you here? You collecting for the IRA—ha, ha! Them hunger strikers about ready for a
decent meal, yeah?"

Francis was a bit taken aback that a fellow Mick would make
light of the plight of Irish Republican prisoners, heroes to most.
"Uh, no, Phil, not collecting and those guys all died of starvation
back in eighty-one. Maze Prison, a hell-hole that we can't even imagine. Why I'm here, you remember I told you what I do for a living?"

Immediately, Phil grew circumspect, glanced up and down the
street for a squad car. "Some kind of legal work. Repo man?"

"Nah, you can get shot doing that. I'm a process server. I serve
papers, and I've got one for you." He took the Show Cause Order
from his back pocket and handed it over.

Phil saw what it was, his name and the daunting words You Are
Hereby Summoned. "Oh, come on! I don't want this. Just say you
can't find me."

"You know, I thought of saying to the lawyer, 'I can't do this, Phil's
my buddy.' But then I thought: Well, I have to and he'll thank me for
it. You know why?"

"Oh, Jesus. Why?"

"Because if it wasn't me it'd be some other fool and he wouldn't be
as nice as I am."

Francis flipped a coin. Heads he'd go, tails he wouldn't. He was
in the town of Barnhart, a half-hour south of St. Louis, in Jefferson
County. He'd just served a records subpoena on a bank and realized that he was about halfway to Avonhurst, a lovely apple of a

subdivision with a worm inside. Rose had asked him to look into Elizabeth's murder, Francis was reluctant. Rose had pressed eighty bucks into his hand, a token payment to get his butt in gear and find the killer; Francis was less reluctant to take that. Plus, she paid his tab at the bar. Now here he was, poised to actually start the job, and what was keeping him from it? Only fear of the unknown, something he was used to as an intrepid process server. Insinuating himself into dicey situations was almost a specialty. Still, it was natural, even healthy, to worry about what might happen were he to attempt to pry open this can of worms. Murderers, after all, can be pretty determined about not getting caught. They'd been known to lash out severely at any pursuers.

It was 12:30 on a Wednesday, eight days after he'd knocked at Elizabeth's door. Four days after her funeral. The coin toss had come up tails, meaning he was off the hook, no need to go. But he was a contrarian, after all. He bought a couple tall boys, aimed his Escort toward Cedar Hill, and pushed on toward whatever Fate had in store.

He took Highway M up to the next town and from there it was all backroads, agrarian, a combination of ranches and farms. The corn was tall and no longer green, harvested in some places, already in the bin. He'd see a herd of cattle and he'd moo at them. He had the road pretty much to himself and now and then he swerved to avoid roadkill in his lane, not wanting to squish them any more than they already were. Mostly raccoon, but also squirrel and possum and the occasional deer. It was a crying shame, roadkill. Here's this animal, minding its own business, trying to get from one place to another. It has the gall to step out on this asphalt ribbon, and along comes this rolling behemoth, this mechanical monster, and suddenly its life is over. How's that for having a bad day? There was no point to it, Francis mused. Senseless carnage. Allow yourself time to react. For that very reason he rarely went over the limit. No hurry, there's lots worse names to get called than slowpoke.

He could pick up KSHE way out here and he heard the beginning of "Copperhead Road," the bagpipes droning, and he turned it up. It was his favorite song, talking of running moonshine and getting over on the law, just the sort of recklessness that had gotten him into so much trouble in his rooster years. He thought it rang true, the part where the Vietnam vet, the fictional guy whose song it is, says:

> *I volunteered for the army on my birthday*
> *They draft the white trash first, 'round here anyway*

And man, Steve Earle singing with such conviction, like it actually happened to him. Francis related. He, too, had joined the army at eighteen. The Vietnam war on the nightly news, guys he knew over there in the thick of it. Why wait for the draft to claim him? Life in a war zone would be dangerous, sure, but a hell of a lot more interesting than the listless day-to-day in Dogtown. Fate sent him to Germany for a couple years. Medical corpsman, ambulance driver. Gasthauses, schnitzel, pilsener, frauleins. Luck of the draw.

The road would wind and straighten out, wind and straighten out, foothills off in the distance, clear blue sky above. He liked driving, the mild suspense of what's around the next turn, and today was a perfect day for it. He got on Local Hillsboro Road and knew that he must be close. Finally, the entrance, the same well-crafted signboard, AVONHURST, like you were about to enter quite the posh community. He drove up the incline, the missing second gear giving him trouble, first heading toward the offshoot streets that made up the far reaches of the subdivision. He tooled around slowly, this street and that, backtracking, getting the lay of the area, stopping every so often to check the Jeff County street guide. Then he made for Portia Way. For starters, he'd see if any of the closer neighbors would be willing to talk. Then maybe he'd branch out, visit the homes further away. He passed the place where he'd met the probable killer, and for the umpteenth time tried to envision that back plate, those cryptic letters, but all he could conjure was a bowl of alphabet soup. He passed the Schurzinger home. The grass had been mowed, the curtains open. It didn't look like the place of a horrible crime from a little more than a week ago.

Elizabeth's was the second house on Portia Way. For starters,

Francis chose the next house up, a ranch style with a carport that housed an older model Chrysler Newport. As he walked up, a big-ass Rottweiler came around the side of the house, snarling, showing fangs. "Easy, boy," he called, trying not to look at it. Eye contact, he knew, could really set off vicious dogs. They were at a stand-off, Francis stock still, eyes closed, and the Rottweiler ten feet away emitting a low, continuous, anus-puckering growl.

"*Help!*" he shouted.

The house door banged open and a man's voice called, "Here, JoJo, com'ere boy." Francis opened his eyes, saw a man in dungarees and sleeveless T-shirt eyeballing him. The dog went past him and inside the house. "Who are you and what do you want?" he asked, zero cordiality.

Francis replied, "Can I come closer?"

"Halfway, no further," he said, "not until I know what you want."

Francis got closer, taking this short time to choose from several vague options as to how to present himself. He didn't really know what he was doing.

The man stood there in the doorway, arms akimbo, like a stern prelate about to pronounce punishment on some novitiate. "Well?" he said when Francis got closer.

"My name is Francis Lenihan. I'm from St. Louis, and I'm looking into the death of your neighbor, Elizabeth Schurzinger."

"I already gave a statement," he said. "Check with your superior."

"Ah, well, I'm not a cop. I'm a private investigator—"

"Who hired you, that Looney Tunes daughter?"

"Could be. Look, I'll just take a minute of your time. That okay with you?"

"No, it's not okay. What happened over there has been nothing but a drain on my life, my energies. Neighbors coming around, wanting to talk. Cops. Now, you. To put it another way, it's been a goddamn inconvenience, and I'm hoping to put it under the rug."

"So it's all about you, huh?"

The man gave a mirthless chuckle. "Yeah, it's all about me. Who else is there to be concerned about?"

"The killer who's not been found, the guy who's out there laughing at law enforcement."

The man nodded ever so slightly. "Sure, I hope they catch the rotten bastard, but just so you know—what I told the cops, I didn't see nothin' and I don't know nothin'. So leave me the hell alone."

"Oh, well, I guess that does it then. Thanks for the interview."

"Smart ass. You know, Magnum looks like a PI. Jim Rockford looks like a PI. You, not so much. You look like some kinda tramp."

"It's my disguise of the day."

"Come around again, you'll be seeing JoJo first and next time I won't call him off so quick."

Francis got back in his car, reached in the glove compartment and took out a flask. "Screw that guy," he said to the windshield. Tipping the flask to his lips, the Tullamore Dew burning his throat like a Banshee in heat.

He drove on to the next house, on the opposite side of the street. Beat up-looking Ford Fiesta in the drive, the front door open. The woman was in her fifties, tall, a towering stack of blonde hair, rouge on her cheeks, earrings that looked like lures from a tackle box. Thin red dress reaching to mid-thigh. He explained himself, she invited him in. She offered him a Coke. He accepted. They talked at the kitchen table. Such a nice person, she began, such a shame what happened. Yes, she was home that day. No, she hadn't seen any unusual activity in the area, but there had been some Ameren trucks in the subdivision last month when that hellacious thunderstorm knocked out the power. But never mind all that, would he like to see something worth seeing? A new tattoo, right here, pointing to her flank. I have to pull up my dress to show you. You're a big boy, you can handle that, can't you? She stood and hiked up her dress. No panties. There, on her bony hip, an inked rendering of Satan, horns and all. Wicked gleam in his eye. A caption that said THE DEVIL MADE ME DO IT.

Francis crossed himself and looked away.

"What do you think?"

"Ah ... it's nice. Look, I've got to be going. Lot of ground to cover."

"Stick around. Why not? I've got some Jack to go with that Coke."

"I'll bet you say that to all the boys."

He doubled back and went to the first home on the street; no one home. Then back up the hill to a fourth house and a fifth. No luck at any of them. That was it for Portia Way but Portia fed into another Shakespearian thoroughfare, Bolingbroke. First house was shuttered, no vehicles visible. Second house looked promising. Ranch house, stucco walls, stone chimney, bicycle in the yard. Day lillies leading to the front door. He was getting further and further from the crime scene, but, hey, give it a shot.

* * *

Detective Bernie LaRocca was taking notes as the clerk at the Conoco told how the woman in the black Camaro had driven off without paying for a full tank of gas. No, he didn't get the plate, but she'd be hard to miss with that bright red mohawk. From his car nearby, LaRocca heard his call signal come over the radio.

"Just a minute," said LaRocca to the clerk.

"LaRocca here," he said into the mic.

"Where are you?" asked Jim Benton, the dispatcher.

"Morse Mill," he answered.

"Good, you're not far. I just got a call from a female resident at that subdivision where the Schurzinger woman was killed. There's a suspicious character, a white male, solo, driving around with no apparent purpose. Black Ford Escort, station wagon. A junker, she called it. This was twenty minutes ago, she spotted him."

"Copy that, Jim. I'm on my way."

* * *

A teenage girl answered the door, chewing something, a copy of

Cosmo in her hand. "Yeah?" she said. Francis sensed a tough cookie.

"I'm not selling anything," he started off, "I'm just going house to house trying to get some info on the murder of your neighbor down the way. Did you know her?"

She swallowed whatever she'd been chewing, said, "Nope, only seen her now and then. And who are you?"

"Francis Lenihan, friend of the family. Look, I've got just a few questions, won't take but a minute."

"The cops were already here. They talked to everyone."

"Well, I'm just double-checking. Sometimes people remember stuff after they've been questioned."

She looked him over and he her. Brown hair worn pixie-style but dyed on top, magenta or some such color, teased into little peaks or spikes here and there, pale complexion, a nose ring, mischievous brown eyes caked in mascara, crooked teeth, and a fresh hickey on her neck. He took her for thirteen or fourteen. "Fire away," she said. "If I can't answer your questions I'll consult the Magic Eight Ball."

"Ah, but that's for fortune telling. I need the skinny on past events, like the day of the crime. Did you happen to be around?"

"I was here in the morning and then I went out and was gone until evening."

"Busy day, huh? You're not old enough to drive. You get picked up?"

A dark cloud passed over her face. "What's that got to do with anything?"

"Absolutely nothing. Sorry, I don't need to get into your business. It's just that I'm new at this and I don't always know what to say. So … um, you ever see a blue Challenger around here? Muscle car? White guy around forty driving?"

"If I had seen anything suspicious I would've told the cops. But they didn't talk to me anyway. They talked to my dad."

"Oh, your dad. Did he have anything useful to tell them, do you know?"

She chuckled, said, "That old fart wouldn't volunteer any information to anyone, not unless you paid him first. To give something out for free goes against his nature. Be like trying to turn a snake into a vegetarian," chuckling some more.

"He around?"

"You see a truck? That's a good thing 'cause if he were here he'd run you off quicker n' shit."

"Okay. Just one more thing. You probably pass by her house fairly often, Schurzinger I'm talking about, did you ever see—"

"Holy shit, here we go now."

Francis turned in the direction that she was looking and saw a Sheriff patrol car approaching. It rolled up and LaRocca got out, all serious and authoritative. He had the departmental ride, a black-and-white Ford Mustang Special Service Package, but still the civilian attire. He walked up and nodded to the both of them.

"Afternoon," he said.

"It is," she said.

He addressed Francis, aggravation barely concealed. "I see you're taking a real interest in this case. What exactly are you doing out here?"

"You two know each other?" she inserted.

"Oh yeah," smiled Francis, "Detective LaRocca has been over to my place in the city. He's even used my commode and made friends with my parakeet. Ask him."

LaRocca didn't find this amusing at all. "I'll ask you to stop what you're doing and step out to the street. I want to have a word with you in private."

"Should I turn off my tape recorder?"

"That would be preferable."

"Kidding," said Francis. He looked at the girl, raised one eyebrow. "Well, *Cosmo* girl, thanks for the swell conversation. Be seeing you ... oh, hey, what's your name?"

"Eve," she answered.

Again, out in the street, LaRocca asked Francis what he was

doing. Francis told him the truth. LaRocca asked him why he was getting involved in a capital murder case that's under active investigation. Francis said he didn't have anything better to do. LaRocca admonished him some more, saying he had damn well better let the officers of the law do what they're being paid to do. Then he asked him what had he learned in his half-assed attempt at playing detective this day. That not everyone is a good egg, Francis informed.

"You bring a notebook? Let me see it," he said.

"I don't think so," countered Francis.

"How about that license plate, the one you couldn't remember? Did that come to you yet?"

"No, man, and I'm sincere about that. I'm not holding back. I have tried and tried to remember. I even arranged letters on paper, moved them around, different combinations like a word puzzle you see in the funny papers. Hey, I'm trying to remember but it's foggy. It won't come to me. Sorry."

The request to the Department of Revenue had come back with a list of 19 Dodge Challengers with vanity plates, and this was statewide. It was a full blown, multi-jurisdictional investigation tracking down all of the owners, interviewing them, establishing whereabouts on the day of the murder. It could take a couple of months.

"I see," said LaRocca dubiously. He came in closer and sniffed at his person, theatrically, a sort of comic pantomime which very much alarmed Francis. "Is that booze I smell on your breath? You been drinking?"

"I might've had one at lunch. Other than that, no."

"Bullshit," said LaRocca, walking the six feet from where they stood over to Francis' ride, sticking his head in the open window. He leaned way in and came out with two cans of Busch, the 24- ounce Tallboys Francis had bought earlier and drained en route. "You really should dispose of your empties," a sly grin forming on his otherwise dour face, "these things can get you in trouble."

"Hey, I—"

"Unh, uh," LaRocca waving an index finger at him, "Don't interrupt."

"I'm listening."

He set the Tallboys on the pavement. "I really want to know that plate, it's what's keeping us from wrapping this thing up. A capital crime committed in a respectable community, and we can't find the killer? Really? People are starting to talk, starting to think the Jefferson County Sheriff Department are the fucking Keystone Cops. So I want you to search your brain and visualize that plate that you saw on the suspect's car. You can do it. Right here, right now."

"I've tried."

"Not hard enough," cop eyes drilling into him. "I'll ask you one more time."

"It's no use, I just can't."

"You know, it's lucky that I'm driving a squad car today. My Continental is in the shop, busted side mirror."

"That's lucky?"

"Yeah, because the squad car has a cage that separates the arresting office from the prisoner in the back seat." Taking out the cuffs, "You have the right to remain silent. Anything you say can and will be used against you ..."

— 13 —

FRANCIS WAS NOT WITHOUT A LOVE LIFE. Besides the very occasional one-night stand, he had a woman over on The Hill, what some would call a love interest. He had met Janie Ventimiglia on one of those Walks For A Cure in Forest Park, a fundraiser for MS or MD, Francis couldn't recall which, except that his Aunt Nan had conscripted him for the day. In those kinds of events, groups of walkers mingle with other walkers, and common cause camaraderie happens. Francis found himself walking long stretches with Janie and her friends, enjoying the morning, the exercise, the friendly banter. But most of all he enjoyed watching this lovely woman strolling along, long wavy black hair flouncing with each athletic stride, great calves and thighs, good health just radiating off her. She worked at an ad agency in the city, wrote copy for car dealers and supermarkets. She had a Boston Terrier named Vito, who was back at the apartment just now because he didn't do well in crowds of people. They got near the finish, almost three miles of getting-to-know-you, and she mentioned that there was a coffee shop in her neighborhood where she liked to go before work, a great place, and would he like to join her there some bright morning? Love to, said Francis, electric with anticipation, feeling like he was back in grade school when Mary Pat Noonan slipped him a note with little Xs and Os on it.

It wasn't a courtship, it was more like hanging out with someone you really like except that at some point—be it a corner booth in some quaint *ristorante* on The Hill or on the water in a paddleboat rented from The Boathouse in Forest Park—they would stop talking and make out heavily. She thought him a fine specimen of a man. Stalwart, handsome, brave. He thought she would have liked his mother. They found they had several important things in common. A love of Italian food, number one. A penchant for movies found in the THRILLERS aisle of the local Blockbuster. And a firm belief that men and women should not cohabitate, a testimony to the old saw that familiarity breeds contempt. But spending the night once or twice a month was all right.

So these simple enjoyments came together one Thursday morning in mid-September when Janie called with a proposal.

"There's this movie, *Manhunter*, I rented from the video store. It's got a cunning serial killer, a forensic investigator with the FBI, another serial killer—a cannibal!—in prison and orchestrating events. It's right up our alley. I'm making *tortellini en brodo* for two—my nana's recipe—and I'd like to pop the movie in around seven. How's about you bring the wine and join me?"

"Oh darn, I've got yoga class this evening."

"Yeah, right, yoga for barflies. Try to touch your toes with a beer bottle. Dinner and a movie and who knows what later on. What do you say, Bonzo?"

"You talked me into it."

"Oh, and bring a couple bottles, both red and white. We'll see which goes best with tortellini."

"Why does his name have to be Francis? That sucks. I mean, look at him. He looks like a guy who'd eat light bulbs for breakfast. Come on." Francis and Janie were nestled on the couch, his arm around her, she leaning into him. Except for the poor choice of the character's name it was a good movie. William Peterson played the FBI profiler Will Graham, who is scratching his head for much of the movie trying to figure out what these murdered families had in common with each other. It's driving him nuts. Brian Cox plays the diabolical serial killer Hannibal Lektor who, during his free-roaming bloodlust days, had nearly done Graham in. Today, Lektor is a prisoner, no less devious even behind bars, and he has found a way to communicate with the Tooth Fairy, the dark moniker given to the current Psycho du Jour that the FBI is striving to locate.

Now it was near the end, a real nail-biter. Francis Dollarhyde a.k.a. the Tooth Fairy works in a St. Louis film-processing lab. The fact that he is big and scary-looking is lost on blind coworker Reba whom he offers a ride home. Instead they go to Dollarhyde's place where Reba is oblivious to him watching home movies of his next victims. They kiss and have sex which confuses Dollarhyde—until now his pathetic life devoid of affection—and spares Reba from a bad end. But that will come another day, for Francis just has to kill somebody every so often.

"Don't the blind have extra-sensory perception?" asked Janie. "Can't she tell that he's he sicko just by osmosis or something?"

"She's caught up in the moment," offered Francis, "probably hasn't gotten any for a blue moon."

"So she's just grateful for getting laid, she can't think beyond that, huh?"

"Yeah, maybe."

"Men. Sheesh."

In a sudden revelation, Graham knows the connection between the murdered families: someone has seen their home movies. In fact, Dollarhyde has been casing the victim's homes by way of remote viewing. He then goes to the city or town where they live and does his terrible thing.

Graham and associates deduce where the films were processed, and fly to St. Louis post-haste. There was a shot of them landing at Lambert International.

"This freak lives in St. Louis!" exclaimed Francis.

En route, on the plane, Graham sifts through a list of film lab employees and finds one that matches the profile they've developed. He gets Dollarhyde's home address. From Lambert they rush to his home where Francis holds Reba, whom he has abducted. A shot shows them on I-70 crossing the Missouri River into neighboring St. Charles County.

The FBI agents meet local police at the house, which is somewhat secluded. The scenes go back and forth from what's going on outside, police surrounding the house, and what's happening inside, Francis about to kill Reba. Ominous music plays as Francis strives to overcome his feelings for Reba so that he can do her like the cold-blooded killer he is. It is a very tense moment. As the law closes in on Francis Dollarhyde, the music, gothic in tone, swelling in volume, strikes a chord with Francis Lenihan.

"I know that song," Francis said. "It's uh … um—"

"Iron Butterfly. 'In-A-Gadda-Da-Vida,'" said Janie. "Now shush, all hell's about to break loose."

"That's it! That's it! The plate I saw. The killer. That's his plate."

She hit the remote, stopped the movie in mid-scene, Graham crashing through a plate glass window. She looked at Francis and saw exhilaration. "This is big, whatever it is. I get it, but can you wait a couple minutes until the credits roll?"

"Yeah, sure. God, I'm glad you chose this movie."

With a flick of the remote, the action resumed. Graham completing his launch through the window into the Tooth Fairy's living room. A gun battle ensues, two cops are killed, and Crawford, Graham's partner, is wounded. Dollarhyde is shot and killed by Graham. Reba is shaken but unharmed. Vows never to date any more creepy coworkers. The end.

Janie swirled the last of the Merlot in her glass, made it disappear. She said, "I'll think twice before using any more film labs, you know? Strangers see your personal stuff, get weird ideas. Ick. Now what were you saying about some plates?"

The next morning Francis was up early. He never slept soundly in Janie's bed anyway, his feet sticking out over the frame at the foot. She got up with him and made him breakfast. It was way early for her, but they sat there at her little dinette near a window, both aglow from having coupled the night before, and watched the sun come up on a new day. Janie studied the man across from her, asking herself what was so special about him. The answer did not lend itself to linear thinking. Brown wavy hair that fell halfway to his shoulders, full lips, Roman nose, hazel eyes that twinkled. Francis was handsome but that wasn't it, although it didn't hurt. Francis was unpretentious, a straight-shooter, perpetually disheveled, a bit goofy, but overall a good-natured, regular guy. To Janie, Francis was a pillar of dependability, and come what may Francis would always be Francis. His unaffected simplicity had the effect of grounding the network of complex thoughts and feelings that was Janie.

Francis looked at Janie, carefully spreading orange marmalade on her toast. He felt lucky that she let him in her life. He liked the arrangement they had and hoped he wouldn't do anything to screw it up. This one was a good one.

She kissed him goodbye. He thanked her for the nice dinner, and promised to take her out before long. He drove straight to his office and sat at his desk, phone in front of him. At 8:01 he called the Department of Revenue in Jefferson City. If you called any time after, say, nine, you'd be put on a queue, holding until the twenty people ahead of you were taken care of. But now he heard the call go straight through to a real live clerk.

"Department of Revenue," she confirmed in a nice enough voice, "how may I help you?"

"I'm a process server in St. Louis with a security access code. I'd like to get the name and address of the owner of a vehicle. Someone

I'm trying to serve. I have the plate." She asked for his code and the name associated with the code. He complied.

Half a minute later he heard, "Okay, what is the license plate?"

"It's a vanity," he told her. "Innagada, spelled N-A-G-A-D-A."

"Nuh-gadda? Sounds Japanese."

"No, it's a song title. Iron Butterfly. The sixties. Heavy metal."

"Spell it again, please."

"N as in Nancy, A as in apple, G as in, uh ... gadget—no, make that gizmo—A as in apple, D as in dictaphone, A as in Andy as in Amos n' Andy." Click-clack click-clack, her fingers at the keyboard one hundred thirty miles away.

"Okay, I have it. The plates go to one Clarence L. Jackson with an address of 5870 Elm Springs Road, Dittmer, Missouri."

Bingo.

"Does it say what sort of car it is?"

"I thought you knew that."

"No ... well, I may know that, but I want to be sure."

"Sure, you want all the information you can legally get. That particular plate goes to a 1974 Dodge Challenger."

"White racing stripe down the middle?"

"My records don't have that sort of detail, sir."

Francis thanked her and hung up. He sat there drumming his fingertips on the desk. He lit a smoke, contemplating, a feeling of trepidation coming over him. A random encounter, a violent crime, a killer at large, and he being sucked in to it all. Now, a turn in events, an opportunity to act, to actually do something about it. Was he up to it?

Before Dogtown there was Kerry Patch, the original St. Louis enclave of Irish-American culture. From the mid-19th Century to the 1920s, no area was more celebrated for the beauty of its churches and the spirit of its people than this neighborhood northwest of Downtown. Now it is difficult to picture among the warehouses, apartment projects, and weed-filled vacant lots the close-knit Irish colony with its houses shoulder to shoulder, the lace-curtained windows looking out on gas-lit streets, the corner taverns, the dance halls, the meeting rooms of fraternal societies, and more.

But as the Irish dispersed throughout the metro area, a successor to Kerry Patch arose south of Forest Park. First known by the grand name of Cheltenham, because of a nearby clay quarry which put many a fellow to work, the area became known as Dogtown, a not-so-obvious elevated plat bounded by McCausland, Oakland, Hampton and Manchester. There are two theories as to how the colorful moniker originated. One, espoused by Red Rush, has it that the name Dogtown stems from the St. Louis 1904 World's Fair when poor Irish squatters living in makeshift shanties in Forest Park were forced by the Fair to move, and chose the neighboring lands across the highway to make their new home. But how does that explain the name? Just use your imagination, Red would say.

Another explanation found in the small, handsomely-bound *A History Of Dogtown* put out by the Dogtown Historical Society also has to do with the 1904 World's Fair, when the city hosted the centennial celebration of the Louisiana Purchase. On the fairgrounds that summer were an aboriginal band of Phillipines, the Igorots. One of the mainstays of the Igorot diet was dog. Legend has it that these pygmies, as the Igorots were mistakenly called, would make clandestine forays into the nearest settlement and snatch dogs for their cooking pot. Perhaps one or two of them were caught in the act and beaten half-senseless by a shillelagh-wielding denizen, who knows? But it is a fact that the Igorots got their canine victuals, whether they had to steal them in the cloak of darkness or whether the Mayor's office requisitioned them from the dog pound and had them delivered as a token of American goodwill.

Just as Kerry Patch had its architectural gem, the church of St. Lawrence O'Toole, so the pride of Dogtown is the parish school and church of St. James the Greater, whose slender copper spire lords over the neighborhood from the summit of a hill. Until some thirty years ago, every pastor of the parish had been born on Irish soil and it is not a falsehood to claim that much of the spirit of Dogtownians derives from the stout Hibernian piety of these stalwart and outspoken leaders, men as ready to pronounce on social and political matters as on things spiritual.

Fr. Russell Eagan, pastor of St. James, was one of these, stoop-shouldered, beetle-browed, crabbed with age, piercing blue eyes, wiry white hair not only dusting his balding pate but protruding from nostrils and ears as well. A man steeped in Roman Catholic canon, a patient man not given to rash decisions, a man eager to bestow common sense guidance to anyone who asked, a man adept at delivering mediocre sermons fraught with platitudes and cliches, a man who never took for granted his exalted position in the community, a man who could hoist a pint at the local pub with the best of them.

Many years ago, Eagan had said some unfortunate things at Martin Lenihan's funeral and Francis never really forgave him. He didn't hate the old priest. He would go to mass and take communion from him, but he would not let Eagan hear his confession.

Francis made a practice of going to confession about twice a year, time to let the sins build up. Maybe he didn't totally believe in an afterlife or the existence of a deity that cares about our puny lives—although he dearly wanted to—but he did believe that there was such a thing as sin, which was merely being aware of one's moral transgressions. And really, he reasoned, unless you're amoral, you have to deal with your wrongdoings one way or another. You could get drunk, you could punch a wall, you could pay a shrink a small fortune. Or, if your religion provides, you can go to confession. The poor man's psychotherapy.

Francis always felt better upon leaving the confessional. If anyone had asked him why he felt relieved, he would have said that his soul had been cleansed, would have repeated the analogy that both his mother and Sr. Thomasina used, likening his post-confession soul to freshly washed linen hanging on the line. How had his soul been cleansed? By virtue of expunging guilt and remorse from his psyche and starting afresh. Like a pressure valve on a steam boiler, otherwise virtuous people need a vent for their misdeeds.

Penance was the currency of absolution. With Catholics it is saying a chain of Hail Marys and Our Fathers even after they have become rote and the meaning in danger of being lost. Some, Francis included, even thought the penances today on the light side. He remembered from fifth grade religion class, Fr. Garrigan telling them that during the Middle Ages it was not uncommon for people to go to confession once, preferably toward the end of their lives, and they would get these massive penances that went on and on. Sometimes they had to beg for alms in front of the church, or wear a sack cloth and roll in ashes. Or they went on a pilgrimage like the characters in Geoffrey Chaucer's *Canterbury Tales*. There was some teeth to those penances, Francis mused.

This day, an overcast afternoon in September, Francis found himself near St. John Nepomuk on Bohemian Hill, south of downtown. He parked the Escort on the street, climbed the steps, and rang the rectory bell. The door opened and Fr. John Benda appeared. "Francis, the sight of you brings me cheer," he said. "Come in, come in."

Fr. John was in his late forties, five-foot-nine, stocky in build, with a crop of dark curly hair. He had an athleticism about him that brought to mind a high school football coach who once played the game. He wore, from top to bottom, a black poplin short sleeve shirt, white collar showing, brown leather belt holding up khaki slacks, brown leather loafers. Born and raised in Cleveland, he had entered the priesthood in 1973 at the age of twenty-six. After a stint at Villanova teaching ethics, he'd switched horses and accepted an invitation to come to St. Louis to oversee this beautiful old church, which had stopped being an active parish many years before and was now officially designated a chapel, although there were still masses and baptisms, weddings and funerals. It was a good fit, him being assigned here. Fr. John was Czech on both sides, and St. John Nepomuk was the patron saint of Bohemia, martyred by drowning in the Vitava River at the behest of Wenceslaus, King of the Romans and Bohemia, because John, or *Jan*, had heard the confession of the king's wife.

The priest lived here alone, and had a secretary to help out during the day. Francis had met Fr. John at Soulard Farmer's Market one Saturday morning, both of them having a desire for locally grown tomatoes, ripe and bursting with flavor. They struck up a conversation. That was two summers ago, and now here he was.

"Time to unburden," Francis said. "Please, do you have time?"

"Theresa," he called to someone in the other room. "I'll be upstairs if you need me."

"Okay, Father," came the reply, "all's well on my end."

Fr. John led the way up a winding staircase to the choir loft. They took a pew facing one another, illumined only by the opaque light coming through the stunningly beautiful stained glass windows depicting saints with halos and scenes from the scriptures. None of this confessing to a silhouette behind a veiled screen.

It was just them, but still he whispered, "Bless me Father, for I have sinned. It has been … how long has it been?"

"About six months, I think."

"A half-year since my last confession."

Fr. John looked at him expectantly. "Any time you're ready."

Francis looked the priest in the eye, ready to take the plunge. "There's a lot, you know. This might take a while. Could I just box it all up and say that besides murder, rape, child abuse and sodomy—anything else, you name it, I've done it."

"No," said Father, "I'd like a more detailed account."

"All right," said Francis, "I guess I'll lead off with the venials. Well, um, I've been stealing my neighbor's newspaper. It's morning, still dark. You can picture it. I'm out heading for the bakery to get my coffee and long john, and there it is, lying on the lawn, just delivered, rolled up in yellow plastic. Free for the taking."

"They do cost fifty cents."

"Right. I know it's petty. I know it's wrong, but I also know that the reason I'm taking it has less to do with getting a free paper and more to do with wanting to punish these neighbors."

"Punish them? Why?"

"Because a preacher and his wife live there. They have a church and food pantry over on Berthold, ministering to the poor and yet they live like kings. I was in there once, neighborhood block party, open doors up and down the street, the place looked like the centerfold from *Better Homes and Gardens*. They were serving steak tartar on Bremner Wafers, none of this food pantry crap. The both of them smiling and just so very fine, living in luxury while their congregation, if you can call it that, sit in their tenements with the heat and water turned off. Shameful, you ask me. I think that's why I steal their newspaper."

Fr. John regarded him, the trace of a smile on his lips. He turned away and put his hand over his mouth. Was he chuckling or coughing? He turned back, that sage look beaming through. He said, "You know, Francis, we all have to live our lives within the structure of our own conscience and these people are probably well aware of their fortunate position. If a condition of, shall we say, hypocrisy exists between the mission of their ministry and their upscale lifestyle at home then they will have to come to terms with that. It isn't right for you to do that for them. Taking their newspaper is one thing, passing judgment on them is another. Do you think you could stop doing both?"

"Sure, I'll try," said Francis. Okay, next thing. Ready?"

"Shoot."

"I put a potato in the tailpipe of this guy's car, a guy who pushed me off his porch when I was trying to serve him a summons. I came back later, just shoved it in there."

"What does that do?"

"The car can't get compression. It won't start and he won't know why."

Fr. John shook his head dubiously. "That's a prank, not actually a sin."

"Really? I've got to start coming to confession more often."

Father agreed. "Next."

Francis went on to whisper his sins to the the priest, the times he'd lied to this one and made fun of that one—in his mind, anyway.

How he'd tendered a five at the market and gotten change back for a ten and didn't correct the cashier, just pocketed the ill-gotten funds. How he'd snuck into the Mojo Nixon show—the side door when security wasn't looking—instead of going through the front and paying the five buck cover like everyone else. The impure thoughts he'd experienced at seeing certain women, imagining them naked and he naked with them. Some of these lustful longings were even directed at married women while he was attending mass. There was more. How he'd made a glutton of himself with chips and dip late one night after coming home from the bar. The whole bag gone in ten minutes. And speaking of bars, he'd drank to excess at least one hundred and sixty times since his last confession.

"How can you be so exact?" asked Fr. John.

Francis stroked his chin, said, "Well, you said it's been a half-year, which is like one-hundred eighty-two days, so if I'm in the bar nearly every day, which I am, and what with people carrying on and buying drinks and me not wanting to leave until I feel that rosy glow. So, take away about twenty days that either I couldn't get to the bar because I was on a stake-out or the bars were closed for holidays or I was laid up with the flu or something and you end up with one-hundred sixty. See?"

"You're imbibing every day, that's what you're saying?"

"Yeah, I made a vow years ago that I would do my best to get to a bar every day, have a drink or six. I feel at ease in bars."

"Hangovers?"

"Oh yeah, and some a lot worse than others. I've learned not to mix certain drinks. Beer with whiskey is all right, but beer with wine—Sneaky Pete it's called—that's a killer. I stay away from that. Same with vodka and gin. I leave those to the hard drinkers, the guys whose faces look like they've been scrubbing pots."

"Saint Bibiana," said the priest.

"Yeah? She some drunk in the bible?"

"She's the patroness of hangovers. You could pray to her to ease your suffering the day after."

"Or I could chug a pint of Alka-Seltzer, jump in the shower—

hot, full blast—then the final leg of the regimen: coffee, toast, eggs, and aspirin."

"If you consider this excess a sin," said Fr. John, "and you're an alcoholic, I don't suppose you'll be drinking in moderation any time soon."

"No, Father. I like it too much."

"Well, in that case, I hope you have a strong liver. Okay, what else?"

"Uh, well, there is this thing that's been on my mind. It's not a sin because I haven't acted on it. Just mulling it over but I'm in a quandary, you see." He paused. The choir loft profoundly silent.

"Yes, yes, go on," encouraged Father.

"Yeah, well, it seems … um, what happened is that I accidentally got caught up in a murder investigation. I was on my way to serve a paper in some remote area, and I was almost there, in this subdivision, when I ran into a guy leaving the scene, a guy who had to be the killer. Only I didn't know that someone had just been murdered or that he was the one. So we talked for a minute and he tried to tell me not to go to the house, that the lady was out of town. But of course I had to try anyway, I'd driven all that way. So, like the guy had said, no answer. I left my card on the door, hoping she'd call and we'd arrange a time. Next thing I know there's two uniforms at my door, asking me all kinds of questions. Not threatening me with anything, just trying to learn what I saw that day."

"And you cooperated fully?" asked the priest.

"Yeah, I told them everything, physical description, what he said, everything except the guy's license plate which I couldn't remember. And, boy, were they pissed—upset, I mean—they really wanted that plate. It's the key to finding the killer." Francis looked to Fr. John, assessing his reaction thus far. Attentive was the word for it.

"Okay, so where does the conflict come in?"

"This happened three weeks ago. I didn't remember then, but now I do. I have what the police want and I'm balking at giving it to them. Not sure why, except … I don't know, maybe it's because I've been hired to find the killer myself."

"Oh, I see," said Fr. John. "Yes, that's a serious problem, both from an ethical standpoint and a legal one. You know that withholding evidence is a crime?"

"Yeah, and I definitely don't want to go to jail. No such thing as happy hour there."

The priest gave a light chuckle, said, "This person who hired you, would he or she be just as satisfied if the police were to bring this killer to justice as opposed to you doing it on your own? Possibly risking grave danger along the way. In other words, the end result would be the same, yes?"

"Well, yeah, but she hired me, the dead woman's daughter, and she gave me a down payment. I feel like I owe it to her to see it through. Once I start a job, it's like I have to finish it. I don't have a choice, the thing's been decided for me."

"That's called monomania," said the priest, "an unhealthy preoccupation with one thing, or, in your case, a series of things. The jobs you take on. You say you *have to* finish it. Actually, you really don't have to. It's okay to let go of this, relinquish control. How much have you done so far? No matter, you have to tell yourself it's okay to turn over the reins. There's plenty of other cases that need your attention."

Francis listened intently at Fr. John's heartfelt delivery, nodding in understanding as the priest spoke. In turn, Fr. John read Francis' body language, receptive, and felt that he'd gotten through to him.

"I don't know," said Francis, scratching his scalp. "What you say makes sense, but my brain is sort of contrary and doesn't always like things that make sense."

"Understood," said Fr. John. "you'll have to ponder this at length until you arrive at a sensible decision. It is no small matter, and, in a way, this is a crucible for you, a test of your mettle, your honor, your integrity. Few people have an opportunity to make such a monumental decision. I will pray for you, that you're up to the task."

"Okay, all right then," said Francis. "I feel better now. I'm ready for my penance."

"I absolve you of all sins confessed. Just reflect on what we've talked about here," directed Fr. John.

"I will, but could I still get some Hail Marys and Our Fathers?"

"How many would you like?"

"Better load me up, I've got lots of dirty linen to wash clean."

Francis concluded with an Act of Contrition while Fr. John sat there musing about something. As they rose to leave, the priest said, "Have you been to this bar over near the farmer's market? The Gold Rush it's called. They have a heck of a happy hour, buck-fifty pints, free peanuts in the shell. And the bartender, she wears this loose low-cut sweatshirt and every time she bends down to get something from the cooler," he winked—"let's just say the Lord was kind to this one."

"Sounds great! Let's go."

"Any day after four," he answered. "Just call me a half-hour in advance."

— 15 —

"IF ONLY YOU KNEW how much I detest that notion, you would not have asked the question," said Francis to a pimply-faced kid in the third row. It was 10:30 on a Tuesday, and Francis had the floor. Having delivered a twenty-minute talk on A Day In The Life Of A Process Server to the students in Shirley Yount's Legal Systems in American Society class, he was now in the Q and A segment. The kid squirmed in his seat and Francis wished he hadn't been so harsh. It was just a question, after all—an annoying question based on ignorance of the real world, but a question nevertheless.

Until now he had answered their previous questions with sincerity and good humor, questions like Do you ever wear disguises and do they work? Answer: No, I'm too lazy to bother with disguises and, besides, my normal everyday wardrobe is a disguise. He modeled his thrift store attire for the class—baggy cargo shorts, hiking boots, beige wool socks, gray T-shirt with green lettering that said

GIRL SCOUTS OF AMERICA. Do I look like a process server to you? he queried. They laughed.

Back to the thing that had him flustered. "Sorry," said Francis to the class as a whole, "that came out more critical than intended. I guess this is what you call a hot button issue with me. And I'd like to know where this actually started, the idea that the client doesn't have to pay if the process server doesn't get the paper served. That's ridiculous on several levels. One, tons more work goes into the paper that *did not* get served than the one that did, say, on the first or second try. That difficult paper often becomes an investigation right off the bat. The person doesn't live there, the occupant never heard of him or her. Then, there are certain things I can do to try to find the defendant or witness—not a lot of things, but they are time-consuming and a pain in the butt. Or, the person to be served has a weird schedule and I just can't seem to catch him at home or work. Or, they know you're trying to serve them and they're avoiding you, not answering the door or having someone else tell you that they're out of town for a month. So, you see, we have to get paid for trying. I've had papers that got served at the very last minute. After what amounted to banging my head on the wall for a couple weeks, I got a break, caught the guy in the yard or something like that."

"Plumbers, carpenters, mechanics all guarantee their work," interjected a doe-eyed girl in the front row. The insinuation being he was not up to their standards.

Francis gave an exasperated sigh. "That's different, can't you see that? Those guys are working with concrete, identifiable problems that can be fixed and if they cannot be fixed the tradesman will say so and replace the problem part. Their work is cut-and-dried. Ours is definitely not. We're dealing with human beings, not malfunctioning parts, and human beings have a knack of throwing the proverbial monkey wrench into the works. Listen, this is one profession where failure and frustration are built in to the job. That's right, as I said earlier, you learn to deal with constant disappointment and try not to let it get to you."

He saw Joe Lennon in his security officer uniform slip through the door and take an empty seat in the last row. Joe gave him a small wave. Francis nodded back. He was feeling the need for a cigarette and hoping that Joe would soon join him.

"What happens if the summons doesn't get served?" asked the pimply-face kid.

"What do you think happens?" asked Francis.

"You get another one and try again?"

"Right-o. All these papers have deadlines, as I said, and if the deadline passes without the summons being served, the lawyer can apply for what's called an Alias Summons. But before the lawyer does that, he or she will talk to the client and discuss if it's worth the extra money. Whether they decide to continue the effort depends on how 'getable' they think the defendant is. And that's what we're known for, Specials, going the extra mile, serving those who are hard to get to. Some process servers will tell you that anyone can be served if you throw enough money at it. It may mean hours of surveillance, sitting in your car staring at a door, or following someone in traffic, maybe hiring two process servers. The bill could come to a thousand bucks—although I've never turned in a bill even close to that—and *still* you may not have gotten service. But keep in mind, the case doesn't move forward, isn't engaged, until that summons is served. Can't stress that enough. Lawyers will say, You've *got to* get this guy served. And I'll give it my very best try, pulling out that old adage, Where there's a will there's a way. It's a cliché, but it's true."

Shirley Yount in a pretty blue dress, entered stage left. "I think that about does it for today," she announced in her classroom voice. "Please give Mr. Lenihan a round of applause and head to your next class. Don't forget to study chapter six, there's a test on Friday."

Francis took a slight bow, thanked Shirley, and headed to the back of the room. "Bravo," said Joe, grinning.

"You should've heard their reaction when I told them I served Liza Minelli backstage at the Fox Theater."

"Wow! For real? Is that true?"

"Nah. Let's go outside."

Joe blew a series of small smoke rings in the still morning air, his jaw snapping with each one. You could tell he really enjoyed smoking. "So how 'bout it, man? You said you'd take me out, a ride-along, that was like weeks ago." Joe was direct like that. He waited for an answer.

"I did say that and I will," said Francis, dragging on his cig. They were standing on a veranda that overlooked the campus quad, students going to and fro like so many ants on a log. "Fact, I've got something this afternoon, I could use your company. It's out in the boonies. I need to do some checking, don't know what I'll encounter. It's so different than the city. I don't expect any trouble, but you never know."

"Aw jeez! I'd love to go, you know that, but I can't just leave work. Besides we're short a guy today. Can't you go tomorrow or better yet, the next day? I can get off with one day's notice. Sound good?"

"Nah, I've got it in my head to do this today. There'll be other times, brother. We'll do it, promise."

Joe ground out his smoke on the concrete. "I'm holding you to it, man."

Francis punched him playfully on the arm. "It's as good as done. You'll see."

Early afternoon he set out for the tiny burg of Dittmer, which had no center just a few buildings nestled on the south side of the two-lane Highway 30. There was a gas station with a soda and ice machine, an accountant's office which advertised tax preparation, a barber shop with an American flag on the porch, and a tow garage with a twenty-foot metal man wielding a sledgehammer stationed out front. Someone's sculpture. And that was Dittmer.

He did not buy beer for the trip like the last time he'd come out this way. The time a couple weeks back when that detective rudely cuffed him and basically abducted him because he couldn't give him the information he wanted. LaRocca—stupid name, thought Francis, sounds like some sort of *bon bon*—LaRocca had pulled a bluff on him, tried to make him think he was being arrested for

DUI when in fact he was just screwing with him. What he did, he drove to a crossroads about four miles from where he'd picked him up, where he uncuffed him and let him out, saying how he can walk back to his car and sober up along the way. Francis wasn't used to walking such distances; it took him two hours to get back.

From Dittmer he turned on Highway J and headed in a south-westerly direction for five miles or so and then came to Sawmill Road, followed that another two miles, mostly woods, but here and there fenced-in pastures, cows munching on a green, rolling carpet. He came to a T and it was Elm Springs Road. He glanced at the directions he'd scribbled earlier. Left or right? There were damn few homes out this way. He tried right and about a mile down the road he figured the addresses were going up when he needed them to go down. He did a Y-turn and backtracked.

As he neared the destination, he felt his pulse quicken. He had courage, loads of it, and it had been tested time and time again. But this was out in nowhereland. Bad shit could happen out here and no one would know. If Clarence Jackson was home, either alone or with friends, it would be his ass for the kicking. He didn't even have a good plan in the event he'd come face to face with Jackson. He wasn't skilled at being cagey, couldn't think up any convincing story to mask the real reason why he'd driven out here. And besides, this Clarence Jackson would probably recall him from their brief encounter that day in the subdivision. He was half-hoping the guy wouldn't be home.

As announced by the falling-off-its-post mailbox, 5870 was a dirt driveway leading about one-hundred yards back to a decrepit filthy trailer with a veneer of sick-looking gray-green mold or maybe moss. He parked, got out. Total silence. The place dredged up feelings of every bad dream he'd ever had. Empty beer cans all around and several sets of antlers strewn about. Over there, a carcass of some animal, headless, ribcage exposed. Deer it looked to be. Off to the side of the side of the trailer, two cars, busted headlights, flat tires, one with the hood up, weeds growing up through the engine block. He ascended the rusted step ladder that led to the door. He knocked, knowing no answer would come.

The door was slightly ajar, and he opened it a bit more, peeked in. What a mess. He pivoted and scanned the premises for any movement, signs of life. Nothing. He went in.

It smelled weird, rancid garbage and cooking oil layered with something else. He stood there looking around, trying to think what he might find and where it might be in this pig pen. He kicked at the junk on the floor, making a path to the rear, the kitchenette and sleeping area.

Flies buzzing in the late-summer heat. He studied the countertops, the table where Clarence ate, food and utensils laying out, Francis sensing that nothing here had been disturbed for some time. An ashtray with Virginia Slims butts. A newspaper dated August 29th. Calendar on the wall with a notation ST. FRANCOIS COUNTY RACEWAY jotted over Labor Day Weekend. He turned to the drawers beneath the countertop next to the sink with the pile of dirty dishes. He opened the first, utensils and more utensils. Then he heard a tiny sound, a movement, a faint scratching, coming from the next drawer over. Definitely something in there. He quickly pulled open the drawer and a mouse jumped out, fell to the floor.

"AHHHH!" He watched the creature scamper off, and then felt foolish. If you're that scared of a tiny mouse, chiding himself, what will you do when Clarence comes back?

He went over to the unmade single bed, grungy sheets exposed. He saw a small notebook on the nightstand, spiral-bound, pocket sized. He picked it up, began reading. At least the guy had decent handwriting. It was a list, a reminder of things to be done. At the top was TIRE ROTATION, followed by PLUMBING SUPPLY – 2" PIPE, CLAMPS, BALL VALVES followed by GET WITH DEKE, followed by FRESH MART – ZUCCHINI, MELONS, TOMATOES, OKRA. Deke, huh. Now, we're getting somewhere. He pocketed the notebook, and returned to the dining area.

A minute later he heard voices. He went to the window, saw two guys approaching, boots and jeans and T-shirts and hair, one with a Red Man ball cap and one holding what looked to be a pipe, gleaming, two feet long. Their car was parked about twenty-five yards back, probably the point at which they saw his car. They'd blocked him in, and now they were coming to call.

"Jesus, Mary, and Joseph," he whispered and he went out, back down the step ladder to meet them, mind racing for an explanation. He and they stood about ten feet apart, the space between them thick with tension.

"Howdy," the one with the pipe called. Tall, lanky, unshaven, dark hair in a ponytail halfway to his ass, Charles "Slim" Westermann could have passed for one of the Manson Family.

"Howdy back," said Francis.

"What y'all doin' here?" said the other, a Harry Dean Stanton lookalike, working his jaw like a cow chewing cud. Orel Flowers Jr.— "June"—was an assembly mechanic at the wire factory in Doe Run. He made sixteen dollars an hour and spent much of it on meth.

Here it is, thought Francis, right now. It's going to go one way or the other. "Uh, I was in the area and I thought I'd see if Clarence was home."

"Clarence?" Harry Dean guffawed. "Who calls him Clarence?"

"Ain't nobody calls him Clarence," drawled the other. "You two must be real good friends, you call him by his given name and go into his trailer without an invite."

They moved in closer, menace written all over them. "Say what?" from Harry Dean, head cocked, palm cupped over one ear.

He said, "Would you guys excuse me for a minute, I have to go to my car."

"And why's that, you fucking thief?" the tall man pointing his way with the pipe.

"Uh, heartburn, burritos for lunch. I need my Tums."

"Oh, I think that can wait," tall man grinning nastily, slapping the pipe into his open palm. "We gonna have us a party first, and you're the guest of honor."

Uh-oh.

"Look fellas, you can believe me or not believe me, but I was only seeing if Clarence was around. I never took anything, didn't mess with anything. Now, I've got to get going. Good meeting you."

Harry Dean twisted his mouth into a sneer. "You're a lyin' sack of shit. You oughta know better 'n that. Lyin' gets you in trouble. Ain't that right, Slim?"

"Fuckin-A right," nodded Slim, moving the pipe from side to side in front of him. "Stoney goes missing for three weeks and now this dickweed shows up, sayin' he's a friend when we know who Stoney's friends are and you ain't one of 'em."

"Okay, jeez, you got me," Francis, palms out in appeasement. "I wasn't going to bring it up because it's, you know, on the sly, but Deke sent me. Asked me to fetch Clarence—Stoney—to him."

Harry Dean snorted derisively. "Bullshit! Why would Deke send a fuckwad like you?"

"Because I'm trustworthy, trustworthy and reliable."

"Who the hell is Deke?" asked Slim.

"Later," said Harry Dean.

From the side of his mouth Harry Dean jettisoned a brown sluice to the dirt. "Okay, Mister Reliable. Take out your wallet, let's see who you are."

"That's right," said Francis, holding out a hand for the shaking. "We haven't been properly introduced. I'm … outta here!" He made a mad dash for his car, but he had to get through them. Harry Dean grabbed him by the shirt and spun him around. He took a swing, a roundhouse looping in from the side, but Francis ducked easily and tried to run again. Slim had flanked him and came in fast, grabbing him from behind. He put the pipe around Francis' neck, and with elbows out he started to tighten the hold with both hands, building pressure on his throat. In one horrifying moment Francis saw the life being taken from him. He reached up behind him and grabbed for something, anything. Nostrils, he had his fingers in the guy's nostrils and he dug them in as far as they'd go and then he dug them in some more. He yanked outward with everything he had. Slim yowled, dropped the pipe.

Francis went to grab the pipe when a fist slammed into his jaw.

He tasted blood. Harry Dean picked up the pipe and tossed it to his partner, six feet away, massaging his nose, whimpering. Slim wasn't ready and the pipe hit him in the face with a *thunk*.

"Damn you!" roared Slim to either Harry Dean or Francis or both.

Francis knew the flight part of the fight or flight option was closed. He kicked hard and caught Harry Dean on the knee and he buckled. Now it was his turn to yell, but he had enough fight in him to lunge for Francis. He had him around the ankles, and Francis went down kicking like hell at Harry Dean's head and shoulders, the Red Man cap flying away. Francis got loose, rolled away, and sprang to his feet. Harry Dean still on the ground about to get up, but where was Slim? Something moved in his peripheral vision. He spun fast, blocked the pipe's arc with his forearm. Slim, eyes wide, face bloodied, was swinging hard and throwing himself off balance.

Francis, playing a desperate game of hopscotch, trying to avoid the blows, managed to say something. "Why don't you put that thing down and fight fair."

Slim halted in mid-swing. "Oh, I like that. Fight fair. Round here fair's whatever you kin get away with."

Francis took this opportunity to turn on Slim, punching him first on the point of his chin and then mashing the heel of his palm upward to connect with the man's already tender nose. Slim dropped the pipe, let out an agonized groan, but a second later managed to grab Francis and take him to the ground. The two rolled over and over, trading punches, thrashing wildly. He got hold of Slim's pony-tail and yanked hard a few times, Slim's head jerking like an epileptic marionette. "No, you—don't *do* that!" cried Slim.

"No such thing as a fair fight," Francis reminded.

Then, Francis got free and had just gotten his legs under him when he felt this incredible white pain in his flank.

"Take that, motherfucker." Harry Dean.

"*Unhh!*" he cried, clutching his side, and then another blow, this time on the left shoulder. By now, Slim was back and together they made short work of Francis—pipe blow to the torso and then, after he was prostrate and helpless, choice kicks to the upper body and head.

"Take his wallet," said Slim, breathing heavily from the exertion. Harry Dean rolled Francis over and took the wallet from the back pocket of his shorts. Francis moaned, gasped for breath, tried to spit the dirt out of his mouth. He gathered himself as best he could, propped himself up with one elbow, wondering what now.

They both stood over him, hunters posing with their fallen prey. "Well, looky here," said Slim, holding up a driver's license. "Francis X. Lenihan, age thirty-six, 6410 West Park Avenue, St. Louie, Missouri. A city boy! How 'bout that? We love city boys out this way, ain't that right, June?"

"Love to fuck with 'em," answered June with the side of his mouth, brown spittle dribbling out.

Slim hunkered down so he was more on Francis' level. "How 'bout it, boy, you love having the shit kicked outta you?"

Wincing at the sparks in his side, Francis managed a half-grin. "I've always been told that I was full of shit, guess you guys took care of that."

"Guy's a comedian, even now," said June.

Slim nudged Francis with a kick to his leg. "Damn your ass. I'm outta patience. You wanna tell us what you're doing out here, skulking around my buddy's trailer?"

Francis wiped at the blood on his face, no clue where it was leaking from. "I told you, man, Deke sent me. Shit, what do I have to do, swear it on an affidavit?" His cracked ribs protested as he took a shallow breath. "And don't think he won't be royally pissed when he finds out how you guys treated me." The effort of trying to talk was just too much right now. He rested the back of his head on the ground and closed his eyes.

Slim stood up, shook his head in disgust. "Oh, for fuck's sake, this guy's pathetic." He checked the wallet for anything else. "What's this? Department of Veterans Affairs Medical ID, got your name and address but no picture." He snapped his fingers. "Hey, I just might need me some medical attention at the VA hospital someday." He put the card in his back pocket. Then, he flung the driver's license off in the weeds and tossed Francis' wallet on the ground beside him.

To June, "We know his address if we want to talk with him later on. Let's just go."

They turned to leave when June said, "Hold up, one more for good measure." He walked over and gave Francis a walloping kick in the balls. "Thanks for your service, man."

Fifteen minutes later, long minutes of contemplating the damage inflicted on his body and waiting for his testicles to find peace, he stood and limped over to his car. He could barely walk and he found he couldn't use his left arm at all; it just hung useless at his side. He slid into the driver's seat, got his key in the ignition, turned it over. With his right hand he lifted his left hand up on the steering wheel. He sat there with the engine idling, feeling about as foolish as he had ever felt, coming out here, taking no precautions—what's the sense of carrying a baseball bat if you don't have it when you need it?—and voluntarily letting himself in for a world of hurt. He lit a smoke, took a good long drag. "Nothing like getting clobbered on a Tuesday afternoon," he said to the dashboard. He uttered similar recriminations for a while longer and then examined himself in the side rear-view. He clenched his teeth and showed them to the mirror. Blood-stained they were, and lips starting to swell. He looked like a chimp that had walked into a wall. He worked his jaw to see if it was out of set. He tested a couple teeth that might have been loosened, wiggling them slightly. Seemed all right. He smiled at himself in the small mirror, a grimace passing for a smile. "Hey, handsome, you're looking good today."

He shifted the Escort into reverse and backed out, his left arm practically useless. It was a long drive home.

"Look at the state of you!" called Red Rush to the sight of an obviously battered Francis bumping through the door and hobbling across the floor. It was around five o' clock and the joint was buzzing with activity. Red's exclamation got everyone's attention and all eyes were on Francis as he moved to the rail and called for a Guinness. They gathered round as he stood on unsteady legs, and they waited in growing suspense to find out what had happened. Red Rush, however, remained on his stool at the elbow of the bar, watching the thing unfold.

On the return back, Francis had stopped at the first convenience mart he'd seen and bought a half-pint of Jim Beam, the only whiskey they had. By now the "medicine" was working and the pain was at a nearly tolerable plateau.

"A bus," someone said. "He's been hit by a bus. Reckless maniacs! How many times have I said that those drivers are an accident just waiting to happen?"

"No," asserted another, "he's been in a fight, can't you tell? Look at his clothes, torn. His face caked with blood and swelling up as we speak. Probably got knots on his noggin that we can't even see. That it, Francis, you been fighting?"

Tommy brought Francis a shot of single malt while the pour was in progress. It takes a while to execute a perfect pour of Guinness and the thoughtful barkeep didn't want Francis to go without. Francis took it in his right hand, held it up. "Sláinte," he pronounced, and downed it solemnly.

He looked around at the faces, saw the concern, the curiosity. "Yeah," he said, softly, "it was a fight, and one that I certainly didn't ask for," his speech noticeably thick. "They outnumbered me and they had weapons, but I summoned the lion within, and, well ... you should see the other guys!"

"Really?" they asked, hopeful.

"No, actually I got my ass handed to me. Those suckers don't think nothing of kicking a guy when he's down. I mean, literally."

His Guinness came, he drank, wiped the foam from his lips. Tommy handed him a clean towel, run with warm water from the sink. Francis began to dab at the blood on his face. "I can't remember the last time I got into a fight," he shared, "probably army boot camp with this farm boy from Kentucky. It was Sunday, and some of us were going to mass. This guy took offense to Catholics, said we worship a monkey in Rome—"

"Aw, go on," said one.

Francis raised an eyebrow. "Hard to believe, I know, but they're out there."

"What religion were these guys, the ones who beat you? Protestants, I'll bet."

"Hey, watch it!"

"Heathen, I suppose. Look, here's the thing, I've never thought of myself as tough. I've often joked—you've heard me—that I fight with my hat. If there's trouble, I put it on and leave."

"But you don't wear hats, Francis," frowned one fellow.

"It's a whatchamacallit," declared another, "a figger of speech."

"I think it's a metaphor," clarified a fellow with a flat cap, "like the hat is a, uh, um—what was Ghandi?"

"Indian dude, looked like the ninety-seven pound weakling in the Charles Atlas ads," offered another barfly.

"No, pacifist, he was a pacifist," insisted flat cap. "So the hat is a pacifist and whoever wears it is one, too." Several barflies nodded understandingly.

Francis shook his head, dubiously. "I'm just saying it's not like me to be throwing punches with some yokels in the boonies. From now on I'm gonna stay right here in the city where the natives are restless, to be sure, but you know what you're up against."

"And where you've got a posse to back you up," proclaimed Red from his stool. The gathered all voiced affirmation at this. Red slapped the bar top in front of him. "Come down here, boy. Let's have a look at you."

Francis limped down there and the others followed. Somewhat

clinically, Red looked him over, Francis standing there, feeling fool-ish. "Where's it hurt?" asked the old hooligan.

"Here," said Francis, stroking his ribcage, "got hit with a pipe. And here," he added, touching the shoulder above. "Same pipe."

"You need to get to the ER," declared Red, "the sooner the better. Today, if you can walk outta here. Cracked or broken ribs can mean puncture to the lungs, damage to other organs, some of 'em impor-tant. I know, I've broken many ribs in my career"—he gave a wink—"not my own, mind you."

Francis nodded agreement. "Who am I to ignore the doctor's ad-vice? I'll do it tomorrow, a fun way to pass the time with a five alarm hangover."

Red got serious then. "Who did this to you, boy?"

"I don't know who they are. Two guys who came up on me while I was snooping in someone else's business. It was my risk to take," he admitted sheepishly, "I knew things could get dicey when I went there."

"Breaking and entering?" queried Red, hopefully.

"The door was open, no one around."

"Find what you were looking for?"

"Yeah, matter of fact, I did. A clue to a mystery."

"Ah. Does this have something to do with that poor woman mur-dered out in Cedar Hill?"

"How did—"

"You were there that day, on the job, the coppers came here to the neighborhood to question you. Everyone knows about it."

"That's right," echoed someone in the background.

"We know you didn't do it," injected another.

"You have any idea how to find these devils?" Red, rubbing his paws together. "We'd like to call on them, stuff their heads into their assholes.

"I don't feel so hot," said Francis, swaying, a wave of nausea pass-ing through him, holding onto the bar to keep from falling. Some-one grabbed him by the armpits and sat him in a chair.

"What can we do for you, boy?" asked Red.

Francis leaned over and puked on the floor. He sat back up, looking at everyone looking at him. "Call Janie," he said. "I'll give you the number. Tell her I need her to come over and tuck me in."

— 17 —

"OHHH ... OOOH," FRANCIS EMITTED A LONG, PITIFUL MOAN as wakeful consciousness greeted him in a landslide of misery. His brain throbbed, and there was a deep ache in his shoulder. His ribs, his thorax, well, not so terribly bad until he had to breathe. He gazed around without turning his head. At least he was in his own bed, and Janie there beside him. "Aspirin," he croaked.

Janie opened her eyes. Her arm reached over and lightly caressed his furry belly. It felt nice. "Today is the worst," she said, "after this it'll get better little by little."

"Right now, I can't imagine better. I'm stuck in 'worse'. Even my hair hurts."

"I'm your nurse," she told him. "I took the day off. Whatever you need, I'm here. You want to go to the hospital, I'll take you. You want to stay put, just rest, I'll tend to your needs."

"You're an angel."

She rolled over, got up. She wore red panties and that was all. He was in his birthday suit. "Be right back," she said, and padded down the hall. He heard the sound of a toilet flush, some pots being rattled in the kitchen, a tea kettle whistling. He got up, made his way to the bathroom. His pee tinged the water pink, a bit disconcerting. Soon she was back with a tray of sustenance—coffee, buttered toast, a sliced apple, and a glass of water. "You must be out of peanut butter," she said.

She held an opened container of aspirin, shook it, took out two. "Unh-uh," he said. "Four."

She propped him up at the headboard, pillows at his back. She lay there at his side, watching him eat, toast crumbs falling onto his chest. "You always slurp your coffee like that?" she asked.

"Only when I have an audience."

His left eye was partly shut, discolored, a nice shiner coming on. Fat lower lip, too. "You look like Rocky after Apollo Creed got done with him," she said.

"Then you must be Adrienne."

"Nurse Adrienne to you."

He set the tray on the nightstand nearby. Having her in bed with him, all but nude, had the effect of making him forget his injuries. "All right, let's get this over with."

"Get what over with?"

He smiled impishly. "Aren't you going to examine me?"

"Your poor testicles," she said, " all swollen, and look! One of them lower than the other."

"It's supposed to be that way," he said.

"Still," she said, "it looks painful." He was lying flat on the mattress, hands clasped behind his head because it felt better that way.

"What about this thing here? Is this all right?" She stroked his thing and it sprang to action.

"Yikes, it's alive!" She arched her eyebrows a few times, Groucho Marx style, and went down on him, head bobbing, eagerly taking in the length of him. This went on a for a minute or two while Francis moaned, although not from pain.

She came up for air. "Feel better?"

"Is this part of my therapy?"

"Wanna see what's next?" She slipped off her red panties and straddled him, her breasts like grapefruits but not yellow or bumpy, practically staring him in the face.

"I don't think I can be on top," he cautioned.

"No worries, I got you covered," and slowly, tantalizingly she lowered herself onto him.

They spent the day watching TV and pigging out on snacks. Janie went to the market and bought peanuts and corn for popping, chips and dip, cheese and crackers, beer and soda. She gave Francis a light massage and a hot bath afterwards. He worked his shoulder, slowly, by small increments, not too much at a time, trying to improve the range of motion. It would take weeks, if not months for it to get back to baseline. She spoke with her cousin, a nurse at Alexian Brothers, and learned about treating cracked ribs; it was mostly about what you shouldn't do. She went home to get ACE wraps and some of those adhesive heat patches and to check on Vito, her terrier. She rustled up the makings for *pasta carbonara* and returned to Francis' apartment. Francis was teaching Petey the parakeet a new trick, to circle the room twice and then land on his head for a treat.

Around 4:15, as they sat to dinner, the phone rang. Janie brought the phone to him. It was Joe Lennon. "Hey man, thanks for getting back to me. What I called about, you've wanted to come along, see how I do things. Learn the ropes, yeah?"

"You know it, brother."

"Well, yesterday, after we talked, I got hurt. Nothing to cry over, but driving is going to be a challenge for a while and I'm wondering if you'd be so kind as to chauffeur me around serving papers."

"Yeah, sounds good. I've got some time off coming, I'll put in for it right now."

"Knew I could count on you. Okay then, get here by eight, we'll get some coffee and head out."

"Thanks, brother, you won't regret it. See you then."

Francis hung up. He ruminated momentarily. His was a solo operation, from knocking on strange doors to ferreting out wily defendants avoiding service to typing up bills and affidavits, but in times of trouble like this it was a real boon to have back-up. Good to have friends. I'm lucky all around, he thought, and he went back to his pasta.

"WATCH OUT FOR THAT VAN!" Francis cried as Joe easily veered around a floral delivery van double-parked in their lane.

"Are you going to stop driving from the passenger seat or do I need to put you in the trunk?"

"Yeah, sorry, I'm just not used to being driven. It's kind of ... I don't know, perplexing or humiliating, something like that."

"You got two days to get used to it, you'll manage," said Joe. They had been in Joe's Camaro for less than a half-hour, Joe turning down Francis' offer of his Escort, dismissing the old school stick shift as "too much frigging work." Just as well, since this was a good time for Phelim to tear out the transmission, restore that pesky second gear.

They were heading to the Southside down around Carondelet Park. First stop, a summons and petition to be served on one Kent Koehler, involved in a car accident.

"This guy know it's coming, the papers we're going to give him?"

"I doubt it," said Francis, "the accident was five years ago."

"What? Really? How come it's just being served now?"

Francis took a drag on his Marlboro, exhaled thoughtfully. "It is a curiosity why some of these papers are so delayed. Years after the incident, you think it's all behind you, then there's a knock at your door, 'Hello, Mr. Defendant, the person you hit long ago has decided to get a lawyer and sue you for damages, and as luck would have it they filed the lawsuit just under the deadline before the statute of limitations ran out.'"

"That would suck," said Joe. "Won't the guy's insurance take care of it?"

"Maybe they did pay out something at the time it happened, but the plaintiff and his sharp lawyer will claim that it wasn't near enough, new ailments are popping up, quality of life is diminishing to the point of despair, and now, years later, the other driver is still on the hook, and has to pay through the nose."

"These claims are all backed up by doctors and medical charts, right? I mean, the victim can't just say, 'Oh, I threw my back out. Oh, these migraines—must be the result of that car accident way back when.'"

"Take a right on Bates," said Francis, referencing the *Wunnenberg's* in his lap, "then up three blocks to Leona. To answer your question: these lawyers are very good at drafting petitions that would convince anyone that their client is a pitiful invalid because of the defendant's careless driving. Here's an example, listen to this, you'll get a good laugh." He turned to page two of the petition, began reading, " 'That as a direct and proximate result of the carelessness, negligence and recklessness of the defendant, plaintiff sustained injuries to her back and neck, chest, left arm and left leg, that she suffered headaches, and all the muscles, ligaments, tendons and nerves associated with the parts of her body which were injured were caused to be severely bruised, contused, lacerated, torn, sprained, strained, dislocated and rendered swollen and inflamed, and that—' "

"Oh, my god!" said Joe, laughing like hell, "get this woman a wheelchair." Joe kept on laughing, wiping tears from his eyes, and Francis started laughing, too. "That's hilarious," said Joe, "you don't think this lawyer's exaggerating the situation, do you?"

"I think they teach this sort of thing in law school, Creative Exaggeration One-Oh-One. But there's more ... 'and that the function of all the said areas of plaintiff's body are impaired and diminished, and all of plaintiff's injuries and the effects and results thereof are permanent and progressive, that any pre-existing injuries and conditions are now aggravated and intensified, that Plaintiff is now more susceptible to injury in the future as the parts of her body that have been injured and damaged are now weaker and more susceptible to injury and that her ability to enjoy life as she did before this collision has been impaired and reduced.' And there you have it," he concluded, "the magic words that'll put the plaintiff on Easy Street for a while."

"Put me on the jury," said Joe, still chuckling, "I'll award her a million bucks. Too bad she's only got a few weeks to live."

"I think the ceiling is twenty-five grand," said Francis. "Here we are, Leona. Fifty-three ten should be a few doors up. They parked in front of the red brick bungalow, the front door open halfway on a balmy September morning. "That's a good sign," said Francis, "someone's there." Joe got out first and came around to Francis' side. He took the papers from Francis as Francis climbed out gingerly, using the top of the door frame as a handrail. It was just two days after the beating and he was still quite stiff and sore. Together they strode up the walkway leading to the door. Joe wore jeans, penny loafers, and a rugby jersey; Francis, cargo shorts, Converse sneakers, and a REO Speedwagon 1987 Summer Tour T. They looked more like a couple guys looking for yard work than they did process servers.

"I'll do the talking," said Francis as he rapped at the door. An elderly man with white bushy hair and thick black eyebrows came to the door, a small yapping dog at his feet. "Mr. Koehler? I'm a process server and I have—"

"Just a moment," rasped the man. He couldn't have been a day under eighty-five. "Just wait here, Trixie," he said to the dog as he stepped out on the small concrete porch and shut the door behind him. He looked up at Joe and Francis, both towering over him. "All right, go ahead," he said. "What is it about?"

"We're process servers," explained Francis, "and we have a summons for you. It involves a car accident you were in a few years ago." Koehler was astonished at this news, but he took the papers willingly. He began reading the summons and then the complaint, making *tsk-tsk* sounds. Joe and Francis stood there, waiting out of politeness more than anything else.

"Actually, our job is done," said Francis. "We're the delivery boys, you might say, and the summons has been delivered. Have a nice day, Mr. Koehler," and they began to walk down the steps of the porch."

"Don't I have to sign anything?" asked Koehler.

"No, that's not necessary," said Joe, "we know who you are."

Francis gave him a look. "How did you know that's exactly what I would've said?"

"Can I tell you something?" the old man asked.

"Sure."

"This accident, it wasn't any more than a fender bender, hardly even that. I was in the supermarket parking lot, starting to back out of my space when this person in the space behind me had apparently already started to back out. Our bumpers bumped, we weren't even moving faster than a walk!" He shook his head in dismay, held up the summons theatrically. "It's impossible that she could have suffered such injuries listed here. From that puny mishap—impossible!"

Francis had seen it countless times, the delayed reaction of anger and scorn that often comes with being served an unexpected lawsuit. "We feel for you," said Francis for lack of anything else to say.

"Where to now, boss?" asked Joe back in the car.

"Downtown," replied Francis, "subpoena to the board of education, and then up north, a protection order to a jilted lover. Then, finally, a summons over on Portland Place in the West End. I'm not going to ask you how you like it, not yet, because the day is still fresh."

"I think my answer would be the same now as it would be at three o' clock," said Joe, pulling out from the curb. "I like it fine. It's interesting, getting to see how people react, driving to all different parts of town, not knowing what you'll find."

"Hurdling obstacles all the time," added Francis, "having to think on your feet, having to make snap judgment calls, some of them the wrong call."

"Like what?"

"The biggest one I can think of is the decision to go ahead and serve someone even though they're telling you they're not who you're looking for. And you get that all the time, people saying, 'He don't live here, he moved away,' or 'That's my cousin, man, he stay over on Hodiamont. No, I don't know the address. Red brick house, you can't miss it.' Anything to throw off the process server, right? Sometimes I have a description of the character, could be a sketchy description but sometimes there's a hunch to go with it."

"A hunch, yeah, like a sixth sense."

"That's right, like this one dude out front of the house, he's working on a car in the street. Only information I have is black male, mid to late twenties. That fits this guy working on his car. I talk with him, show him the papers, he's delinquent on child support. Only I got the wrong guy. The guy I want is a friend of his sister's, comes around every so often. But I notice two things: the guy is very interested in what these papers are about, that, and he has two big eyes tattooed on the back of his neck. I know that the baby mama would be able to confirm or deny that the deadbeat dad has these markings, so I serve him under protest and walk away, him cursing me out. Our counterparts, the deputy sheriffs who serve papers, wouldn't have done that, they're always going to err on the side of caution. But the special, every now and then he takes a calculated risk despite rule number one, that the one thing you don't want to do is serve the wrong guy and say it was the right guy."

"Well, did your hunch play out right?"

"It did," said Francis. "I got the number of the petitioner, called her and told her about the eyes. She said, 'Yep, that's him all right. He likes to say he's got eyes in the back of his head, and now he can prove it.' Now, if my hunch had been wrong, I wouldn't have called it good service. I would've talked to the lawyer and I'd've gotten another copy of the papers and kept on looking. You see?"

"Yeah," said Joe. "You weren't going to let that asswipe get over on you."

"I guess you could put it that way. Head down Bates and jump on the Interstate north, okay?"

Joe glanced over at Francis, watching some kids in a schoolyard play kickball. "You ever think about getting on with the sheriff department?"

"I could if I wanted. I've got a buddy in administration there, he'd like to see me come on board, but I like being the Lone Ranger, making my own hours, no supervisor to report to. What a drag that'd be. And besides, that polyester beige uniform would make me look frumpy."

"My work uniform is beige," said Joe. "No one ever called me frumpy."

"It's just a matter of time," Francis sallied.

"Yeah, yeah. So ... you gonna talk about what happened now, or are you still being secretive?"

"Hmm? Oh, the story behind my injuries? Just a little misunderstanding in a backwoods setting, two against one, and no cavalry on the way. You ever been beaten with a lead pipe? It leaves some pretty bruises. I got bruises on top of bruises—you wanna count 'em?"

"You're allowed to carry but you choose not to," Joe frowning, "wouldn't this beat-down qualify as a good reason to change your mind about that?"

"Maybe so, but I still can't feel comfortable, natural, carrying around a loaded piece. And if it's in my glove compartment while I'm knocking at a door and suddenly I need it ..." trailing off.

"I'd love to carry a weapon on my job, but they won't let us, saying it would intimidate the students. So they keep the rifles and handguns under lock and key. Bunch of liberal morons."

"I've got my ammonia-filled squirt gun," he said, "what do I need a gun for?"

"A squirt gun. That'll have them running for cover."

Francis coaxed a Marlboro from his pack, lit it, adjusted his position, groaning again while stroking his side. Joe looked over. "Ribs hurt, huh? I ever tell you I broke a guy's ribs?"

"You? In a fight were you?"

"Nah, some guy in the campus cafeteria had a pork chop stuck in his throat. I tried to do the Heimlich ... WWF style."

Francis laughed, then winced, said, "Please don't make me laugh."

"I know," said Joe, "I'm such a card. Hey, why is it that I never hear you curse or swear? Just curious. Like you could've said, 'Just a little misunderstanding between me and some fucking asshole hillbillies who thought to wail on me.' Did your ma wash out your mouth with soap one too many times when you were a kid?"

Francis smiled. "No, not my mom. It was Sr. Thomasina. She said that profanity is the effort of a feeble mind trying to express itself forcibly. I took that saying to heart, that's all it is."

"Sr. Thomasina, huh? She was before my time. We had Sr. Bernadette, the queen of corporal punishment. Any infraction of the rules, and there were many, she'd make you kneel in the hallway outside the classroom, that marble floor just doing a number on your knees."

Francis, warming to the subject, "Oh, I pulled that punishment a few times, and if you dare to complain they tell you to give it up, your suffering, give it up for the poor souls in purgatory."

They got on 55 North, headed for downtown. Joe had the radio set to some classic rock station. "Money For Nothing" came on, and Joe turned it full volume, singing along. "The little faggot with the earring and the make-up ..." slapping the dashboard, keeping time, " .. that little *faggot* got his own jet airplane, that little *faggot* he's a millionaire." Joe looked to Francis, big grin, now pretending like he was holding a mic, and really belting it out. "We gotta move these refrigerators, we gotta move these color TVees." Francis having fun, too, watching this goofball ham it up.

"Damn! I love that song, how they get to say 'faggot' on the radio," said Joe when it was over, but before he could finish "Dreamweaver" come on and he shut it down. "And I hate that one," he said. "Hey, did you hear about the two Irish queers?"

"They met at Dairy Queen?" guessed Francis.

"Hah, good try. No, the two Irish queers, you know 'em. Tom Fitzpatrick and Patrick Fits Tom." Francis began to laugh and, again, it woke up the pain in his side, a reminder of his infirmity and why he was in the passenger seat. "I asked you, man. Laughing's great, but not right now."

"I've got lots of jokes, most of 'em dirty," Joe went on, "if you want a way to pass the time."

"Don't tell them all at once or they'll lose their effect."

"Some of them are really sick, you probably don't wanna hear those."

"Why not?"

"Because you're wholesome, so it seems. Virtuous, maybe devout even. You're not a sick joke kind of guy."

"You'd be surprised," said Francis. "You didn't know me when I was in high school and after that. Loved to raise hell—drinking, vandalizing, racing down on Hall Street, maniacs behind the wheel, running all night. Hoodlum in training. It was so much fun I had to join the army to get away from it all. But you're right about the sick jokes. Even back then I didn't care for them."

"We both go to mass," offered Joe. "I guess there's some hope for salvation." Francis was silent. "That's sarcasm," he added, "I'm just making conversation."

"Mass is all right," Francis remarked, "you pay attention, which, I admit, is hard sometimes with Fr. Eagan's monotone, pay attention and some of that stuff rubs off on you, maybe cause you to become a better person."

"You know why I go? Claire Delaney. She attends on Tuesdays and I'm trying to get close to her. Sometimes we sit together in the pew. If no one's nearby, no prying eyes, I'll put my hand up her dress."

"You do not!"

"Well, maybe not. But I can have fantasies, can't I?"

"Horndog." Francis shaking his head, chuckling.

"So, here's a question," said Joe. "If you walked up to a hundred women on the street, random women between, say, twenty and forty, and you asked them this one question: Would you like to have sex with me? How many do you think would say yes?"

Francis stroked his chin. "I think it would make a big difference where you are. If you're at a outdoor music festival with plenty of trees and bushes around, the answer might be ten or even twenty. If you're out in Clayton with all the pretty secretaries at lunchtime, the answer might be closer to zero. But you'd be red-faced by the time you're done."

"From embarrassment?"

"No, from being slapped silly by all the women who took offense at your solicitation."

"Oh, bunch of prudes out there, huh? I think if you presented yourself as a cool dude and you came on confident and charming and asked real polite-like, not like you're begging or anything, you could score with at least a half-dozen."

"A half dozen women who'd go to bed with a total stranger just because he asked nicely?"

"Why not? Men are always horny, that's a known fact. Women are the same way, they want it—need it—just like we do. You just have to find the key to unlock their initial reluctance."

"Look at you," said Francis, "Doctor Ruth."

"I know you get your pipes cleaned every so often, who's the lucky girl?"

Francis shot back, "Go ahead, keep egging me on, I'll give you a wedgie at our next stop."

There was a backup in traffic as they approached downtown. Joe took the time to light a smoke. "Come on, we're guys. We can talk like this. Me, I've got this girl over on Berthold, lives with her brother. The brother works second shift at Chrysler so I go there after work, we got the place to ourselves. I'll bring a bottle of wine, MD Twenty Twenty or some other fancy label, just to impress her, you know? And before that bottle's gone we've gotten down to it. I mean, every which way—"

"Wait, what about Claire Delaney? Isn't she in the picture.?"

Joe looked hurt. "Yeah, of course she's still in the picture, but I'm saving myself for *her*. So this other girl, Joyce, we're like what you call fuck buddies, and, as I say, we're doing it six ways from Sunday but, get this, she won't let me in the old snatcheroo. Stroke jobs, blowjobs, even up the back chute, that's all right. But no vaginal penetration, that's her rule."

"Yeah, okay, a bit strange, I'll admit. She'll take you to paradise but leave you at the gate. So, what is it? What's her deal?"

Joe blew a cloud of smoke out the window. "To have regular sex she'd have to use a contraceptive like a diaphragm or the Pill or else I'd wear a rubber. But we can't use contraceptives because— you're not gonna believe this—because the church says birth control is a sin."

They served a subpoena at the board of education, academic and disciplinary records on a student, a pawn in a bitter divorce. They had to wait around for the in-house counsel to get out of a meeting. When the lawyer finally came out, looking like one of those Farrakhan followers who hawk newspapers in the middle of busy intersections, he examined the subpoena most carefully, all four pages of it, and declared that he would accept it.

From there they headed to the Northside, an order of protection to a guy who wasn't ready to break up with his girlfriend. They drove up West Florissant to Natural Bridge and on up to Harris, the homes getting more and more ramshackle, some actually succumbing to gravity, crumbling and falling down. Then they were in the busier neighborhoods, stores and shops, people out and about, waiting for buses, standing on corners. It was just after ten. They came to a stop sign and there was a girl, about twenty, brown as a walnut, short shorts, tube top, high heels, standing in the entrance of a chop suey joint that had not yet opened. She was eating Vienna Sausage from the can with her fingers. She stopped, licked a finger, and gave them the once-over.

"Look, she's licking her lips at us," said Joe.

"Very observant, Sherlock. That's their new thing," said Francis, "their come-on. It's a lot more subtle than flagging down cars the way they used to."

"So that's what a hooker looks like. I'll be damned. You don't see any of those in Dogtown. This is great!" Joe gave her a friendly honk: *beep beep.* He leaned toward the open window where Francis sat and called out, "Show us what you got." The girl looked this way and that, see if anyone was watching, then she lifted her tube top and presented a pair of hefty boobs, more long than round. She shimmied just a little so they jiggled with a life of their own.

"*Woooo-eeee!*" cried Joe. "Nice rack. Ain't that a helluva rack, Francis?"

"Not bad," said Francis back.

She nestled her boobs back into their sling, and sashayed the twenty feet to the Camaro. She hunkered down and looked inside, palms on her thighs, looking for something to go on. She said, "You guys cops?"

Joe jumped on this. "Us? Heck no. I mean, *hell* no. We're process servers. Just out for a drive."

A car behind them gave an annoyed blast of the horn. Joe waved him around.

The driver pulled up, a black guy with dreads, taking in all three of them, shaking his head, sadly. "Stupid white boys in the city," he said, "go back to your big lawns and Walmarts. All this black pussy gonna do is give you the clap."

Joe turned to Francis. "You think that's true?"

They watched the driver pull away. Then, the hooker, impatient, said, "I gave you the opening act, you wanna see the rest of the show?"

"She's asking," said Joe to Francis or maybe himself. "This is the part where I say 'How much?'"

"I don't like the sound of this," said the girl, backing away, "sounds like a trap."

"No, no," called Joe. "Come back, I might be interested." She stood there three feet away, trying to decide if these guys were vice or just unschooled in streetwalker protocol.

"Just drive," said Francis.

"She's not bad looking. How much you think she wants?"

Francis rolled his eyes. "Are you gonna drive?"

Joe got out his wallet. She was still looking, eyeing them with suspicion. He waved a bill at her. "Here's a ten," he called loudly enough for any pedestrian to hear, "what'll you do for a ten?" The girl about-faced and walked off, high heels clicking on the sidewalk.

"Now will you go?" asked Francis.

"It could've been beautiful," lamented Joe.

They found Lamar Bedford, the respondent on the Order of Protection, sitting on the stoop in front of his crib. He was smoking a joint and talking on a cordless phone. "I come to you," he was saying, "it ain't no big thing. You just be sure you got the product weighed and bagged up ..." He saw their shadows before he heard their voices. "Gotta go, blood," he told the cordless, "call you back in a flash."

He flicked the roach off into some shrubs. "S'up?" he said, rising. He wore baggy shorts with lots of pockets and a black nylon tank top. Hair done in corn rows and a gold front tooth glinting in the sun.

"Hey Lamar," said Francis standing before him, Joe off to the side, "we're process servers with the city courts with some important documents to hand you."

Lamar frowned mightily. "What it be?"

"Here, take a look," and he held out the sheaf of papers.

Lamar hesitated, then he accepted the papers. He studied the face of the document, big bold letters PROTECTION ORDER AND JUDGMENT. He recognized his own name and that of the petitioner. He guffawed. "What she sayin'?" he asked. "Whatever it is, it's bullshit." He pronounced it "bool-*shit*."

"I didn't read it," Francis said, "but you should. And look, here's a court date. She's alleging that you did this or that, but right now it's only her word. You have a chance to go before a judge and tell your side. Meantime you're to stay away from her, got it?"

Lamar showed off his gold with an insincere smile. "Shee-it, you think this piece of paper gonna keep me away from that girl? That be the day."

"That's on you," said Francis. "You violate this order and they take you into custody."

"Just so you know," chimed Joe.

"Wouldn't be the first time," said Lamar. He held up the cordless, there was business at hand. "We done here?"

Now they were heading to the toney Central West End—sidewalk cafes, art galleries, fashion-conscious boulevardiers, cops with mousse in their hair, buskers, plein air painters, housewife joggers pushing Land's End strollers. Some said Euclid Avenue and Maryland Plaza reminded them of Baltimore; others said New Orleans. Joe, oblivious to the genteel surroundings, was still going on about the hooker back there.

"Where do you think she would've taken me, you know, to get it on?"

"Probably some nearby trash-filled alley where you'd step on a nail and end up in the ER waiting for a tetanus shot."

"Jeez, man, you don't need to be so negative."

"And you don't need to pretend that she's the hottest thing since Madonna in her boosti-ay."

"Madonna? Yuk! Hey, did you ever get offered sex from some hot chick in trade for your services? You told me that some of your papers come directly from, like, regular people, and not always the lawyers. I mean, it's not crazy to imagine some woman saying, I'll do you, Big Boy, in return for serving my no-good future ex-husband. That ever happen?"

"No," said Francis, "but I have had several come to the door in just their underwear or with really scanty attire, usually rubbing the sleep out of their eyes. You make a lot of calls early in the morning, that happens."

"And you didn't take advantage of that?" asked Joe.

"Lose my license for a wham-bam-thank you, ma'am? I don't think so. Most of them, I averted my eyes. They weren't remotely sexy."

The last stop was Portland Place, two long blocks of fabulous turn-of-the century homes on a private tree-lined street across from the landmark Chase Hotel on Kingshighway. The private watchman from the security company marking time in his patrol car eyed them as they drove past; Francis nodded. The sum total of wealth on this street alone was probably enough to run a small country like Lichtenstein for a decade. "One thing you'll find about this job," Francis was saying as they rolled up to the gray mansion with the carriage house in back, "is how amazingly diverse the experiences are. I mean, in the span of a half hour, you go from urban decay to the lap of luxury, from the hovels of the have-nots to the palaces of the have-all-they-wants."

"Yeah, I'm taking it all in right now. So what'd this person do that we're serving him?"

"Contracted with some company to come out and put in shades and blinds and now he won't pay. I guess even the wealthy aren't above stiffing the working man."

"Especially the wealthy," put in Joe.

Joe came around to get the door for Francis, help him with that first step out. "What's this guy's name?" asked Joe as they walked up to the expansive front porch with hanging ferns and a pair of stone lions guarding the entrance.

"Edward James Tarkington, no description, nothing else to go on. Just a name."

"Well, Eddie, prepare to meet Joe and Francis, your friendly process servers."

Joe helped Francis up the tile mosaic steps. Francis rang the bell. They could hear it inside, chimes going off. Nothing. Joe lifted the big brass knocker on the door, let it thunk on its plate. Joe pointed to a closed-circuit lens positioned over and to the side of the door, pointing right at them.

"Smile, you're on Candid Camera," said Joe.

"Who is it?" asked a high falsetto in sing-song fashion. The voice surprised them because nobody was around. "I said who is it?" the falsetto again.

"It's coming from this intercom," said Francis, pointing to a little rectangular box on the wall nearby. He pushed speaker button. "Hello?"

"Hello yourself," said the fey voice, somewhat flirtatiously.

"It's a put on," said Joe, "the guy's putting us on!"

"Uh, we're here on your porch, process servers with a summons for Edward Tarkington. Could you send him down, please?"

"Edward is indisposed," the voice replied.

"I can't keep talking to the wall," said Francis, "will you please come to the door so we can talk in person?"

"I don't think that would be a good idea," the voice cracking just a little.

"Why not?" asked Francis.

"I'm not decent," said the voice.

Now Joe intervened, hitting the talk button. "Ed, why don't you cut the crap and come out here and take your papers like a man."

"But I'm not a man," assured the falsetto voice, "I'm the cleaning lady, Beatrice."

"Open this door, right now!" demanded Joe, anger flashing.

"Or what?" wondered the voice. "Will you huff and puff and break it down? Are you big bad wolves?"

"You get your ass down here now!"

Francis edged him away from the intercom, said, "Unh-uh. We can't do that. It's still America, we can't make them open their door." Joe turned his back on this admonishment. He lit a smoke and stared off somewhere.

"Have it your way," Francis told anonymous, "today you win. But we'll be back, again and again, as many times as it takes. You can't hide forever, you're as good as served." He waited for a cute reply but none came.

As they walked back to the car, feeling played, Joe said, "I hate intercoms."

"Yeah, well," said Francis, "there's always tomorrow."

"That asswipe is in there right now, watching us walk away with our tails between our legs. He's laughing at us, Francis, hooting it up at our expense. I'd love to punch his lights out."

"I hear you, Joe. It's aggravating as can be. But it does happen, people knowing that if they don't come to the door then they won't get served." Still walking, he put a consoling hand on Joe's shoulder. "All I can say is you can't take it personal." Francis felt the hypocrite inside him exulting, for he did take it personal and vowed he would get that weasel Edward Tarkington no matter what.

— 19 —

Grunts emanated from the bathroom stall, the guttural
sounds of animals rutting. But these animals were human and
though they were rutting no offspring would ever come of it. The
stall was one of four at a rest stop on Highway WW, just south of
Grubville. It was maintained by the Big River Saddle Club and it
had several amenities that other rest stops lacked such as double-ply
toilet paper and hooks for the hanging of garments. Two men in one
stall, one bent over with his pants on the floor beside him, legs apart,
both palms braced against the rim of the toilet bowl, head partway
in the bowl so that his long hair nearly touched the water. The other
stood behind him. He had removed his pants as well, and he was
earnestly thrusting his erection into the man's fundament. He held
tight to the bony hips as leverage in order to drive his tool more
deeply, as far as it would go. In out, in out.

The rest stop was a known hangout for men wanting to hook
up with other men of like mind. Ronnie Dalton, twenty-nine, an
out-of-work grocery store bagger, had been there for almost an hour
before Derrick Johnson showed up in his heavy duty cargo truck
with a company name written on the sides. It was 3:30 and Derrick
had just finished his route. The two had never met or even seen each
other, yet very soon they would be carnal mates. When asked, How
do you like it? Ronnie smiled and pointed to his rear end. That was
the extent of their conversation. The long-haired Ronnie was a bit
too swishy for Derrick's taste—he liked the lumberjack type—but
he would do for now.

From Ronnie's perspective, Derrick looked brutish and he reeked
of something. Raw sewage maybe, rotting carcasses. Whatever it
was, it was putrid. But Ronnie knew he'd see it through, because it
had been a week and he was desperate for dick.

They went into the facility, Ronnie leading the way. Once in the
stall and the action about to commence, Ronnie said, "Hold up."
From his pants pocket he took a container of Vaseline, and with two
fingers he scooped up a nice dollop and swabbed both the rim of his

anus and the inside of his rectum. "Delicate tissue," he said by way of explanation.

Now, five minutes later, Derrick pulled out, his hard eight-inch penis making a sucking sound. "What are you doing?"asked Ronnie, voice echoing in the toilet bowl. "You're not done, I didn't feel you come."

"Turn around," said Derrick.

"Why? What for?" alarm in his voice.

"I said turn around."

Ronnie lifted himself from the bowl and turned around, Derrick's imposing member staring him in the face. "Suck it," ordered Derrick.

Ronnie saw that Derrick's hard-on was smeared with mucus and shit. He cringed and backed away.

"Go ahead," said Derrick, grabbing him by the hair and pulling him in closer, "get a taste of yourself."

"Ah, no way," said Ronnie, "I can't do that. It's … it's just too gross."

"You insulting my cock, you little pissant?" Ronnie was on his knees, sniveling. Derrick pulled the hair on the back of Ron's head tighter and made him look up. Teeth clenched, he said, "You know what, man, you know what?" Ronnie gazed up at his tormentor, the bulldog face, his mighty boner curving upward like a scimitar, and he trembled. "Lemme tell you what. The only thing I like better than drilling some ass is beating the living shit outta some fuckhead who doesn't do as I say. Now, fucking suck it."

"Could you wash it first?" cried Ronnie as Derrick drew him in.

Later Derrick found himself at the Honey Don't, a no frills cinder block tavern over on Jones Creek Road. He often stopped here on his way home to knock back a few. Certain days there was barely a full set of teeth in the place, and today was one of them. Six rumpots present and they all sat at the bar. Derrick sat apart at the end of the bar by the jar of pickled eggs, partly because the others were friends and they liked to keep to themselves but also because

Derrick reeked and his demeanor was not at all inviting. That was okay with Derrick. It wasn't like he didn't have friends. He did, and when they got together—watch out. But right now he was content to drink by himself and pass the time reading the labels on the bottles arranged in elevated rows on the back bar. There was Old Crow and Jim Beam and Johnny Walker Red, yeah, he knew those. One shelf held just vodka, like six different flavors—something new, he guessed, but what was wrong with plain old vodka? Then there was Grand Marnier, a liqueur, orange flavored. He recalled that once in a bar a guy bought the house drinks but the drinkers didn't get to choose because the guy buying decided that everyone had to try this Grand Marnier stuff. He must've really liked it to buy a round for everyone. And they had a name for it, what was it? Grammaw, that's it, they called it Grammaw. He remembered one guy saying, "She's quite the lady at night, but a real bitch in the morning."

The door opened, two guys came in. As happens in a bar, everyone looked to see who it was and then went back to what they were doing. To get drinks the two went to the only spot open at the bar, next to Derrick. One was tall and lanky, long black hair in a ponytail, banded every so many inches. He wore a denim jacket with cut-off sleeves and the name SLIM embroidered over the left front pocket. The other was older, maybe forty, limp brown hair peeking out from under an American flag doo-rag. Crow's feet around his eyes, brown chaw stains around his lips. The bartender came back with their order, Miller High Lifes and shots of Jack Daniels.

"I'll move if you guys wanna sit down," said Derrick in an unusual act of courtesy.

"Nah," said the one in the denim jacket. "We been drivin' for a spell, it's good to stand."

The other guy looked at Derrick for the first time. "Say, ain't you Deke's boy? I met you and your daddy at the meat shoot last fall over in House Springs, the VF-dubya. Darryl is it?"

"Derrick," he corrected. "Yeah, I remember you. Didn't you win the money round?"

"Yeah, the money round, sixty bucks, *and* the pork steaks round.

That old Mossberg Five Hundred keeps doin' it for me." He held out a hand. "I'm June and this here's Slim."

They shook hands and clinked bottles. "June and Slim, huh? Not bad. Maybe I need me a cool nickname. Chopper or Killer, somethin' like that."

"Tell you what," said Slim, "before we leave here we'll give you a name and you'll like it."

"Meanwhile, said June, "I need to tell you something."

"Yeah?"

"Yeah, and it's something Deke should know."

"I'm all ears, go ahead."

"Well," started June, "I know that Deke's pals with Stoney—you know Stoney, right? Been missing now for about a month."

"Yeah, a mystery there," said Derrick.

"Yeah, so here's a clue to that mystery. We're pals with Stoney, too, and we went by his place, oh, 'bout ten days ago, see if he might've showed up. Well, Stoney wasn't there, and I don't think he's ever gonna be there again. Something bad happened to him. But there was someone at Stoney's and he wasn't a friend."

Slim nodded. "We saw his car in the drive and we snuck up on him, he was in the trailer snooping around. A guy from St. Louis way out here, gettin' into Stoney's shit."

"A cop?"

"No," answered June, getting into it now, "he weren't no cop. And we done beat the shit outta him, worked him over with a pipe." He gave a demented chuckle. "He won't be gettin' into people's shit for a while, I tell you that. But here's the thing, this guy, Francis Lenihan by name, he told us that Deke sent him."

"What!"

"Yeah," said Slim, "he said it twice and he swore that it was true and that we shouldn't spank him because he had Deke's permission to be there."

"We didn't believe him," said June, "because he just didn't look like the kinda guy that Deke would associate with."

"You did right," said Derrick. He held up his beer and in fraternal solidarity they clinked bottles again. "You said his name, what— Francis? Goddamn pussy-sounding name."

"He can fight, but not good enough," informed Slim.

"You happen to learn where this guy lives? Maybe we'll pay him a visit, see how well he knows my dad."

Slim and June looked at one another, grinning. "Hell yeah," said June, "his full name and address."

They had three more beers and some shots, thick as thieves they were now. At one point, Slim raised a palm, a sign to be quiet. He addressed Derrick. "Okay, man, I told you we'd come up with a handle for you and I've got it, finally. It took some thinkin' but here you go. You ready?"

"Yeah, lay it on me."

"Skunk."

"Skunk?"

"Yeah, Skunk."

Derrick shrugged and held out his bottle to be clinked. "Works for me," he said.

— 20 —

"WE'VE GOT IT DOWN TO two decent possibles in that subdivision," Detective Bernie LaRocca was saying to Chief of Detectives Vincent Stockman. "The first is a Richard Johnson, 782 Bolingbroke, fairly close to the Schurzinger place, age fifty-two, no known means of income. His priors include a four-year stretch in Potosi for passing counterfeit bills, a whole lot of them over a period of three months or more. That was in '79. He was offered a plea if he'd reveal his connection, his source, but he kept mum and did the time and got out. He had one arrest before that, in '75, for a bogus check to the tune of four-hundred bucks." LaRocca, standing before Stockman seated at his desk, paused.

"Hmm, not exactly your violent criminal," said the chief. "Just a guy trying to get over on the system, probably never did a day's work in his life. But still ... who else you got?"

"One Terrance Boynton, forty-four, lives four streets over from Schurzinger, works third shift at a twenty-four hour Moto Mart over in St. Clair—"

"You may as well pull up a chair," said Stockman, "you're making me nervous standing there."

LaRocca sat in the chair as directed. He adjusted his tie and smoothed out his roomy sport coat, far too big on him thanks to his wife not knowing his right size. He consulted the notebook in his lap. "This Boynton, his only prior being assault with a deadly weapon. Seems he attacked a utility worker who came to shut off the gas at his home because of non-payment. Put the guy in the hospital with a broken arm and a concussion. The weapon? An ax handle. Imagine what he'd have done if he'd had the blade. He did two years for that in Eastern Missouri Correctional over in Pacific. Nothing since."

"A hothead, huh? And he works nights so he was likely home that day." Stockman swiveled his chair so that he was looking out the window at the bail bonds office across the street. It was his only source of distraction in this otherwise dull office on the third floor of the sheriff department. The jail was on the first and second floors of this building and the courthouse was next door, and so Hazel Hammonds Bail Bondsman did a very brisk trade day-in, day-out. It was like having a Kool-Aid stand in the Mojave Desert.

Still looking out the window, Stockman said, "Both these guys live alone or what?"

"Johnson has a teenage daughter lives with him, record of truancy at Northwest High School. He also has a son, older, who may or may not live there. No known wife or significant other. Boynton lives alone."

Stockman watched what looked to be a family of four coming out of the office across the way. They walked toward Old State 21, the main drag of Hillsboro, two blocks to the south. He swiveled his chair back around to face LaRocca, a wry smile on his jowly face. "We put 'em in and, before you know it, ol' Hazel bonds 'em out. Ain't that the way?"

"You got that right, chief. It's like a game of musical chairs."

"Something like that." He ran a hand over the rug of his crew cut. "And you've been out to see them?"

"Johnson and Boynton? Just the initial canvass on that Friday of Labor Day weekend. Johnson was forthcoming enough, said he'd been doing errands that day. Boynton acted somewhat cagey, said he was home, didn't hear or see anything unusual, claimed he was working on his car."

"Okay, go back out there, take Pilchow with you. Talk to both of them at length even if they've told you all they claim to know. Push 'em around a little, keep it going long enough to make it uncomfortable. Mention a search warrant. Ask for names of close associates, maybe one of them had visitors that day. Full court press, we've got to get this thing in the win column."

There was a knock at the door which was open anyway. Detective Anna Riggs with some papers in her hand. "You wanted to see me?"

Stockman smiled at the welcome intrusion. "Come in, come in. I'd offer you a seat, but Bernie here has the only one."

LaRocca jumped up from his chair and bid Riggs to take it. Riggs was dressed in a navy blue pantsuit, white linen shirt with wide pointed collars draped over the lapels. Generally, she tried to be all business, and that meant accepting no special treatment because of her gender. She answered cordially, "I'd rather stand, you don't mind. But thanks anyway."

LaRocca remained standing and the chair sat empty.

"I was just briefing Bernie here about the Schurzinger case. We've zeroed in on two persons in that subdivision with previous arrests. We also have a good lead on the owner of the Challenger seen by Lenihan at the scene."

"I hadn't heard that," said LaRocca.

"I was just gonna tell you," said Stockman. "It took a good long while to look at every Dodge Challenger with a vanity plate registered in the State of Missouri. It was like playing some kind of board game with all the possibilities and guesswork, especially since we didn't know how the plate read. And all the while I'm thinking what if this Lenihan doesn't know his cars and it's actually a Charger and not a Challenger. Then we'd be barking up the wrong tree, see?"

"It happens," put in LaRocca.

"Yeah, and maybe Lenihan does know one model from another because there's a Clarence Jackson over near Dittmer with a '74 Challenger, and vanities that read N-A-G-A-D-A. You recall that Lenihan said there was a 'G' in it."

"He did," affirmed LaRocca.

"Wonder what it means," from Riggs.

Stockman shrugged. "Some quirky phrase known only to the driver. Who knows? But here's the clincher." He took a sheet from the top of a pile of paper on his desk, a muddy-looking xerox of a man's face. The guy looked stunned, like a sneak thief caught in the act. He passed it over to LaRocca.

"Clarence Jackson's drivers license photo."

"Well, I'll be. It's the guy in the artist sketch."

"Yeah, it's finally coming together. So, here's the plan. I want Bernie and Pilchow to go back to Avonhurst and put it to the two residents with priors. I mean really put it to them, make them hear the clank of the cell door if they don't spit something out worth our time. Obviously, a confession is the holy grail, but the next best thing? Fingering an associate, someone who was there that day. A friend, an accomplice, someone who doesn't live there but comes around. And maybe this Clarence Jackson is that person who comes around, maybe that was him that day who was seen leaving the scene all fucked up." He looked at Riggs standing there, arms folded across her chest. "So, Anna, I want you and Berlinger to pay this Jackson a visit. I don't have to tell you to use extreme caution. We're only there to talk with him, but if he turns belligerent or tries to run, then go ahead bring him in."

"Understood," said Riggs, "but it's Saturday, Vince. Berlinger doesn't come in 'til three."

"Oh, that's right," said Stockman. "We're down to three. Then you and Pilchow go see Jackson while Bernie goes to Avonhurst."

"I can handle it on my own," said Riggs, a trace of superiority in her tone.

Stockman shook his head no. "Jackson is the more perilous of the two assignments. Two detectives go out, two detectives come back. Got it?"

Riggs was forty-one and one tough cookie, the thyroid condition notwithstanding. She had medium-length auburn hair and smokey brown eyes. She'd been a detective on the force longer than any of the others except LaRocca. It was this sort of patronizing treatment that really galled her. How she had to work twice as hard and be twice as smart as her chums in the Old Boys' Club. One of these days she would vent, tell off Vince Stockman and anyone else who thought to suppress her ability to perform the mission and do it as well or better than any man. But for now she kept her mouth shut and accepted the status quo like the bitter pill it was.

— 21 —

"How's your grits?" she asked.

He thought for a moment while chewing. "Salty and on the bland side. That how they're supposed to be? Unflavorful?"

"You can put things on them," she said, "add flavor. Things like honey and walnuts and raisins. We'll call the waitress, I'm sure she can make you happy with your grits."

Francis waved away that idea. "It's all right, I'll take it as given. Au natural, as they say."

"Who says that?" Rose wondered.

"The Three Bears," he answered. "Isn't this the same thing they eat for breakfast. This is what they call porridge in that story, I know it."

They were in a booth at the Rise N' Shine Diner in Cedar Hill. It was nine on a Saturday morning, and they were planning a foray into Avonhurst, where Rose once lived. He wore sneakers, faded

jeans with a red bandanna sticking out of the back pocket, and a
navy blue cotton pullover with the Old Warson Country Club crest,
a multi-hued acorn with a golf club bisecting it, something he'd
found in a thrift shop. Her attire was nothing if not original: gray
tights with loose-fitting beige socks rumpled down over the tops of
combat boots, and a linen-embroidered off shoulder peasant blouse.
String-like braids of hair framed her face, a sterling silver stud
punctuated the side of her nose. Different look and style than the
last sighting; either way she would stand out in a crowd. He thought
she looked great, and wondered if he was enamored of her. The day
before he had called the number she'd given, and then waited nearly
an hour for her to call back. A new development, he'd said, can you
meet me out your way in the morning? He had filled her in over coffee as they waited for their order. How he'd remembered the license
plate and then obtained a name and address.

She listened as he told her about the empty trailer, what he'd
learned, and the reception he got there. Told her how a few days
later he called a Domino's in the nearest sizable town and paid by
credit card to have a pizza delivered to the trailer. Call me if there's
any problem, he told the kid on the phone. In his apartment Francis
waited by the phone; it rang ninety minutes later. The delivery guy
had returned with the pizza, a Hawaiian, said the place was deserted. Creepy and deserted. What do you want me to do with the
pizza? asked the delivery guy. Give it to Don Ho, he said.

"So allow me to summarize," Rose was saying. "We know the
identity of the probable killer, but it's quite possible that this Clarence or Stoney is out of the picture. Missing. Skipped out on his
own or ... or lying in some ditch, little Xs in his eyes, maggots eating
him from the inside out. And that would be pure karma. But we
have another name, a likely suspect, maybe they acted together in
killing mom." She raised a brow in satisfaction, said, "This is getting
good. I like playing detective."

Francis lit a Marlboro and slid sideways in the booth, lounging
with one leg up.

"You can smoke in here?" she wondered, doubtful.

"Yeah, this is the smoking section. The chain-smoking section's over there at the counter. Go on," he urged, "you're doing great."

"Okay. We still don't know who Deke is and that would be a key piece to the puzzle. We deduce—I like that word—we deduce it could be someone in the subdivision where mom lived. Stoney had business with Deke that day."

"And how do we learn who Deke is?"

"We go to the site and ask around," she said.

"You ready?"

"Ready Freddie, just let me pee."

Early October, overcast, cool, the sun trying to burn through the clouds. Most driveways had vehicles in them, but the residents were in their homes. Yard work would go on later when it turned warmer. They were hoping to make inquiries without having to walk up to the homes and ring doorbells, Francis having told Rose what happened the last time he was here.

"Maybe we should put this off for an hour or two," he said, "wait for people to come out. These folks are already on the alert for suspicious characters."

"You couldn't be any more suspicious if you had three-foot antenna coming out of your head. Me, I'm just a local girl," she said.

They were in her old Toyota, Rose driving. They went past the home where Elizabeth breathed her last and Rose said, "We've *got* to find this son of a bitch, and we will." They kept on up a slowly rising incline to Mercurio, turned in and came back out without seeing anyone. It was a short street, only four homes. They continued on up Portia Way and came to Bolingbroke.

"I've been here," said Francis. "This is where LaRocca caught up with me."

They kept on going, mopering along, watching for any activity. They veered off Bolingbroke onto Reynaldo. Suddenly Rose straightened up, motioned off to the left. "Look over there, a woman walking a dog."

Rose crossed over onto the opposite side of the street and pulled up alongside the woman. "'Scuse me," she called out the open window, "we're trying to find someone and we've been given the wrong address. Maybe you know this person, name of Deke."

The woman took a few steps toward the Toyota, she hunkered down a little to see the occupants within. They saw that both she and the dog were quite old. "Could you repeat that name, honey? I'm a bit hard of hearing."

Rose said the name again. "Deke Johnson? Sure thing, honey. Try the ranch house with the chimney just past that fork you come from. If he's home you'll see a green-and white pickup truck parked out front."

"Great!" said Rose. "Thanks a lot."

"Y'all have a blessed day," she returned and walked on.

"What do you know, it's the same place I was before," he said as the stone chimney came into sight. "I was talking to a girl there, early teens, when LaRocca rolled up and whisked me away."

She said, "I don't see a truck so I guess this Deke's gone somewhere. Wonder where he is on a Saturday morning."

"I had an Uncle Deke," said Francis. "He got through the Korean War only to be shot outside a strip club on the East Side."

"Tough break," she said.

"Yeah, he used to take me bowling, and buy me popcorn and soda."

They had parked down the street fifty yards from the house. "What if Deke loaned out his truck," Rose puzzled, "and he is there, then what do we do? I mean, we know who he is now. Did you see him when you were here?"

"No, just the daughter home and she was all right. Sassy and coming on too cool for words like teens will do. But she was all right, I could tell. Her name is Eve."

"Should we go up and talk to them, whoever's home?"

"What's the goal here," he asked. "What's the bottom line of this mission?"

"Find mom's killer and see that he fries."

"Missouri's got lethal injection."

"Whatever, just so he suffers."

"Once again, let's lay it out. Your mom's killer, most likely Stoney Jackson, is MIA. Deke is one removed with some connection to Stoney, but we don't know what exactly. Let's say they are in cahoots. Let's say that Deke knows Stoney murdered your mom, so he's complicit. What can we do with that? Not much, because it's just a hunch." He looked to her, shrugged. "Maybe we've reached the point where we've gotten what there is to get and we decide to let the police take it from here." He looked for a reaction. She was fingering the thin braids of her hair, gazing at the house.

"Look how far we've come," she said, "you put on your detective hat and in one month you come up with two scum-sucking suspects—not one, but two. That's pretty fucking impressive. Also, you took a beating for the cause, and I am forever in your debt. One of these bastards may be dead, but the other's alive and kickin'. We're more effective than the cops. I say we keep on keepin' on, see what more we can learn so that this Deke's role in mom's killing is more than just a hunch. You down with that?"

Francis nodded slowly. "I can be down with it if that's what you want. Look, I've already been there. I think it's better if you go up and make contact. You're the hope here, I'm the disappointment. If it's the girl, she'll just get sassy with me again."

"That's fine, I'll ask about her father, try to get a picture of who he is and what he does. What will you be doing?"

"I'll move the car up closer and have a smoke. Anything goes down I can be right there."

Again, Eve answered the door. She wore flannel pajama bottoms and a T-shirt with a Panda and St Louis Zoo. She must have been sleeping—make-up smeared around the eyes, her two-tone hair all mussed up. She scratched an itch on her neck with fingernails painted black.

Goth? Punk? "Sorry, if I woke you ..." Rose began.

From a nimbus of smoke Francis watched them, encouraged because several minutes had passed and they were still there in the doorway gabbing.

"I've seen you around," ventured Rose, after a bit of hemming and hawing, "don't you go to that skate park over in Hillsboro, hang with all the skater boys?" This was just a guess based on the girl's look and demeanor. Rose knew about the skate park and, well, it was worth a try.

Eve brightened up. "Yeah, you go there too? That's cool. Yeah, you do look familiar." She studied the older woman—not that much older, nine-ten years—and she liked what she saw. What certain adults would call a free spirit, but to her a latter-day hippie. Far out. "And you're here at my door, why?"

"I told you. That was my mom got killed down the road. They still haven't found the killer. I'm just going around to the neighbors introducing myself, see if I can shake anything loose."

"First the cops, then that guy from the city, now you."

"Yeah, well—"

"I'm really sorry about your mom," Eve said.

"That's kind of you to say." She gave Eve a radiant smile and put a hand on her shoulder. Eve smiled back and almost purred at the touch. They both felt a palpable connection.

Rose scanned the yard, saw a concrete birdbath and a bicycle. "Just you today? Where are the others?"

"My dad and my brother went to the Rural King, they'll be back in a while."

"What kinda business is your dad in?" she asked.

"You can ask him that directly," replied Eve, "'cause here they come right now."

The F-150 pulled up and Deke and Derrick got out. They began to walk across the yard, both frowning at what they saw. "Here, take this," said Rose, and she slipped Eve a card.

Then they stood a few feet away, fixing them with hard looks.

Deke said, "You wanna tell me what this is all about?" He could have been addressing either one of them, or both.

"We're just talking," said Eve, "ain't nothin' to get riled over."

"You get your ass back inside," Deke told her, sternly, "we'll take care of this."

"Ain't nothin' to take care of," she spoke back.

"Do as I say!"

Eve looked at him with obvious disdain. "You give ogres a bad name, you know that?" She turned and went inside.

Right there without any preamble, father and son began to question her, and none too kindly. Who are you? What's your business? What did you say to Eve? Rose said she had nothing to hide, and she began to tell them the truth.

"Let's see some identification," demanded Derrick.

She looked at the both of them, serious disapproval in her eyes. "I'm done with this," she said, and started to walk off.

Deke grabbed her by the arm. "Hold it, Missy."

"Get your fucking paws offa me!" boomed Rose, trying to jerk free.

Seeing this, Francis rushed over, thinking to calm the situation. Now there were four, and two of them hostile. Deke gave a fractured smile and released Rose. "I see you got your bodyguard, huh? He come to save you from the big bad ogre?" Deke turned on Francis, and Derrick stepped up as well, fists balled. Francis was out of breath from his sprint. They listened to him huffing. They waited. "Well?" said Deke, all impatient.

Francis reached out and took Rose in close. He held her hand, and tried to compose himself. "I'm sure she already told you," he said, "we're investigating the murder of Elizabeth Shurzinger, and we're asking the same questions of everyone in the subdivision."

This evoked a scornful chuckle from Derrick. "That why you were hiding in that Jap car over there?"

Deke took him in, and something clicked. "You that fella was nosin' around Stoney's trailer?"

"That was me," affirmed Francis.

"I heard you used my name, told them boys 'Deke sent me.' Where'd you learn my name?" Francis declined to answer that. Deke filled the silence. "Them boys did a number on you, didn't they?"

"I left my squirt gun in the car," explained Francis.

Deke didn't find this amusing. He said, "You got a pair on you, dontcha? You know who I am—other than some nickname you learned?"

"No sir, I don't."

"I'm the son of a bitch who's gonna kick your ass into next week, you come out here again."

Francis nodded acknowledgment. He looked Deke straight in the eye. "Then I'm the guy who'll have his ass kicked into next week, 'cause we're not done yet. I'll be back."

"Well," said Francis to Rose on the way out, "now we know who Deke is. What next?"

— 22 —

Later that day a detective came to call. Deke remembered the guy from before—olive complexion, dark hair combed straight back, brown eyes almost black, some kind of Greek or Italian. He stood there at the door, plainclothes, expectant, saying his name and title and asking if they could talk.

"You can talk and maybe I'll listen," said Deke. "This about the woman down the road again?"

"I mean," said LaRocca, "we have a two-way conversation about the events of August twenty-seventh. Another way to say it is that we lay our cards on the table, because you've been holding back your hand and I'm here to call you on it. Now, you gonna invite me in or do we have to stand out here?"

Deke led him into the living room to a sofa and a coffee table with magazines arranged in rows. For a guy who made his living as a burglar and sneak thief, Deke lived fairly modestly. LaRocca took the sofa while Deke plopped into a recliner angled away from the sofa. With a grunt, he turned it around to face his guest.

"You mind turning that off?" asked LaRocca, chin-pointing at the TV. It was tuned to some wrestling show, beefy ballerinas in spandex trunks throwing each other around. "That's better," he said. "We alone?"

"That's right," said Deke. "Say what you gotta say."

LaRocca studied the man for a second, looking for signs of nervousness. He seemed calm, collected. For now. Maybe the anxiety would surface later when the water got hot. LaRocca led off by stating the current status of the investigation, embellishing here and there to suit his purpose as he went along. We haven't made an arrest yet, he was saying, but we have a person—or persons—of interest. This person was seen in this subdivision on the afternoon of the murder. We have reason to believe he was visiting someone here, someone such as yourself." He paused for dramatic effect. "Would you care to elaborate on what I'm saying?"

"That day you mention," said Deke, "I'm pretty sure that was the day I was out running errands. I told you before I didn't get back until late afternoon and I sure didn't have any visitor that day." He reached over to a stand and took a sip of a highball he'd been drinking before LaRocca came knocking.

LaRocca raised his brows and nodded. "That's the way you wanna play it, huh? You're not under oath right now so you can lie with impunity, but we hook you up to a lie detector then it's another story."

"Lie detector doesn't stand up in court, that's what I heard."

"That's right," shot back LaRocca, snapping his fingers, "you'd know about such things, legal matters and loopholes, what you can get away with, how far you can take it without the cuffs being slapped on."

"I don't follow you," said Deke.

LaRocca leaned forward, elbows on his knees. "You're a jailbird. I know you did time, and once a jailbird there's always that prison mentality that says How can I get over on the system? What's in it for me? Why work when I can steal and plunder? Why tell the truth when I can lie? You see? The criminal is just under the surface, it's embedded in your personality. Why don't you just tell me what really happened that day?"

Deke rose from the recliner, took his drink and downed it. He stood there, hands on hips, looking at LaRocca. "You come into my home and insult me like that? Unbelievable. Yeah, I did time and it had a big effect on me. It made me promise I'd never again do anything that would land me back in there. I've kept that promise. I'm clean as a whistle, don't do anything criminal and don't associate with criminals. I am one fucking upright citizen."

"Nice speech," said LaRocca, "just the right amount of indignity. But I happen to know that you're lying through your teeth, because you do associate with criminals. That police sketch I showed you the first time I came calling? That's Clarence Jackson, a real dirtbag. You associate with Clarence Jackson and don't try to deny it." He waited for Deke's reaction.

No feathers ruffled.

"That your person of interest?" he said disinterestedly. "Well, I don't know anyone by that name, never heard of him."

LaRocca got up off the couch. He took two steps toward Deke so that they were nose to nose. "We'll see," he said, "we'll see what the lie detector has to say about it." He held Deke's glower. "And, oh, you don't mind if I come back with a few more detectives and a search warrant? Now don't you go concealing any evidence before we get back, hear?"

Deke saw him to the door. "You don't believe me," he said, evenly. "I can't do a thing about that. So you do what you got to do, I'm not worried. You'll see I'm just a guy trying to get through life with a minimum of hassle. The old ways are gone."

That night Deke had a fitful sleep, tossing so that the sheets were twisted and damp with sweat. He was in the throes of a bad dream. He was down below the quarry, walking toward the sinkhole but against his will. It was daylight. There was the opening, the ravenous maw of some monster, with noses of cars sticking out. He didn't want to see the sinkhole. His legs were taking him closer, but his mind was fighting it. It was like he was being pushed along by some unseen person. He got to the rim and looked in. Just then the ground shook and the sinkhole belched, its contents upchucked.

* * *

It was a drive from Hillsboro to Dittmer and the AM-FM didn't work on Pilchow's unit. They watched the scenery flying past and spoke of things they had in common. Like cop shows. Pilchow said that he liked the shows about private eyes better than the ones about cops because the cop shows were just too close to home and he was always watching for mistakes that they made.

"Some of those cop detectives—*T.J. Hooker* for one—couldn't investigate a dogbite much less a robbery or a kidnapping," he said with scorn. "The private detectives are more interesting. *Spenser: For Hire* is pretty good and, of course, *Magnum P.I.* Tom Selleck is the best." He looked over at Riggs in the passenger seat. "In my humble opinion," he added.

"I like *Cagney and Lacey*," she said. "You get to see their lives on the job and at home. They're real people with real everyday problems."

"Well, yeah, they gotta have at least one female cop show for the chicks. And I watched it a few times, but that brunette—what's her name?"

"Tyne Daly."

"Yeah, that Tyne Daly can really come on like a ballbuster. Kind of a bitch, don't you think?"

"Oh, I see," said Riggs. "She's doing a traditional male job, and, when she grows a pair to keep up with the boys then she's a bitch."

"Aw, don't take it personal."

"How about Spenser and Magnum, your buddies? When they pull out the stops going after the bad guys, maybe shake down one or two, crack a few skulls. Then what are they? If Tyne Daly's a bitch then they must be pricks. You agree?"

"I see your point. Forget I ever said that, okay?"

"You were right about one thing, though."

"What's that?"

"*T. J. Hooker*. Shatner should've stayed on board the *Enterprise*, fighting Klingons and porking space babes. His cop persona is not very convincing."

"I think you drove past it," said Riggs, paying close attention to the roadside. "That mailbox back there, looked like someone lit an M-80 and tossed it in."

"I'll turn around," he said.

The mailbox bore the address in faint hieroglyphics. They drove up the gravel drive, and a trailer came into view. If it was a house it would be a shack. Some of the vinyl trim was dangling, falling away, the flat roof was covered with leaves and branches, and the sides— more vinyl—were coated with slimy green flora. Cast-off appliances in the yard, if you could call it that, and a couple of rusted-out junkers completed the picture of Hillbilly Haven.

"Disgusting," said Riggs, stepping around an open bag of garbage, flies buzzing. Weapons drawn, pointed downward—just like their cop show counterparts—they approached the door of the trailer which was wide open. It was procedure, although they both knew with near certainty the place was vacant. Then Riggs stood facing the door, weapon held out with both hands, while Pilchow stood off to the side, weapon also pointed at the door. They both carried department-issued semi-automatic nine millimeter Glocks, which carried fifteen rounds in the magazine; they were half-hoping to use them.

"Clarence Jackson, you in there?" she called in her field voice. Nothing. "This is the Jefferson County Sheriff Department," authoritatively, "we're coming in."

"Guy's not the best housekeeper," said Pilchow, kicking at an opened box on the floor, uncooked fish sticks scattered on the grungy carpet.

"Or the maid has taken the decade off," commented Riggs, poking around the small dining table. On the tabletop, there were mouse turds and morsels of food with tiny teeth marks everywhere.

"What're we looking for anyway?" he asked rhetorically.

"Clues, detective, clues to help solve the crime of the year," she answered half-sarcastically.

"Never mind that we're in here without a warrant," he said, "give me an example of a good clue that we might find."

She left the dining area for what passed as a den—a small couch, an end table and a portable TV on a stand, aluminum foil on the antenna. "Some article of the victim's," she called back, "clothing or personal effects or some object from the home. A lot of these guys like to take souvenirs from their victims."

"That sounds great in theory," he said, "but come on, we wouldn't know whether it's a souvenir taken on the fly as he's leaving the vic's house or whether it's something he got at the Goodwill. The best thing we could turn up, the holy grail, as good old Vince would say, is some blood-stained panties with 'Elizabeth' written on them."

"Wonder where he keeps his tools," she said, studying a plaque on the wall. FIRST PLACE – MUSCLE CAR CATEGORY – FARMINGTON CAR SHOW 1987.

They walked around the trailer, skirted a freshly dug hole, a pile of dirt beside it, found a shed in the back, tall weeds all around. It held all sorts of implements and tools—a sledgehammer, a rake, gas cans, shovels, some chains, even a Christmas tree stand. Nothing to get excited over. They made another circuit of the premises, stepping around deer carcasses, some with heads and some without.

"If it turns out that this guy's not good for murder one, then at least we'll get him for poaching," said Pilchow. "You ever had venison?"

"Eat bambi? I don't think so," she answered, stooping to pick up something. "Hello, what's this?"

Pilchow walked over and looked at it with her. A Missouri driver license. Current. He let out a mild chuckle of surprise. "That guy sure gets around, doesn't he?"

— 23 —

SGT. BRIAN SCANLAN WAITED IMPATIENTLY for another cop to get off the phone. He stood nearby drumming his fingertips on a file cabinet and staring at the rookie patrolman obviously talking to some woman, calling her honey and making a spectacle of himself. And the conversation sounded pretty important, something about him picking up groceries on the way home. They were in the squad room where there were just two common phones and the other was being used by a fellow sergeant for proper business. Scanlan had just returned after three days off, three days of much needed relaxation after pulling eight days straight. There was a note on his locker, CALL DET. LAROCCA - HILLSBORO, and the phone number beginning with the 636 area code. The note was dated, too. Three days before. Just after roll call and briefing he went to make the call, wondering whether LaRocca was as impatient as he was. Probably thinks I'm blowing him off, thought Scanlan.

"He's out in the field right now," said the female dispatcher on the receiving end. "I can take a message."

"Tell him Sgt. Scanlan returned his call, and the best time to reach me is—"

"Oh, he just walked in. Bernie, you've got a call."

Then LaRocca was on the line. "Hey, thanks for getting back to me. Took long enough, you must be slammed with work. Hey, the reason I called, just wanted to update you on the Schurzinger case. At long last we finally located the owner of the Dodge Challenger that your boy saw that day leaving the scene. We're pretty sure it's a man out in Dittmer, Clarence Jackson. No apparent record, employment unknown, associates unknown. Only problem is we can't find him to question him. We had a couple detectives out there on Saturday and the place was deserted. No suspect, no Dodge Challenger.

We did turn up one interesting thing, though."

"Yeah? What's that?"

"Your boy, Lenihan. His driver's license on the ground near Jackson's trailer."

Scanlan whistled through the phone lines. "You think he was out there before you guys or someone got hold of his license and dropped it there, either by accident or deliberate, make it look like he was there?"

"I'm inclined to *not* give him the benefit of the doubt," rejoined LaRocca. "I think he's involved in this. He knew about Jackson before we did and he didn't say a word. I'm not saying he's in with the killer. I'm saying he's acting on his own or someone hired him—and I have a hunch who—to dig into this separate from our investigation and he's found out some things. Long and short, he's withholding information pertinent to a criminal investigation, and you know the consequences of that."

"I'll talk with him," said Scanlan, already thinking there was some logical explanation for the license being there. "It'll be interesting to see what he says. I'll get back to you tomorrow, and sorry for the delay in returning this call. I was off for three days, took a trip down to Branson."

"Oh, you take in some shows?"

"Yeah, they got a Japanese guy there, plays the fiddle like you wouldn't believe."

"I believe it. Foreigners about to infiltrate every part of our culture. Sports, entertainment, you name it."

"Hell, we were foreigners once."

"Yeah, but not like these foreigners nowadays."

Scanlan left that alone. "Will you send me Lenihan's license? I'll see that he gets it."

"Check your box there at the station," said LaRocca. "I mailed it a few days ago."

* * *

Francis drove west on Lindell Boulevard, the showcase thorough-fare of the City of St. Louis. He had just passed the landmark spire of the The College Church at Grand Avenue, the cornerstone of the sprawling Jesuit-run Saint Louis University. Soon after that, at Spring, he passed the truly awesome Masonic Temple, its facade and massive columns looking like something out of a history book on Ancient Rome. There was an inscription at the top, along the hori-zontal stone beam to which the columns joined. It was placed by the Freemasons back in 1926 when the edifice was built. It was in Latin and it had taken many drive-bys to translate with his murky recol-lection of grade school instruction, but finally he thought he had it. *Ad Gloriam Architecti Mundi et Hominem Fraternitatum* it read: To the Glory of the Architect of the World and to the Brotherhood of Man. Francis liked that, how it kind of pulled everything together.

Two more blocks up was the Cathedral Basilica of Saint Louis, the crown jewel of the archdiocese and the office of the archbishop. As a kid, he and his family would go there to hear the concerts over Christmas. He remembered being impressed at what was on display at a side altar. The final resting place of two Cardinals, interred under the marble floors, the area roped off. Look up at the ornate ceiling, and see the red hats with wide brims that they wore in life suspended by tassels. It was said that those red hats would hang there until the day they fell.

He could see the Chase Hotel further up, another landmark and one that you could see for miles around if nothing else was in the way. It had something like thirty stories, and at the top was the Starlight Room, *the* place to be on New Years' Eve or for any reason. Drinks, music, dancing. Pretty darn romantic up there at night, and he'd kissed a few girls out on the veranda overlooking the city.

The Chase was at Kingshighway and Lindell, the verdant expanse of Forest Park across the way. The first street after Kingshighway still heading west on Lindell, was Lake, which led into the private streets Westmoreland and Portland Places, where his quarry, Ed-ward Tarkington, was ensconced in his castle.

Now he was at the light on Kingshighway, singing along with Marvin to "What's Going On," and watching valets from the Chase in the turnaround, schlepping guest's luggage to the lobby. Beside him, in the lane to his right, a silver Beamer, window halfway down, plumes of white issuing out. Francis saw the smoke was coming from a stogie planted in the driver's mouth. The driver was a man in a suit, somewhere south of forty, dark hair slicked back and a diamond stud in his earlobe. The guy had Hotshot written all over him. Being in the car much of the day, Francis always kept things to munch on. In that way, his car was like a lunch wagon. He reached down and popped the lid of a small cooler. He took out a nice-sized carrot, and put it to his lips, the fat end jutting out. Now he was smoking an orange stogie. He turned to the Beamer. Mr. Hotshot looking straight ahead, willing the light to change. He gave a little beep and the driver looked over. Francis made a show of smoking the pretend stogie, pantomiming a deep satisfying draw and a long luxurious exhale. The driver watching him, Francis took the carrot from his mouth, held it up longingly, and puffed on it some more. The light went green. He looked to Mr. Hotshot; the man just shook his head sadly and drove on, cigar smoke trailing behind. Francis began laughing and he kept it up all the way to Portland Place. He could crack himself up like that.

He walked up to the great oaken door with the ornate brass knocker wondering what it would be today. Last time here with Joe, this goof made fools of them. He let the brass knocker do its work. He stood there waiting, just him and the two stone lions nearby. He tried the bell, and he could hear it chime inside the mansion. At length the voice came over the intercom. "Yahsss?"

Francis hit the TALK button. "Process server. Summons for Tarkington."

"Oh non, Monsieur. Meestair Tarkington he ees—oh, how you say? Een-disposed. He ees een-disposed."

Though he felt he should be upset, Francis found himself amused and decided to play along. "Where's Beatrice, the cleaning lady? What have you done with her?"

"Ah, la femme! She ees here. I have already—how you say?—had my way weeth hair thees day. Non, I am Pierre, ze butlair."

"I'm not buying the accent," Francis told him, "I've heard better from the waiters at La Maison." Francis had never set foot in this fancy restaurant, but he thought that it might get a rise out of Tarkington.

"Okay, how about this accent?" a new voice asked. "Straight up American. Why don't you turn around, get into your jalopy, and head back to the hole you crawled out of. Now get off my porch, peon."

"My," said Francis, "how easily we change nationalities. Get off your porch or what? You'll call the cops? I'd like that, so please be my guest."

Francis heard a huff, and the intercom clicked off.

It was 2:45 on a cloudy day. Second week in October, the mugginess finally gone. Since this morning, he'd served two summonses, four depo subpoenas, and a landlord-tenant summons, which was SERVE AND POST. This last one, after handing the summons and notice to the grumpy defendant/renter, he duct-taped another copy to the door as the woman watched, scowling and muttering. These landlord-tenant summonses, what folly. Half the time he'd find the domicile empty, the premises vacated. Professional skip rents, they know exactly how long they can stay unpaid until the 'lord sics the process server on them.

One of the depo subpoenas had gone to a small insurance agency, three employees typing away at their desks.

"What name do you have on that paper?" one asked.

"No individual name," replied Francis. "Only the business, Kraus Insurance, and Custodian of Records."

"That would be Mr. Kraus," answered the woman, "and he's in Baltimore until … when's he coming back, Norma?"

"The convention ends Friday, so he'll be here Monday morning," answered Norma helpfully. The women looked at him, blinking like owls. They seemed to think that settled it.

"Then I'll serve the office manager, someone in charge."

They, all three, looked at one another, puzzled. The one who hadn't spoken yet, an old guy in a brown tweed sport coat, said, "Why, none of us are in charge."

Francis still had some patience left. "One of you is in charge while the boss is away," he told them.

The other two concurred with the old man, no one was in charge and no one was authorized to accept the subpoena. There would be trouble if they did.

"Well, someone here is going to take it," he insisted. There were times when you just had to be assertive, and this was one. Hearing this ultimatum, they began to grow uneasy.

"Shall I phone the police?" asked Norma. People were always threatening to call the police, thinking the process server was somehow breaking the law, acting the vigilante. But, in fact, almost always, the cops, if they did show up before he left, were willing to back him up.

"Go ahead," he nodded, "and while you've got them on the phone tell them that a legitimate place of business is obligated by law to accept a subpoena for records. That there's no putting it off until Mister So-And-So gets back from vacation." He looked down at the woman at the desk nearest him. There were business cards in a holder; he took one. "Mary Holthaus, Agent," he read aloud. He handed her the subpoena, she took it grudgingly. "Thank you, Mary," he said. And looking around the drab office in which they frittered away their lives, he added, "You've got a nice establishment here, I'll say that. Tell Mr. Kraus for me that you're all doing a great job."

Now he was heading for Murphy's, the thought of that first draft going down so inviting. Coming from South County, he cut through South City and came into Dutchtown. Red brick homes set close together, small front yards, immaculate concrete stoops with folding chairs. Wending his way through several distinct neighborhoods, he got on Oakland at Kingshighway, drove west, the giant Amoco sign in view. The thing was a true landmark, marking a rise in the landscape called Hi-Pointe, and it was illuminated at night with bats swirling around it. They weren't really bats, but birds of some kind, though everyone liked to say they were bats. He came to the busy intersection at Hampton, a big Imo's Pizza sign with a caricature of a chef holding a steaming pie. Almost there, he could see Tommy pouring that beautiful pint. He was at the red, first to go. The light turned, he began to drive when a sedan whizzed past coming from his left, running the red, not even swerving around him but on his merry way somewhere down the line. Another second, he thought, that would've been the end. I had the green, it didn't matter. Life in the Big City.

He had stomped on his brakes and now he was stopped in the busy intersection, creating havoc, horns honking Get Outta The Way! He crossed himself and moved cautiously into safety.

Francis sat on a barstool looking at the handmade notice posted on the wall behind the bar. The notice and its significance was pure Dogtown, Francis mused, a blacklist of rascals and reprobates singled out for misbehavior on these premises. On white poster-board there was a decently drawn picture of a doghouse with a sad-looking hound. In The Doghouse, it read, and below it the names of persons who were banned from Murphy's. There must been have fifteen names, and some of them were crossed off meaning they had served their sentence and were now in good graces—until the next misadventure. Charlie Dunne was listed several times, and Francis remembered one particular instance when he was given the boot. The time Charlie, as a joke, had brought a baby possum in under his folded coat and released it behind the bar. The last entry for Charlie read: Charlie Dunne Okay As Of 7-30-89. Then there were the Grogans, the scourge of Dogtown. As grade-schoolers, they had pelted the pastor's car with hand-crafted iceballs, and, in summer, used slingshots to shoot lit cherry bombs into the open windows of the library. They had their own section on the notice, occupying the lower right quadrant. James Grogan, it read, and below that, in succession, Gerry Grogan, Sean Grogan, Aloysius "Al" Gro-gan, and, finally, the entire clan of miscreants circled in black with bold lettering No Grogans!

Francis sat there for quite a while, getting his drink on, thinking about this and that. Others would come up and ask about his day, and he would regale them with some amusing anecdote, perhaps something that happened long ago but he told it as if it happened just hours ago. Toward five he was getting that bloated feeling and he began to slow down on the beer. When they asked him to sing "The Minstrel Boy," he obliged but had to wait until he had burped the carbonation out of his belly; he didn't want to ruin the song. He finished the song and took a bow. They held up their drinks his way and bought him another round, camaraderie running high. An old man that Francis did not know appeared before him like a supplicant and asked him to sing "Mother Machree."

"Me mother used to sing me asleep to that song," he said, sentiment welling up, rheumy blue eyes blinking. "Please, it would bring back such memories."

But Francis was bound to disappoint. "I'm a one-trick pony, and I've already done that one trick. But here, pal, I'll get you a drink," and he motioned for Tommy.

Behind him, Francis heard a tenor voice, rich in tone, as it sang, "*I kiss the dear fingers so toil worn for me. Oh God bless you and keep you, Mother Machree.*" A first-rate delivery. He turned to see Sgt. Brain Scanlan in uniform.

"Not bad, quite decent," said Francis. "Will you finish it?"

"Later," said the officer. "I've been looking to catch up with you, have a talk."

"That's easy enough," answered Francis. "Here or there?" He motioned toward some tables in the back. Then, calling out, "Tommy, would you please get Sgt. Scanlan a Coke or a Seven-Up—what'll it be?"

"Mountain Dew," said Scanlan.

The jukebox was playing The Pogues' "Dirty Old Town" as they leaned in close and talked.

"Let me see your license," he said right off.

Francis fished his wallet from his back pocket, took out a folded piece of paper. "All I've got's this temporary," he said, "a new one's on the way."

"What happened to the old one?"

"I lost it," he said, the import of the questions beginning to dawn.

Scanlan gave him a look usually reserved for lying thieving perps. "I see, and where pray tell did you lose it? And as long as you're about to tell me the truth, what's with the bruise on your face? It's all but healed now, but I'll bet it was a doozy when it was fresh."

"I need a refill," said Francis, draining the last of his schooner.

"You'll sit here until I've had an explanation," he declared.

"I'm two sheets to the wind," he smiled. "Just one more will get me to three. And then I'll tell you some things, okay?"

When Francis returned minutes later with a schooner of Busch in each hand, the jukebox was playing "Raglan Road" from the album *Irish Heartbeat*, a collaboration by Van Morrison and The Chieftains. "I played this song," said Scanlan, "even though it chokes me up."

"Tugs at the heartstrings," agreed Francis.

"Van Morrison just kills it," said Scanlan, caught up in some reverie. "Hear it now."

They listened together:

*"On a quiet street where old ghosts meet I see her walking now
away from me so hurriedly my reason must allow ..."*

Fully, Scanlan chimed in, mouthing the final verse and looking to Francis as if here were singing to him and him alone.

*"... that I had loved not as I should a creature made of clay –
when the angel woos the clay, he'll lose his wings at the dawn of day"*

With a forefinger Scanlan dabbed the corner of his eye. Then he got serious. "Your license was found at the home of the primary suspect in the murder of Elizabeth Schurzinger. It was on the ground outside the guy's trailer. Jefferson County homicide would like to know how you knew to go there before they did."

"Ah, um, that vanity plate that I couldn't remember? I remembered."

"And you took it upon yourself to investigate? You think you know what you're doing? You think you know better how to handle a murder investigation? You might've fucked up the very evidence that would've brought that guy to Death Row." Shaking his head in dismay. "We'll never know because he can't be found."

"I don't know why I didn't tell you guys," he said, sheepishly. "The daughter, Elizabeth's daughter, Rose, hired me to look into it. I was on assignment, I wanted to solve the crime. I've never solved a crime before."

Scanlan gave a weary chuckle. "You want to solve crimes? You apply to the Police Academy, you get accepted, you graduate, you walk a beat for ten years and if—*if* you show promise then you get promoted to Sergeant Detective. Then you can start solving crimes."

"That ship has probably sailed," said Francis. "I'll just stick to serving papers."

Scanlan squinting hard at him, "What else do you know that you're keeping secret? Huh? It's not even my case, but you'd better not withhold evidence in Schurzinger because by God I'll have you in the slammer quicker'n you can say 'I wish to hell I'd come clean.' And you can say goodbye to serving papers for any court."

"I don't know what I'd do if my license got pulled. There's no other profession that would have me."

"Then out with it, man, what else you got?"

Francis finished the one schooner and began to work on the second. He belched and rubbed his belly in satisfaction. "Hey, remember I told you that there was some question about my father's death, supposedly suspicious? Is there some way you could look into it? Martin Lenihan *requiescat in pace* November 18th, 1965."

"It's been so many years now," Scanlan said, scrunching up his mouth. "I don't know. We'll see. Now back to the task at hand. You were about to tell me what else you know."

"Well, um, you see there's ..." He was maybe going to bring up the matter of Deke Johnson, his mind at war with itself, when the door burst open and Darlene Kennedy, his neighbor three doors down, shouted out for all to hear, "It's Phelim! He's been attacked in his own place! They broke his fingers!"

THEY WENT STRAIGHT TO DEACONESS HOSPITAL just around the corner and up the hill on Oakland. Scanlan drove with Francis and a friend of Phelim's, Del Twohey, in the back seat, because it wouldn't look good, a civilian riding up front in the passenger seat. The charge nurse in the ER said that Phelim had been attended to and discharged. It wasn't serious, broken fingers on the one hand, and he had decided to walk home. You're driving you'll probably beat him there, she said, he left but ten minutes ago.

It was a two-family with doors side by side on the wooden front porch. Phelim had the first floor of the house while Francis had the second. The small party rapped at the door on the left for a second time. At last a voice from within croaked, "Come in, come in—damn you!"

They walked through a hallway into a kitchen and there sat Phelim Burke in his Carhartt overalls at the table, a bottle of Paddy's in front of him. The whiskey paired with a six-ounce beer glass, GRANITE CITY AUTO PARTS written on the side. Next to the bottle, a small open container, white safety lid beside it, and several white tablets in sight. His right hand was bandaged, three middle digits in splints sticking out of an ACE bandage. Phelim held out the glass in a salute and drank with his good left hand. They gathered around him, one sitting and two standing at the table.

"What the hell happened?" asked Del.

"Did you make a report yet?" wondered Scanlan.

"You got a beer handy?" said Francis.

At their urging, Phelim began to tell what had happened. How he was in the garage under the hood of a sick Buick and suddenly he saw two sets of legs on either side of him. He rolled out on his creeper and saw a pair of goons, one meaty but not fat with blunt features and a buzz cut. The other one big and muscle-bound like the friggin' Hulk, head shaved on the sides but full on top, twisted into some kind of topknot—never saw nothing like it outside of a wrestling ring. Oh yeah, he had a harelip, too. Both of them white boys, in their twenties probably, and mean as a boil. He had a wrench in his hand and the first thing they did, they took that away.

"Then they began to ask questions," Phelim recounted, "like where do they find my upstairs neighbor, meaning you"—he looked to Francis, sipping at a can of Stag—"and when I didn't have the answers they wanted, they acted like they were sad and how it was really a shame that they'd missed you. They said they really had their hearts set on my neighbor, but that I would do in a pinch." He took a hit of Paddy. "I knew right then it was gonna hurt."

He held up his damaged hand. "So the rest is pretty damn obvious, right? The big one held me while ol' Buzz bent my fingers back until they snapped. The whole time he's smiling and saying weird things like 'This shouldn't hurt too much,' and 'Is this the finger you use to diddle your girlfriend?' Hell, man, you talk about pain, I damn near passed out."

"We're gonna get these guys," said Scanlan, sitting at the table across from Phelim with a small spiral notebook. "With just a little more information we're gonna bust their asses." The cop definitely had his Irish up. "Now, did you hear either one of them say a name, one calling the other by name?"

"Well, yeah," said Phelim, looking at his poor hand, "Buzz, he called the other lunkhead 'Brun' or 'Bun,' something like that."

Francis had a feeling that Buzz was Deke's son, whatever his name was.

"Okay, that's a start," said Scanlan, jotting in his notebook. "Did you happen to see what they were driving?"

"Well, no," said Phelim, "I was too busy having my poor fingers broke."

"Anything else about them?" pressed Scanlan.

Phelim brought the glass to his lips and up-ended it, the whiskey going down smooth. "Ahhh," holding the glass before him, gazing with admiration, "best pain killer there is. Del, hand me that ashtray over there, will you?" Del took an overflowing ashtray from the countertop, dumped the stale butts into a trash container nearby, and placed it in front of Phelim. "Top left pocket," said Phelim, and

Del fished out a pack of Pall Malls. He shook one out and gave it to Phelim who held it expectantly between his lips. In an instant Del had his Zippo out and put flame to the cig. Again, a contented sigh, Phelim leaning back, puffing away.

Scanlan drummed the tabletop with his fingers. "Well?"

"Well what?" acting now as if he can't be bothered.

"Anything else about them that you remember, something that stands out from the ordinary?"

Phelim nodded in the affirmative. "They weren't from around here. I know that because they had accents like you hear out in the country. Hard to describe, kind of a drawl, a sort of lazy way of talking yet they run their words together—not that I really wanted to understand what they were saying, the dirty potlickers."

Now Francis was sure that Buzz was Deke's boy.

Scanlan was studying what he'd written in his notebook, pondering what else to bring up.

"What were you thinking?" asked Francis, mild rebuke in his tone. "I mean, you knew where I was, over at Murphy's like I am every day at that time. You could've saved yourself some suffering, not to mention loss of work, if only you'd simply told them where to find me."

"Yeah," said Del, "they would've come there and we would've taken care of them."

"I did tell them where you were," said Phelim, matter-of-factly, "but only after they threatened to break the fingers on my other hand."

* * *

"He said it was one block down and three blocks over," said Brunt.

"No, other way around, Doofus. He said three blocks down and one over."

"But which way is over, left or right?"

They were in Derrick's Regal, tooling through Dogtown, looking for the bar where the old man had said Lenihan would be. Derrick's passenger was Randy Bruntraeger—Brunt—a lifelong pal and unquestioning partner in crime, the perfect sidekick. Brunt was a laborer on a highway department crew; all day long, for years now, he cleared ditches, cutting away brush and honeysuckle that choked the ditches and impeded water flow. Even in bad weather he liked the work and pretended that he was on a prison road gang, like in *Cool Hand Luke*. Brunt was six-three and weighed at least two-fifty. He could lift three-hundred and instead of regulation weights he used hydraulic jacks and steel girders and other things he found lying around the MoDOT facility where they clocked in each day. His head was shaved on the sides up to the crown and then there was a lengthy crop of hair on top tied into a cluster, sort of like a sheaf of wheat you'd see in some old book on farming. At times he wished he could grow a mustache to cover his harelip, but his partly Native American lineage didn't provide much facial hair.

"There's a bar over there," said Brunt, pointing to a two-story on a corner, red-and-black letters spelling out GRIESEDIECK BROS. BEER on the side of the building.

Derrick looked for a name somewhere on the facade. "That says O' Rourke's, we're looking for Murphy's."

"These fuckin' Irish and their booze," said Brunt contemptuously. "They're all addicted and they love it. What's that saying? Whiskey was invented so the Irish wouldn't rule the world. You ever hear that?"

"Nah," said Derrick, "I can't be bothered with no sayings. But that geezer back there, you can bet he's feelin' it now." He gave a nasty chuckle. "That look on his face as we were crackin' his knuckles for him. Priceless. You get off on that?"

"Not too much ... it was okay, though."

"I did, I got off on it. I guess I like inflicting pain."

"You enjoy the geezer more'n the bird?"

Derrick thought about that. "Probably. Birds don't stretch it out yelling and screaming in pain, music to my ears. A bird, it's just one surprised squawk or screech—whatever they do—and then it's over."

"There's a name for that," said Brunt.

"Yeah?"

"Yeah, sadist. You're a sadist."

"Good, at least I'm something."

"It was colorful, the bird."

"So's an oilslick."

"Look, there's a guy coming out that bar, let's ask him."

The man was walking along, weaving through some invisible slalom course when they pulled up alongside. "Hey," called Derrick, "you know where Murphy's Bar is?"

"Hell, yes, I know where Murphy's is," he shot back, "but you wouldn't catch me in there. Bunch a losers, don't know shit from Shinola."

Derrick snorted. "We don't care about what you think of the place, just tell us where it is."

"The man, obviously soused, came closer, studying them in the dimming daylight. He shook his overcoat and brushed away some imaginary soot. "Gerry Grogan," he said, "at your service." He took a little bow. "What is it I can do for you gents?"

Brunt got out and opened the back door. "You can get your sorry ass in here and lead us to this Murphy's," he told the drunk.

Grogan shrugged. "Why the hell not?" Two minutes later they were there, a watering hole that had once been a bungalow, home to a family once upon a time. Neon signs in the windows hawked various beers in a warm glow of colors.

"Listen, fellas," said Gerry Grogan from the back seat, "I ain't about to go in there, but I sure could use another drink. How's about yous giving me a couple bucks for a pop at another bar? You know, after I brung you here and all?"

Brunt turned around. He looked at Grogan and Grogan knew the answer. Still, he hesitated, imploring them with this hangdog look. Brunt pointed at the pavement. "You get outta this car, dickweed, before we decide to scramble your brains—"

"Then fuck you in the ass," said Derrick. Brunt glanced at Derrick, sniggering at his own ribald remark. He was pretty sure Derrick was a homo, but he would not bring it up because he would never talk about such things—too personal. So long as Derrick didn't hit on him. Grogan got out and shuffled off into the evening.

"How you wanna work it?" asked Brunt as he climbed back in the car. "I mean, we gonna work him over in the bar? Probably better take him outside."

Derrick was thinking, always a dangerous thing. "Let's just take a look through the windows, see that he's in there and who he's with."

"All right," said Brunt. "So this guy's a thorn in your side, huh? Some barfly in St. Louis causing problems way out in our neck of the woods?"

"You got it," he answered, balling a fist into the palm of the other hand. "He used my dad's name and he's got something to do with Stoney being missing."

"And who's Stoney again? I know you told me, but—"

"Friend of the family, but that don't matter. This guy's bad news, a cog in the machinery and we're gonna fix him good. You with me?"

"You know it, man. Let's fucking do it."

They walked up to one side of the tavern, trampling some pansies below a square mullioned window that afforded a view. They stood there peering through, trying to locate Francis. There were maybe twenty people inside, some with their backs to them and others they couldn't see off in the corners. Then they moved to the entrance, a wooden door with a green shamrock relief in the upper center, opened it just a little. They could see the entire interior now.

"What's he look like?" asked Brunt.

"He looks like that guy at the table over near the jukebox talking to that cop," said Derrick, really bummed.

Brunt looked and saw two guys at the table, one in cargo shorts and a ratty blue sweatshirt, long hair but not hippie long. The other was a square-jawed, blond-haired cop, had the look of a high school jock gone to seed. Brunt's eyes went to the pressed blue uniform with sergeant stripes on the sleeve. "Aw, shit!" he said.

That was an hour and a half ago. Derrick and Brunt had high-tailed it back to Jeff County and were now shooting pool in a smoky bar. Meanwhile, back in Phelim's kitchen they were wrapping it up. The fifth of Paddy's was down to the dregs and Phelim was nodding off. Del had gone back to Murphy's. Scanlan and Francis sat there talking while Phelim snoozed on the table with his head nestled in folded arms.

"I think you know who these palookas are and why they're in our neighborhood," Scanlan voiced accusingly. Francis played dumb. He wasn't into having the third degree just now. Scanlan leaned forward, a hand cupping his chin, stroking that chin thoughtfully. He tried to bore into Francis' skull with his noble sense of justice, as piercing as any drill bit. "You think about this act of violence on your pal, Phelim," his delivery measured and earnest, "you think about it and help me make some sense of it. Does what happened here have something to do with that murder in Jefferson County? I think so, and now those country rhubarbs are leeching into Dogtown and we sure as hell can't have that."

"I want to get to the bottom of it as much as you do," Francis told him, "especially if it's me they're after."

"You just watch yourself, hear? Anything strange, anything out of place, you call me. Got that?"

"Yes, sir."

"Good, now let's put this old boy to bed."

Francis let himself out the front door and ascended the stairs to his apartment. He never locked the outside door because this was Dogtown and break-ins were not fashionable. At the top of the stairs he saw that his door was open. Open and askew, the wood around the doorknob splintered and the door itself partly off its hinges. He entered with a prickly feeling of dread. He switched on the light and saw the place had been tossed, clothes and books and things from the fridge all in a mishmash on the floor. Furniture tipped over, pictures broken, curtains ripped down. He stood there among the sorry mess, anger welling, when suddenly the thought of Petey stabbed his brain and he felt panic. He rushed to the cage, hoping against hope that his friend was all right. The cage door was open and within, at the floor, near his water tray, the lifeless form of Petey the Parakeet lay, his wings torn asunder.

— 25 —

"MORNING MRS. TIERNEY," HE SAID as he passed the old woman scrubbing her stoop with a stiff-bristled broom, a pail of bleach and water nearby. She waved distractedly and went back to her task. Around the corner he came to a playground. It was put there by the city before he was born, and he'd spent many happy hours there as an energetic kid testing the limits of the merry go-round, the slide, the monkey bars and swings. Learning, too, how to get along with other kids. Now there was a woman sitting on a bench reading a book as one child played by herself. "Come on, mommy," she called, "push me on the swing. Please, mommy."

Francis kept walking, heading nowhere in particular, just wanting to be out and enjoying the morning, slightly brisk. He turned on Tamm Avenue and saw Pat Hannan unlocking the door to his barber shop. Pat was old sod, and Francis loved to hear the brogue in his voice, as authentic a souvenir of Ireland as any embroidered finery or commemorative plate or what-have-you that may have made its way to the States in the suitcase of some hopeful immigrant. Pat had been his barber since his mother stopped cutting his hair when he was seven. He'd wait for the others to be done, pretending to be engrossed in the current issue of *Outdoor Life* or *Argosy*, and all the while taking in the conversation around him, every word telling him something about the arcane world of adults, how they think and behave. Finally, it was his turn and Pat would say, "Climb on up here, boy." And he would sit on the throne of the plush Koken chair with its brass foot rest, although his feet couldn't reach that far, as Pat snip-snip-snipped, making small talk and treating him with respect the same as he gave any other customer. When he was finished and the haircut approved—Pat behind him, showing him the back by holding a mirror that reflected off the big mirror on the wall in front of him—Pat would strap on this nifty mechanical glove with an electric cord attached and give him a two-minute shoulder massage, the contraption making this pleasant whirring sound. No other barber was doing anything like that. It was a class act and it gave customer service a new meaning.

Now he stopped at the shop and put his head in the door, Pat making ready for the first customer. "Been meaning to come in and get my ears lowered," he said.

Pat looked up, a fancy bottle of something yellow in his hand. Hair tonic. He smiled. "Ah, Francis, my boy. Anytime, anytime. Even now."

"No, not now, but soon. I'll be seeing you."

"You have a fine day. May the Lord bless you and keep you."

"Thanks, Pat."

He walked on, his mind a camera, capturing every little thing that made this neighborhood unique. Up there, hung from the telephone lines and branches of trees, strands of colorful beads, some with plastic shamrocks attached, remnants of the great Hibernian Parade that thronged Dogtown each March 17th. Over there, a wooden gazebo in a small park out front of the hardware store, the place to be on a summer's night with a cold beer and a pretty girl, expectations high. Some good memories there. He looked across Clayton Avenue and saw Paul Tanner in the parking lot of the TomBoy Market, setting up the custom-built 55-gallon drum that served as a smoker for the brisket and pork steaks and sides of rib that would be ready for sale before noon. Paul owned the market with his brothers and, though he was needed inside, he was given a pass to be out here each morning eight months of the year, wearing an apron with a cartoon image of a happy pig and the caption "King Of The Grill." This was his real love and he, like Francis, was very grateful to Dogtown for letting him live life on his own terms.

More. Celtic Pride Pawn & Jewelry where many an engagement ring had been bought, and, sometimes embarrassingly returned.

Dogtown Liquors where old Pete McCormick behind the counter had sold him beer when he was just eighteen, back when a six was something to crow about. Backyard grottoes featuring a statue of the Blessed Virgin, nestled in the protective shelter of an upright bathtub. Mary on the Halfshell. There, on the side of the hardware store, an ancient sign for Royal Patent Flour, the painted letters now part of the brick, the artistic work of some nameless wall dog back when beer was a nickel. Over there, down that sidestreet, Galvin Funeral Home, where everyone in Dogtown, including his parents, wound up sooner or later. These images and countless more were cataloged in the archives of his mind. Cumulatively they formed a mosaic of a place that gave him a sense of who he was and what he might become, a place that was at once comfortable and unforgiving; friendly, yet narrow-minded; safe, yet insulated. The entire neighborhood somewhat off-kilter in a good way. So how in the world does it happen, he asked himself, that a couple of degenerates—strangers—can waltz in here and create mischief of the worst kind, leaving a blot on the neighborhood. It just wasn't right.

* * *

Deke pushed his plate aside, the ribeye gnawed to the bone, the tater tots and broccoli nothing but crumblets. He went to the cupboard over the sink and got two clean glasses. The Seven Crown was already on the table. He filled both glasses halfway and passed one over to Derrick, just finishing up.

"Now, we'll talk," said Deke, knowing some of it wouldn't be pleasant. Deke and his son looked at one another. Deke knew that Derrick was too big and ornery to chastise, but nevertheless he had to say something, him acting on his own without any restraint.

"What you told me earlier, that took me by surprise, and I gotta say, it didn't sit well with me."

Derrick turned in his chair, looked over his shoulder, wanting to make sure that Eve had left the room. She'd prepared the meal, supped with her father and brother, and, as soon as she was finished, announced she was going to her room. She hadn't said much during the meal, all that noisy masticating driving her batty. "I didn't have to tell you," Derrick remarked. "I coulda kept it to myself, but I thought you'd be pleased."

"You should've talked to me before you went and I might've said, Okay, but what's your plan? More importantly, what's to be gained by it?" He shook his head in exasperation, and tilted the whiskey to his lips.

"I guess I thought I knew you well enough, that you'd be okay with it. And it was kinda spontaneous, I mean, me and Brunt were just sitting around drinking when the idea popped up." Now Derrick took his first taste of the evening. "Hoo!" he blinked, the booze burning his throat. "As for what's to be gained. Well hell, we done put the fear into him and those around him including that hippie-dippy daughter of the lady what was killed—he'll figure it was us, and tell her. I mean, c'mon, them comin' round here, stickin' their noses into our business, talkin' to Eve on the sly. They're trouble."

"Yeah? And what the fuck am I?"

Derrick grinned. "You're double-trouble ... and so am I."

"All right," said Deke, seeming appeased, "let's back up a minute, look at this thing objectively. We're not involved in that woman's murder, we got nothing to hide about that. But these idiots are convinced that we are somehow involved and them nosing around and checking into us has the effect of putting the kibosh on our operation. We can either strike back, which you've already done—without my consent—or we can just ignore them. In other words, those two are not necessarily that big a threat. They're like mosquitoes, annoying, but easily swatted away."

"And if they keep it up?"

"We're private citizens, we got rights. They come back and try to get in our business, I'll go to Hillsboro and take out one of them restraining orders."

Derrick was horrified. "What're you, *trying* to make me look like a pussy? Don't you fuckin' do that! If the guys found out I'd never live it down. They'd say I was afraid of the prick."

Eve, just out of sight, eavesdropping, put her hand to her mouth and stifled a laugh.

Deke was pleased that he hit a chord in his headstrong son. He wanted to rile him up, prick his macho skin. "Ah, forget that. It was just a stray thought. You know we take care of our own problems." He watched Derrick calm down, take another sip of Seven. "You say you found him in a bar, and he was talking with a cop?"

"Yeah, older cop with sergeant stripes on his uniform. They were at a table in the back. It looked like friends talking more than the cop questioning him in some official way."

"You think maybe it had something to do with what's going on out here?"

"Hell, it could. I wouldn't be surprised, I mean, for more'n a month now it's been cops out here, Lenihan and the girl out here, Lenihan at Stoney's place—Christ Almighty, everyone's a fuckin' detective."

"Yeah, and they're not gonna let up until they put the finger on someone. I tell you that this dick from the sheriff office was out here the other day?"

"No, man, you did not."

"Guy's name is LaRocca, Detective Bernard LaRocca, and he's got me in his sights. Only I ain't done nothin'. But this guy he don't care, he don't listen to me when I say the truth, that I got nothin' to do with this woman dead. He says he's coming back with a search warrant and he's gonna hook me up to a lie detector. Bullshit! They're only on me because I did time and I happen to live in the same vicinity as this dead person."

Derrick shook his head in commiseration. "It ain't right. Goddamn cops, it ain't right."

"Fuckin–A it ain't right," he said, holding up his drink for emphasis. Derrick did same. They were well in cahoots. "Well, I ain't worried, because unless they plant some evidence or make up some shit they don't have squat on me."

"They'll do that! Enough time goes by and they ain't made an arrest, they'll get desperate and do a frame-up. It happened to my pal, Johnny."

"Johnny Kingman, lives over in Grubville?"

Nah, Johnny Fortner, a roofer over in DeSoto. You don't know him."

"I take it back," confessed Deke, "I am a bit worried. I hate having this attention from the cops. You ain't done time, you don't know what it's like, being caged up like an animal. And I was only in medium security. Like you say, they control what happens. What if they make up some shit that I can't defend? Man, I can't go back there. I can't and I won't! When I check out it's gonna be in the sunlight, and not some gloomy prison cell."

"I hear you loud and clear," Derrick told him. He reached for the bottle. He filled their glasses again. "So what do we do with this Francis and his sidekick?"

"We're just gonna sit on it," he replied. "Don't do anything right now." He looked hard at Derrick. Chunky build, flat features, beady brown eyes, upturned nose, and thick lips that always seemed to be snarling. Not the most attractive features for a young man to have; Deke felt they had to have come from his wife's side of the family. "Meanwhile," he went on, "what with Stoney gone, I need a hand in taking a load of merchandise to Tulsa for the big swap meet they got in early November. There must be five-thousand bucks of swag in that warehouse, all of it just waiting to be converted. We'll rent a trailer, go down there together, make a weekend of it. And this is a good venue. If the weather ain't horrible there'll be thousands of people flocking that fairground, wallets out, looking to buy."

"Yeah, all right," said Derrick. "I'm in. What's my cut?"

"You don't worry 'bout that, we'll settle up on the way back home."

"I got to have an idea," persisted Derrick. "Is it fifty percent or what? That's what it should be."

Deke gave him a look. "You didn't steal the stuff, you didn't take a risk. All you're doing is loading it and bringing it to market."

"I want the same cut that Stoney would get, all right?" Deke didn't answer. "All right?" Derrick repeated, forcefully. Now Deke was glowering in his direction and Derrick decided to change the subject. "So what do you think happened to Stoney? What's your theory? He hiding under a rock somewhere?"

Deke made some glib comment about Stoney being unstable and how he had talked of going on a long vacation to some tropical place.

Derrick was more than skeptical. "What? I don't think so. I didn't know the guy hardly at all but I can't see him in a Hawaiian shirt and surfboard shorts under a palm tree, sipping a pina colada, watching the sunset. You think that, you're deranged."

Deke shrugged disinterest. "All I know is he didn't tell me that he was booking out. He's gone, his car is gone. Where? Who knows. He just lit out one day to follow his own path … wherever the hell that might lead."

Derrick studied Deke's face, looking for something. "Didn't he disappear right around the time of the murder?"

"I can't rightly say," answered Deke, "I don't know the timeline. We didn't talk but once or twice a month."

"It's a hell of a mystery," said Derrick, "and I don't think he'll turn up."

"You got any weed or other drugs laying around?" asked Deke.

"Nah, you know I ain't into that. I'm a boozer. Why you asking?"

"I told you, LaRocca said he was coming back with a search warrant. I just wanted to give you a heads up."

"No, I'm cool."

"We're both cool," said Deke, holding up his glass in a salute. "Cool as cucumbers."

Quietly Eve walked down the hall and went upstairs to her room. She'd heard enough from her lowlife father and brother. Maybe Deke knew something about Elizabeth's Shurzinger's murder, maybe he didn't. But if he got put away it would certainly change things for her. Would Derrick then be her guardian? Ugh. She'd have to leave, go somewhere she felt comfortable. Maybe one of her friend's families would take her in.

Atop her dresser, a decal-plastered Jambox with a cassette player.

She put in the Pet Shop Boys and began dancing around the room. Faster and faster, doing some crazy whirling Dervish thing, bobbing, weaving, arms outstretched, twirling. The song over, she plopped down on her bed. This next cut wasn't near as good, sounded like a guy imitating a sick cat. She reached over and opened the small drawer on her nightstand. She found the card on top of everything else. She read it again for the tenth time. She liked the way it looked and felt. Thick stock, nothing flimsy about it, pearl finish. A definite shimmer to it. The illustration, done in miniature, was intriguing: A crescent moon and several heavenly bodies set against a cobalt sky with a crooked tree at the bottom illuminated against a soft glow on the horizon. Nice—beautiful!—but what did it mean? On the obverse, in flowing script, it read:

May Rose Schurzinger
Diviner – Healer – Citizen Of The Planet

— 26 —

This was certainly something different, sitting buck naked in a sauna with mostly strangers. Talk about dropping one's inhibitions, Francis reflected, bemused. There were five others in the two-tier wooden structure that looked like a shack from the outside. Beside him on the lower bench, a bearded wonder with steamy John Lennon spectacles on the tip of his beak-like nose. Rainbow. That's all, one name like Tarzan or Cher. Above and behind him, on the upper berth, where supposedly it was hotter, because heat rises, sat Ranald and Darby and their offspring, six-year-old Odin. Every so often Darby would massage Francis' shoulders with her toes. Pretty weird, but it felt good. Young Odin was already on his way to hippiedom with long brown locks braided into pigtails and threaded with colored ribbons that cascaded over his shoulders. It was his task to sprinkle water on the grate of the metal box over in the corner, the rocks hissing and making steam. Every so often Darby would give him a signal, and Odin would scamper down for the water bucket and ladle. Also, every so often, Rainbow would go out and stoke with wood the kiln which heated the room. Over in the upper corner, opposite Francis, sat Rose, leaning back on the wall, eyes closed, her knees apart. Was it rude to stare? He was unsure of sauna etiquette. But, hey, that furry blonde beaver was definitely staring *at him*. They'd been broiling in this hothouse for twenty-five minutes now and all were sweating profusely.

During a recent phone call she'd invited him out for the day, said she wanted him to see her life in this commune. Why not? He drove an hour southwest of St. Louis, having himself a nice adventure on the way, stopping to look at cows and toss stones in creeks that crossed the road. Having finally arrived, he drove along the apple tree-lined gravel drive to the main house, canary yellow with blue shutters and green trim. He blew the horn and Rose emerged from a barn, wearing a knee-length cotton dress the colors of fall, a black crew-neck pullover, gaucho hat, and cowboy boots. She gave him a mama bear hug and introduced him to the others. There were more than these folks who were now in the sauna; there were maybe nine—he didn't meet them all at once—and he wondered which ones were her lovers. A lifelong city boy, he'd never been to a commune. In his somewhat provincial outlook, a commune, that is, the communal life, was about sharing—partners, drugs, work, meals, games and recreation, what-have-you. Having taken the tour and met the folks at their labors—they reminded him of settlers in some 19th century photograph—he decided that his outlook wasn't all that off base.

She took him around the farm, for that's what it was, a working farm with goats and chickens and rabbits and three moo cows. There were two large gardens, one for produce and one for flowering plants—oleander, sunflowers, snapdragon, hydrangea. Except for the pumpkin patch and some zucchini all crops were harvested and the ground lay waiting for spring tilling. The chores rotated, she explained, For instance, one week she would care for the chickens, collect eggs, feed and water them, clean out their coop. The next week someone else would get that job and she would move on to flower cultivation or rabbit husbandry. And so it went until the cycle of chores was completed and she would go back to chickens and start all over. Rabbits, he asked. Why those? There's a market for them, she said. Every Saturday from May to October we go to the Farmer's Market over in DeSoto and we sell our goods. Eggs and cheese, tomatoes, squash, kale, carrots and more. Flowers, too, beautiful arrangements that I myself make. And yeah, slaughtered chickens and rabbits—ever try hasenpfeffer? You do the slaughtering? he asked, intrigued. I do, she answered, although it's not my favorite thing. You get used to them, and some you even grow fond of. You can't help it.

"Probably not a good idea to name them," he said. "'Here, Flopsy, here boy. Don't mind this hatchet in my hand.'"

She smiled at this pretend scenario, not being far from the reality of it. "It's all part of the cycle of life," she said, taking his hand. "Birth, growth, maturity, wisdom, death. We're all just here for the ride, and it only comes around once."

"So hold on for dear life while the merry-go-round is spinning," he said.

"Something like that," she said, laughing. "Come on, I'll show you my yurt."

That was hours ago. He'd visited her yurt, and learned that many famous people had spent time in yurts, Ghengis Khan for one. He'd lain in a hammock, milked a goat, canned some peaches, sampled some dandelion wine—ugh!—turned down her offer to get high, and now they were in the sauna. A conversation had started about a chicken-killing dog that belonged to one of their neighbors. This dog had been making forays into the commune by night and leaving dead fowl in its wake. They knew it was this dog in particular and not a fox, say, because the dog, an Airedale, wore a bright red collar and it was known by them. Plus, someone had seen it jump over the wire fence that enclosed the chickens, heading out, feathers stuck to its nappy muzzle. The members of Peace Haven were to have a tribunal, their word, this very evening to decide what should be done with this animal. They were not going to invite the dog's owner, because they didn't want any unpleasantness. The consensus among these folks here in the sauna was that the dog, on its next visit, would be captured by some clever means and humanely dispatched. This had happened before, and that was the solution then. Once a dog got the taste for chicken, Ranald informed, there was no rehabilitating it. It would go on killing chickens with abandon until stopped in its tracks. If the tribunal did vote to do away with this dog, which it would, the owner would never know what happened to his pet. The dog would just disappear. Let him wonder.

"What if," wondered Francis aloud, "you guys just walk over there and offer him a basket of fresh eggs and ask him nicely to keep his dog tied up? Tell him he gets a dozen eggs every month for doing just that. How about that, huh?"

No one said anything for a while and then Rainbow said he was about poached and was going out to cool off. Then they all went out and stood in the afternoon daylight and doused each other with cold water dipped from a cast-off bathtub. Laughing, clowning, having innocent fun. The scene would have made a nice cover shot for *Nude Lifestyle*. They stood there, steam coming off their bodies, talking for a while longer until Ranald and Darby said they were going back to the main house. Rainbow said he may as well go, too. They didn't put on their clothes, just carried them in their arms and began striding through the grasses.

"Well, that leaves you and me," she said, and they went back in the sauna.

"I went by the address you gave, the trailer over in Dittmer," she said, once they had settled in on the upper berth, "what a hole."

He was flummoxed and alarmed by this announcement. "Why would you do that? I told you what happened to me out there."

"I wanted to see it for myself. If this guy did murder mom I wanted to be in his place, where he dwells. I thought maybe I could pick up some vibe that would tell me who he is, where he is."

They were sitting side by side on the upper berth, starting to sweat once again. There was not much light in there, only an opaque window near the door that dripped condensation.

"And?"

"I think those dead animals on the ground created interference with my radar. When I tried to intuit something—anything—all I got was static. The deer, though, I took that as an omen. The place reeked of death." She looked at him, earnestly. "I'm virtually certain this Stoney character is no longer among us."

She had not mentioned her visit to Stoney's place while walking the farm earlier, when they had gone over it, rehashed the thing for what seemed like the tenth time. Stoney, the likely killer, was missing. Deke has something to do with the murder, but what? If Deke is tight with Stoney then Deke knows Stoney killed Elizabeth, which makes Deke an accessory. If they can't get to Stoney then they have to get to Deke. But getting to Deke had its perils. He filled her in on what had happened in Dogtown, how Deke's son and another had harmed his neighbor and killed his parakeet. In short, this was getting serious.

He also told her that the local cop, Scanlan, knew that he was keeping things from him, that Scanlan had told him emphatically that he must divulge whatever information he had turned up.

"Am I still on the job?" he'd asked. "Because I'll keep going as long as I'm officially on the job."

She'd shrugged and said, "Yeah, you're still on the job, it's just that we have to figure out what to do next. In my mind Deke is just as guilty as Stoney. We have to find a way to prove that Deke is in on it."

He'd walked along in thought. "Scanlan's in touch with LaRocca and he says that the Jeff County detectives are really looking at someone out here, that's got to be Deke. I just don't want to get in the way of what they're doing."

"They've got their methods, we've got ours," she'd replied.

In the sauna, Rose went to sprinkle some water on the hot rocks. She climbed back up. "Maybe the daughter," she said, picking up on a stray thread of their previous conversation, "maybe I can get her alone and see what she knows."

"How would you do that, trail her? That's risky."

"I know a place where she hangs out."

"Give it a try. Talk her up, she'll relate to you."

"That's enough business," she said.

They were close enough that their thighs brushed together. He asked about the tattoo on the small of her back, some sort of hieroglyphic, a stylized "3" with a kind of diagram and little squiggles above and beside it. She said it was the OM and it represented a belief or concept sacred to Hinduism. Oh, he said, dropping it, not wanting to go there. Her breasts hung down on her chest. Not drooping, not at all, but angled to her sides and jutting outward. Magnificent breasts, Amazon woman breasts, all sweaty and glistening. He stole a glance as a drop of sweat began to form on a nipple, pink and protruding. He began to have impure thoughts, very much so. The droplet fell onto her thigh. Now he had an erection—again. He placed his hands on his lap, thinking to cover it up but she was quite aware of it.

"No need to be modest in here," she said, her voice turning even more husky than usual. "We like to let it all hang out, and some of us hang out more than others." She moved even closer. She took his hands away. "Let me see that," she said. She caressed it, fingers lightly tracing the contours of the head. His lust built until he thought he'd burst. He closed in on her, rested a hand on her shoulder and with the other one sculpted a breast. He smothered her mouth, kissing hungrily, tongues probing, and she filled him with craving and wonder. For a stark moment he thought of Janie, but Rose's femininity was overpowering and an instant later there was only Rose. They did it on the wooden plank spanning the upper berth. First, him on top—and she was a big strapping girl, her behind and thighs just massive, giving him quite the ride—and later, she astride him. Her face just over his, her body covering him, her pelvis working the pole. He closed his eyes, he opened them. In the dim light she seemed to be glowing.

"This is Francis. I'm not here right now but please leave a message and I'll get back to you soon. If you just want to tell a joke, feel free, and I'll tell you later if I think it's funny." He pressed the Hear button on the answering machine. "Francis, this is George Lowry, I've got some summonses for you at my office. Two going to South County and one in the city. I'll be in all day, so stop on by. See you." All day was yesterday. He'd make that his first stop. Next, the voice of a man who the world revolves around, his brother Mike. "Hey FX"—Mike the only one who got to call him FX—"what's happening? Haven't seen you for the longest. Still serving those writs and warrants? Risky business, brother, risky business, hope you carry a piece. Hey, I just called to invite you out for Thanksgiving. Linda and the kids would love to see you. Me, eh, I can take it or leave it. Kidding! Dinner with all the trimmings at two, why don't you get here around noon. If you have a girlfriend these days, bring her. Oh, and Thanksgiving's on a Thursday this year. Call me back to confirm, sayonara."

He'd go, he'd make the yearly pilgrimage out to the west county 'burbs, wending his way through the maze of streets with names like Autumn Leaf and Lamplighter and he'd find their home among all the cookie-cutter homes, every one with a perfect family inside. And he'd sit with Mike in the living room, TV tuned to some bowl game, and he'd drink imported beer but not Guinness and listen to his brother boast about how well he was doing at the brokerage, and why didn't he think about some other profession where he could make some real money, maybe real estate or financial planning. It wasn't too late. Had he ever considered going back to school for a business degree? And the two girls would draw near and giggle and ask Uncle Francis why he always came by himself, didn't he have, like, a girlfriend, and the Golden Retriever would sniff his crotch while Mike made some clever remark. Then it was time for the great repast and afterward he would again join Mike for the treat of single-malt Scotch and Linda would prepare for him a large Tupperware container of leftovers, a full weeks' rations and a reminder of the family life he was missing. Then it was goodbye at the door, hugs and well-wishes and See you next year! Yeah, that certainly was something to look forward to.

Next in the message queue was Janie inviting him to meet for drinks after work on Friday. This was Wednesday so there was time to respond, and he wouldn't have the added guilt of feeling like he'd blown her off. "I'm thinking Balaban's," she was saying, "or that new place in Lafayette Square where they have the shrimp and oyster bar during happy hour. Thinking of you, call me back, kisses."

The voice and accompanying image of Janie brought up very strong feelings that he knew were not going away until some thankless resolution came along. Prickly feelings of guilt over having cheated on her with Rose overlaid by more icky feelings of dread that their relationship would soon be ruined because he had succumbed to temptation. Shoot, he more or less instigated it. Of course there was no formal declaration of monogamy, it was tacit. Still, he had to go betray that trust and now he would pay with heart-wrenching recriminations. Life would never be the same. He caught himself. Woe is me, huh? It's Janie who'll be filled with pain and hurt once she finds out. And that was the big and looming question, to tell or not to tell. Could he go on living keeping secret from her his infidelity? But that craven act of dishonesty would be detected by Janie—"What's going on, Francis? Something's on your mind, it's written all over your face"—and their romance would go down the tubes anyway. What a pickle. He couldn't feel worse if he'd been caught red-handed robbing the poor box at church.

The next message was from Joe Lennon wondering when the hell they could go back out and serve some fucking papers.

The last message was one he did not expect. "Francis, this is Sgt. Brian Scanlan. You asked me to look into your father's death, and I did. I'm here at the station, mornings until around nine. Roll call's at seven. You've got my card, call me. Oh, and it's a joke you want? Why can't you borrow money from a leprechaun? ... give up? Because they're always a little short. Ha, ha!"

Francis took the cordless from its cradle and began to pace the room. What did Scanlan have? Did he really want to find out, knowing that it might open the Pandora's Box of intricate feelings and nagging doubt surrounding the demise of Martin Lenihan? So much wondering over the years, now it might become clear. Or clearer. He stood before Petey's empty cage, and the heartless act that befell him once again came to mind. Those pricks. He might not say that word aloud in public, but he could sure think it. Life was good, he truly felt that. But it was cruel, too. Look at all the kids born with some awful disease that kept them from enjoying life. Look at the young people involved in accidents that left them paralyzed. Look at the innocent victims of crime. Maybe he'd learn that Martin Lenihan was the victim of foul play. How would he react? Would he do something stupid, something he'd regret?

He glanced at his Coleman wristwatch: 8:15. He dialed the station number.

"Scanlan here."

"It's Francis Lenihan, good morning."

"The jury's out on that."

"On your message you said—"

"Yeah, so I did my own checking. No autopsy, but the death certificate says Food Poisoning. Then I spoke with Pete Bosley, superintendent at The Workhouse, guy's been there forever. Pete recalls your father, recalls that there were some question marks in the matter. Pete did a little checking, a report on the incident in some musty old file, and it turns out there was another guard with your dad when he took ill. A fella from the neighborhood it turns out, and this fella has retired from Corrections and he's still alive."

"Wow," said Francis, feeling a flutter in his chest, "that's ... that's amazing. Who's the guy?"

"You know," said Scanlan, "my memory seems to've gotten a mite foggy. That name is clouded in mist. How about your memory, boyo? Any luck recalling why those assholes were here looking to fuck you up? You show me yours, I'll show you mine."

"Of course, the old reciprocal thing. All right, here you go." Francis gave him the plate on the Challenger, gave him the name Clarence Jackson alias Stoney and the address out in Dittmer.

Scanlan was not pleased. "That's old news, you know that. Jeff Co homicide's already been there, that's where they found your wallet. Jerkin' my chain, are you? This Jackson's a strong suspect, but he's made himself scarce."

"Sorry, let's try again. What else? Well, um, Stoney, he's a friend, an associate, whatever, with another guy, Deke, lives over in the subdivision where Schurzinger lived. I'll get you his address, and maybe he's the one you should be looking at because they're up to something ... sounds like a couple of cowboys, doesn't it? Deke and Stoney."

"Cowboys at the end of a rope maybe. But again, you're handing me old news. LaRocca already mentioned Deke—or did he? He spoke of a suspect, Johnson, something Johnson ... Richard Johnson—the neighbor, did time, shaky alibi, but no motive for the killing. Maybe that's Deke. I'll pass it on. Still, they're on the guy, something's gonna break loose before long. What else?"

He could hear sounds in the background—a door slamming, someone shouting, chatter from a police radio. "Those guys who came to Dogtown that day, messed up Phelim? I never saw 'em, but from the description I think one was Deke's son. The other, I don't know. Like I said, never saw 'em so it's just conjecture."

"And why would they come here to find you?"

"Because I was out to their place, asking around, and they thought they'd return the favor."

"Ah, I see. Makes sense. You got his name?"

"I don't," said Francis. "Only met him once and we skipped the introductions. Now is it my turn?"

"I don't know," said the cop, a tease in his voice, "the quality of your intel leaves much to be desired."

"Oh, come on!"

He heard Scanlan take a breath. "The name of the man who was with Martin, and it was just them apparently, is, uh, Jackie Delahanty. You've probably seen him around, goes to mass each morning."

Francis had a small balcony in his apartment that overlooked the street below. He went out there and had a smoke. It was a nice day already, the sun shining on the autumn foliage, the Bradford Pears which lined most of the streets in the city having turned a rich orange and red. He looked out on the neighbor's yards and saw cute little cardboard ghosts and witches, pretend graveyards with gag names on the store-bought tombstones. Another lawn feature was vampire coffins, some with a gnarled hand sticking out, waiting for dark to open the lid and prowl the backyards looking for succulent children to drain. Yes, Halloween was just around the corner. He looked to the east, to his right, and saw the sign for Dogtown Liquors; the old man would be there soon, arranging his counter, chock-full of gum and all manner of confections. He probably sold as much candy to the schoolkids as he did booze to their parents. He heard the bell toll over at St. James just around the corner. It tolled four times a day: nine, noon, three when school let out, and six. He thought of his mother who had toiled in the kitchen there for twenty years, a sweet, thoughtful woman who tried to like everyone. If she had one fault it was frugality, a common enough flaw in many Irish women. Many the day she would bring home leftovers from the buffet line—tapioca pudding, stewed tomatoes, rubbery-looking wieners, other shady victuals. Cafeteria castoff, and he and Michael would groan and roll their eyes because they'd already had that and didn't like it the first time.

While Lorraine tended to be stay-at-home, Martin was definitely an out-and-about guy. His father took him and Michael bowling and to parties at the Knights of Columbus Hall. Sunday mornings they went to Wrestling At The Chase and watched Joe Garagiola do color commentary as the legends of pro wrestling battled it out— Lou Thesz, Dick The Bruiser, and the great Bruno Sammartino among them. Sometimes it was women wrestlers and they were just as fierce and/or campy as the men. When Martin died Lorraine had to take on a second job, bookkeeping for a family-run hardware store late afternoons and Saturdays. She was still very pretty although her vivacious nature had been dampened. Men would ask him, pretending to be disinterested , if she was seeing anyone. And men came around, one of them Jackie Delahanty, but she spurned them, saying no one could take the place of his father.

There came a day when she didn't go to work not because she was sick but because she'd given up. She was a homemaker but she wasn't cut out to be the head of a household. Her situation had dragged her down to where she no longer felt like seizing the day. She just sat there at the kitchen table playing solitaire, drinking rum and Cokes, and letting the dishes pile up. Then one day he came home and heard sounds from her bedroom. He went in, she was crying something awful and it scared him. What's wrong, he asked. You wouldn't understand, she said. Try me, he urged. Her face was in her hands. Right then, she looked up and blurted, "I don't know how to lift this burden."

Not much later she caught a cold which turned into pneumonia and she didn't have the strength to fight it. Finally, she saw a doctor but it was too late. She died at home on a Friday in February as the snow was falling and kids were sledding on the hill across the way. Next stop: Galvin Funeral Home, the same as her beloved husband before her.

He was in high school at the the time, and took it real hard. No one loved him like his mother and now, well, the world seemed a lonely and despondent place that held no prospects for him. Michael was already off on his own, and Francis had to move in with an aunt. He began to get in trouble, even more than before. The Vietnam War was on the evening news nightly. He was not particularly patriotic, but he was looking for a ticket out. He left high school three weeks before graduation and joined the Army, a decision which, over time, had the effect of restoring his otherwise sunny temperament. It also saved his life.

Still, it would have been so much different had Martin been around.

He went back inside and thumbed through the phone book. He got to the Ds. There were several. Delahanty, Bryce; Delahanty, Carroll; Delahanty, Helen and Mary; Delahanty, John. That had to be it, on Kraft, just a few blocks over.

Jackie Delahanty answered the door with a butcher knife in his hand. He was hunched over near the top, something wrong with his spine so that he had to crane his neck to see straight. The old man beheld his visitor with either scorn or malevolence, not liking what he saw. "State your business," he said in a voice that sounded like gargling. Francis just stood there in his jeans and sneakers and an old John Hartford concert T shirt, Mark Twang on the front, eyes narrowed, brow furrowed, regarding this gnome-like creature. Being scrutinized in this way set Jackie off even more. He brandished the butcher knife, shaking it inches from Francis' nose. "I'll use this, you better believe it!"

"I'm Francis Lenihan, I need to—"

"I know who the hell you are!" Delahanty barked, but more like chihuahua than a rottweiler. "What is it? What?"

"Can I come in?"

Delahanty curled his lip in a sneer, but lowered the weapon. "Ach!" he uttered and about-faced, leaving the door open. Francis followed him in to the small living room just inside the door. There was a sofa with plush cushions and a cabinet with china, a television on a stand showing some black-and-white Western, sound turned down, and framed pictures on a shelf. Lifelong bachelor, Francis guessed correctly. Delahanty himself was around seventy-five, stunted, as mentioned, with ears that stuck out, and a full head of fine gray hair combed forward in tufts which gave him a fey look.

Delahanty laid the butcher knife on the mantle behind him. "Well, sit if you want. I'll stand."

"This isn't the sort of situation that calls for sitting," he said evenly. "You used to work with my father at the jail."

"Me and forty other guards, so what?"

"You were with him when he got sick, just before he died." A cloud passed over the old man's visage. Francis waited for some defensive remark, none came. "What can you tell me about that, his final minutes?"

Delahanty looked away, eyes focused on something on the wall, a picture. He kept looking as if it would help him out. Francis walked over, took a look. It was the traditional image of St. Patrick, bedecked in resplendent green and gold vestments, bishop's miter on his head, silver hair and beard, a halo behind him. One hand holding an ornate staff with a Celtic cross at the top, the other hand pointing a finger toward a batch of serpents at his feet, green and brown things with red tongues which he apparently had rounded up, and were now in his power. There was a prayer writ beneath the picture. Titled St. Patrick's Breastplate, it began, "I arise today through God's strength to pilot me, God's might to uphold me, God's wisdom to guide me, God's eye to see before me, God's ear to hear me, God's word to speak for me ..."

Coincidence or just plain weird, the same colorful picture had graced the household of the Lenihan family. Francis knew the prayer by heart.

He turned back to Delahanty, who was visibly shaken. "I want to hear it from you, old man. What happened to Martin Lenihan that day? He didn't just up and die from something he ate for lunch. You gave him something. Did you poison him?"

Looking to the carpeted floor, Delahanty shook his head violently, a shudder passing through his entire body. "You don't know shit," he said, vehemently.

Then Francis knew he was right. "But why? Why take another life? You're a Catholic, you go to mass, you know that's a mortal sin."

Delanty looked up, he met Francis' eyes. In those eyes Francis saw a lifetime of loneliness. "You came to our house a couple times," he continued, "sniffing around my mother. I remember you bringing flowers, reeking of cologne. Is that why you did it? Killed my father to open a path to—"

"She made eyes at me, I thought ..."

"She would never do that, not in a million years!"

"Leave me alone, damn you!" Eyes blazing anger, tongue spitting out the words, "I confessed long ago, I did my penance."

Francis went straightaway to St. James rectory. He had some idea of what he was about to do, and he forced it from his mind. He rapped at the door and the secretary answered. He asked for Fr. Eagan, she told him to step inside and wait. She left him in the foyer and he heard her call out somewhere down the hall, "Father, someone here to see you."

She returned a minute later. "He'll see you, follow me." They walked down a hall, her shoes making the softest of sounds on the tiled floor. They came to a wooden door that was open, she motioned him in and left. Eagan was at his desk shuffling papers, a steaming mug of something within reach. He looked up from his work. "Why Francis, what a pleasant surprise." He rose and came around the desk to greet him. Francis ignored his outstretched hand.

Eagan dropped the hand and grew perplexed. "What can I do for you then?"

He cut to the chase. "What knowledge do you have of my father's passing?"

"Only the usual," the priest replied somewhat taken aback. "The arrangements with the funeral home, the wishes of your mother as to what would be said, the arrangements with the cemetery." He paused, reflected, "Such a terrible shame, the man a good provider, salt of the earth, he died far too young."

He would not be placated by glib remarks. "You're right, he died too young. We all know that." He took a step closer so he was eyeball to eyeball. "What I'm getting at, Father, is the knowledge you've been carrying around for years now, the knowledge of who it was that did him in."

"Oh," said Eagan, quite flustered, "you're asking me to reveal a confession that you believe I heard concerning this matter? Even if I had heard such a confession you know very well it cannot be shared with anyone. Sanctity of the confessional, it's a universal precept, and one that I would never break."

Francis grabbed the priest's forearm, putting a vise-grip on it. "You'll tell me," he said, and by the look of his face Eagan knew he was in for it.

"I can't, I won't," protested Eagan, trying to wrest his arm away. "The sins, the offenses against God are told with the utmost confidence. I can't betray that—"

Francis tightened his grip on the arm. "Don't make me hurt you."

"Help!" called Eagan.

Francis grabbed the priest by one ear, and walked him back to his desk. He pushed him down in the chair. He stood over him and said, "Now, *you're* going to do a little confessing—to me."

"Oh, Jesus," Eagan muttered as Francis got behind him and put one hand over his mouth and pinched closed his nostrils. The priest's eyes grew wide and he jerked his body and kicked at his desk, the mug of something—tomato soup it was—spilling all over his papers. With his free hand Francis held him down, pinned to the chair. Thirty seconds passed, the priest's face turning red, his eyes beginning to bulge and tear.

"Blink once if you heard the confession of the man responsible for my father's death."

Eagan, grunting and straining, tried to reach a letter opener on the table. Francis knocked it out of reach. Francis kept tight the seal over Eagan's mouth and nose. He didn't know if he'd go through with it.

"C'mon, blink!"

Eagan blinked, batting his eyelids furiously.

"I said once, blink once." Eagan blinked once, but Francis still held on.

"Now, blink twice if that confession was made by Jackie Delahanty."

On the brink of passing out, Eagan blinked twice. Francis released his hold, and Eagan fell off the chair. He lay there sprawled on the floor and he drew the longest breath he'd ever drawn. Great heaving gasps punctuated by rasping sounds. The gasps turned into sobs and maledictions, and these dramatics were transacted to Francis who also began to blubber. Then the both of them simply broke down, weeping and wailing something terrible.

Francis walked out and made his way down the hall toward the door. Along came the secretary with a tray, a disappointed look on her face. "Leaving so soon? Are you sure? I've some tea and cookies here for you and Father." He nodded, walked past her and let himself out.

— 29 —

Finally, on the third try she showed up. There was no mistaking Eve as she stepped out of the passenger side of a yellow VW Rabbit with cardboard duct-taped over one side window. The driver came out first, young like Eve but old enough to have a drivers license, wearing an unbuttoned flannel shirt, plain black stocking cap topping a head of Gene Wilder blond hair. He carried a skateboard. Eve wore jeans and sneakers, a loose red sweatshirt with something on the front, Rose couldn't make it out. Eve and her friend walked toward the cordoned-off asphalt rink where a half dozen skaters were already doing their thing. They had a way of walking, Rose noticed, that was part shuffle, part jive as if they were moving to some upbeat rhythm.

Over the last week Rose had come to the Hillsboro Skate Park at different times in the afternoon, hoping to find Eve here. It was a drive from Peace Haven Farm in Valle Mines, and she was beginning to think the hell with it. She had passed the time reading the work of G. I. Gurdjieff, the mystic and teacher who had come up with a series of sacred dances, each posture and gesture representing some cosmic truth that the informed observer could supposedly understand. These dances were organized into Movements, of which there were 39, each having its own title. She was taking her time reading the Movements and even trying some out beside her car, for the book was illustrated with various poses. She was on Movement 15, "Tibetan Days of the Week," when they pulled up. Now that Eve was here, the ball was in Rose's court. It was her play, although she still had only a vague idea of how she would go about this, the magic words needed to get the girl to open up.

They were at the rink now, the boy in a crouch, pushing off on his board, Eve standing there, watching. The kid joined others, already out there, skating to tunes blasting from a boombox, doing stunts on wooden ramps. Rose made a brief entreaty to the Great Spirit and walked over.

"Hey," she said, coming alongside, still six feet away, hands in her pockets.

Eve turned, a look of surprise then of questioning. "Hey," she said back.

"You remember me?"

She had a new dye job, the magenta spikes now jet black. Eve ran her fingers through her hair, gave a tentative smile. "Yeah, you came to my door. And now you're here. How come?"

Rose shrugged. "I don't know … maybe 'cause you said you come here sometimes." She moved in closer. Eve chewed on that remark, looking off in the distance, thoughts percolating. She looked to Rose in her button-front striped twill shirt, hemp skirt, and hiking boots and she sensed that, whatever her motives, this was a person worth getting to know. In fact, she'd been thinking about her since that initial encounter, so rudely interrupted by her boorish dad and brother.

"I'm Rose in case you forgot."

"I didn't forget. You ever find out what happened with your mom? I mean, who did it. Why."

Now they were turned facing each other. Rose saw what was on the sweatshirt, an image of Bob Marley, looking Christ-like, and the words ONE LOVE. "Nah, not yet," she answered, "but let's save that for later." She looked out on ramps where the skaters were trying out all sorts of tricks on the ramps, getting airborne for a few seconds, doing one-eighties, dropping into the bowl and sailing back out. Some bailing hard, but getting right back on. The boombox somewhere pounding out a Violent Femmes tune. "How come you're not out there?" she asked.

"Ah, it's not my thing," said Eve. "I'm happy to be the audience.

Besides, I like my elbows and knees, like to keep them movable, unbroken—you know?"

"Yeah, but your friend, he's good."

"Yeah, Chad. He took fifth in the Spring Roll out in Boulder last year. He's met Tony Alva, the original Z Boy."

"Wow. I guess."

Just then he skated over, grabbed up his board, and joined them. He wore pads on his knees. "Did you catch that stoke I did?" asking Eve, but stealing glances at Rose.

"Yeah, I was watching you. Totally sick. You got a name for it?"

"I don't know. Dolphin Flip, whatever you wanna call it. Who's your friend?"

"Chad, this is Rose. Rose, this is Chad." They nodded. It wouldn't be cool to shake hands.

He nodded headbanger fashion and his wavy golden locks flounced. "Okay, cool. I'm going back out there. Watch me some more and tell me how it looks."

"Okay," she watched him go. Then, "You wouldn't have a number on you, would you?"

"Nah, sorry, all out."

"All I've got's these clove cigarettes and they suck."

Rose made a face. "Ugh. I tried those once, like smoking a spice cabinet."

"I don't need to get high, but it's fun once in a while. 'Specially if you're with the right people."

"I know what you mean," said Rose, "you can't underestimate the value of good company."

"Right on. Friends are important, more than family even."

"My mom was the only family I had," she said. "Close family, anyway. There's aunts, uncles and cousins, but I hardly see them."

"Yeah, that's tough, lose your mom. I lost mine, too, only she's out there somewhere. Walked out on us."

"Oh, I'm sorry for you."

"It took me at least a year to deal with it," she confided, "and it still bums me out if I dwell on it too much. I mean, how bad was it that she felt she needed to abandon us, get away altogether?"

"Pretty bad, I suppose. But your dad and brother, they take care of things now?"

She laughed bitterly. "They don't do shit except scratch their asses and think about their next scam. I may as well be a ghost in the attic for all they care."

"You fend for yourself." It was a statement not a question.

"Damn straight, and I'm good at it."

"I'd say that you're as capable as they come. I can tell by looking at you. There is one thing, though."

"Yeah?"

"Yeah, I hope you don't think I'm being too personal, too in your business."

"No," intrigued, "go ahead."

Rose put her hands on the girl's shoulders, peered into her eyes. "I think you need to go easier on the makeup. So much mascara, eye shadow, you look like a raccoon." Eve burst out laughing, Rose laughed with her. "I'm serious," Rose went on, still chuckling. "Have you heard the expression Less is More? It's true."

"Yeah, sometimes I do go a bit overboard. What, you don't do makeup at all? I don't see any."

"I threw away my makeup kit long ago," Rose said, "but I am into scents and fragrances. Today I went with Sandalwood. Can you smell it?"

"Mm, maybe."

"Come closer." Rose hunkered down a little, and offered her bare neck. Eve sniffed at it, nestling her face in there.

This went on for several seconds then Eve broke off. "Yeah, it's nice," she said. "Brings to mind some enchanted forest."

"Elves and pixies around," added Rose.

"A couple wizards, too."

"Where do you get your smells?" Eve wondered. "You have a lab or something, make them yourself?"

"There's a little shop in St. Louis. I'll give you the address before I leave."

Eve looked to Rose, her size and personality humongous. It felt nice to have an older friend, someone who understood her. But wait, there was a catch. There had to be.

She said, "You think my family had something to do with your mom getting killed, don't you?"

Rose looked straight at her and in a low, steady voice replied, "I think that a man named Stoney murdered my mom and that he knows your dad. And he was probably at your place that day."

Even though she'd brought it up, Eve wasn't prepared for that answer. "Wow. Okay. That's news. You like to get right down to it, uh?"

"That guy you saw me with, Francis? That's what he and I have come up with. It's based on real detective work, asking questions, putting two and two together. It's not just something I'm pulling out of my ass."

"But you're not saying that Deke, dear old dad, was in on it, are you?"

"No," said Rose, "not saying that at all. This Stoney probably acted on his own, he may've seen mom outside when he was coming or going to your place. Do you know the guy?"

"Never seen him, only heard of him in passing. Heard Deke mention him once or twice."

The exchange hung there for bit, Rose pondering. The boombox now blasting The Pretenders' "Back On The Chain Gang." Both watching the boarders going airborne out on the ramps.

"What kind of business is Deke in? Are he and Stoney partners?"

Eve said, "Deke's business is basically a mystery, least he never talks about it with me. I think it's something illegal, though. Which doesn't surprise me. But what it is exactly, hard to say. I'm not home enough to know what's going on. And Stoney, the one you've marked down as the killer, yeah, I think maybe he and Deke are teamed up for whatever it is they're doing."

"But Stoney's disappeared," declared Rose. "Did you know that?"

Eve nodded affirmatively. "I heard Deke and my brother talking the other night. They said he's gone, Stoney, a long vacation with no return ticket. Deke wants Derrick to take his place."

"You said they were into scams."

Eve thought for a moment about how much she felt comfortable sharing. Her father and brother were assholes, but they were family. She wouldn't like it if they were broadcasting her business. "Scams probably isn't the best word. Opportunities is more like it."

"You said 'something illegal.'"

"I did say that, but I don't know anything specific … except they're taking some stuff down to Oklahoma to sell."

"You're not going along?"

"No way. I'd go bonkers riding for hours on end with those idiots."

"I appreciate you telling me this," said Rose.

"It's why you tracked me down."

"True, but I felt a connection when first we met and I'm glad we got to build on that."

"Maybe keep it going, huh?"

"Sure, why not. You could come down to the farm, see how the hippies live."

"Yeah, I'd like that."

They watched the boarders for a while, then Eve blurted, "Deke's worried, that much I know. The cops have been to our place a couple times. He's under suspicion and that's got him freaked out. He's coming apart at the thought of doing time, well, *more* time. I mean, he's been to prison and he swears he cannot, will not go back. If they do come for him, I think he'd do something drastic."

"He could give up Stoney."

"But then he'd be admitting he was in on it, like he was lying to them all along. And with Stoney disappeared they'd arrest Deke anyway just for being associated with Stoney."

Rose put her arm around Eve. "Hey. They're going to arrest

someone, and pretty soon I think. They've got to or they look like clowns."

Eve shook her head in frustration. "I wish it were Derrick they had their sights on. Deke's got half a heart, he's basically a decent person. Derrick's the evil one."

— 30 —

"Told you I'd be back," he said, waving the warrant in Deke's face. "I'm as good as my word, and now it's time for a little game of Hide n' Seek," snickering, "you hide evidence and we seek it out. Doesn't mean we'll find it, but we'll sure as hell give it a good try."

Smug bastard, that was Deke's thought, standing in the doorway. And they had him, LaRocca and his sidekick, a guy with a fucking suitcase and a blue nylon parka that said Evidence Tech in bold yellow letters on the back. "Well, you gonna invite us in," said Larocca, tapping him on the chest with the paper, "keep it somewhat civil." Deke just stood there shaking his head in dismay, trying to get a grip on himself. He'd always been careful not to bring any stolen goods into his home, whatever he had here had been purchased honestly. And there definitely was nothing here to tie him to a murder. So, the thought that they would come up empty-handed was consoling, at least. Maybe some weed in Eve's room, but nothing to really land him in hot water. That thought helped to compose him.

LaRocca glanced at his Timex. "Time's a wasting," he clucked, "we've got nooks to explore, crannies to inspect." It was a line he'd heard on *Hunter* and he'd been waiting to use it. "No stone unturned, that's our motto. Look, see here? The judge just signed the warrant this morning. You wanna read it?"

Deke shook his head no, stepped aside, waved them in with a flourish of one hand. "Have at it, boys," he said, "just leave it as you found it."

At first he stood at the kitchen counter, cup of coffee in hand, watching them go through his stuff. They removed all contents from the hutch in the living room, had it scattered on the rug, and were sifting through it. There was a door leading to a small room under the stairs, a space where he kept all sorts of miscellaneous stuff since he didn't have an attic. They switched on the light and were in there for a good ten minutes and came out with nothing.

Again, he thanked his stringent sense of caution for the prohibition against bringing any stolen merchandise home, not even some generic vase or figurine. Everything was out at the place.

"'Scuse me," said LaRocca, as he and the evidence tech brushed past him into the kitchen. Deke watched as they pulled pots and pans from the cupboards, utensils from the drawers, the clanging and clattering driving him outside. He stood on his porch having a smoke while the two of them systematically checked the rest of the house, the laundry room by the kitchen, the mud room on the back porch, the upstairs and downstairs bathrooms, the closets and drawers in three bedrooms, beaming flashlights into dark spaces, down on hands and knees poking around. At length LaRocca came out to the porch holding a contraption that had Deke baffled.

"What's that?" Deke wondered.

"Hookah," said LaRocca. "It was in your daughter's closet under the dirty clothes."

"Figures," said Deke, taking it in hand. There were snake-like extensions coming off the cylinder, and within he could make out some nasty brownish liquid sloshing around. "Must be for smoking, yeah?"

"I'll bet you we find some contraband in this thing here," pointing to a small tar-encrusted bowl at the top.

"I won't take that bet," stated Deke. "Knowing my daughter, you probably will."

"It's a start," said LaRocca, taking back the hookah. He stood there apparently in thought, then said, "Do you go by Deke?"

"To my friends, yeah, but you can call me Mr. Johnson."

"The reason I ask," said the detective, "is that I got a call from St. Louis, an officer I've been working with on this case, and he said that a source told him that someone named Deke is an associate of one Clarence Jackson, who, as I told you the last time we met, is even a bigger person of interest than you."

"I think I know who that source is," said Deke, "and I told you the last time I don't know no Clarence Jackson."

LaRocca nodded tritely, conveying to Deke he didn't believe a word. "So you said. Anyway, I said to Sgt. Scanlan, my counterpart in the city, I said that I didn't know the name Deke, but maybe it's this guy Richard Johnson out in Avonhurst. Guy's done time and he's a neighbor of our victim. Nice coincidence, don't you think? I said to Scanlan that I'd been to see this Richard Johnson and I left unhappy with the meeting. I told him how I felt that Mr. Johnson was less than forthcoming so I was planning on going back, this time with a search warrant. That was yesterday."

"What was?"

"When I spoke with Sgt. Scanlan of the St. Louis Metro Police Department."

"I don't give a shit about some cop in St. Louis, or what he claims."

"See? Now you're getting defensive—that's a sign."

"Oh, Jesus Christ, give me a fucking break."

LaRocca gave him a fake-friendly wink. "We're heading out to the barn now. You wanna come along?"

They were frightening the chickens, and it was annoying the hell out of Deke. He felt he had to say something. "The only thing you're gonna find in that coop is eggs," he told them, "and I already collected 'em earlier."

"You never know," said LaRocca. "You just never know."

"We've found some primo evidence in some very strange places," echoed the evidence tech, his latex-gloved hands buried in straw, probing.

It was a sizable barn built by the previous owner who must have been a rancher to some degree, and it had a tack room, a hayloft, a large open area for parking tractors or machinery or whatever.

Spider webs everywhere, ancient wooden beams overhead, swallows darting to and fro. A cat sat on an upturned grain bucket watching as they went to the stall where the horse lived. Deke rushed into the stall before they could.

"You don't wanna just barge in here," he said. "He don't know you and you might spook him. I just don't want anything to happen." Deke was stroking the creature's flank, saying, "There, there." It was an eight-year-old mare, an auburn Bay with black mane and tail.

"She's a beauty," said LaRocca.

"Name's Danger."

"Good name. Well, we just need a sample of her droppings."

"What?"

"You heard me," said LaRocca, leaning forward. "And there's one right there. Terry, I think you can collect that without actually going in the stall." The evidence tech got down on his knees and reached into the stall, scooped up a sample and placed it into a plastic cup that looked like what they give you at the doctor's office and tell you to pee in. The tech stood up, sealed the lid and placed a label on the side.

Deke had watched with curiosity. "You mind telling me what this is all about? My horse a suspect, now?"

No trace of a smile crossed LaRocca's serious expression. "Sure, I'll tell you. The killer left tracks on the carpet, muddy tracks mixed with horse manure. So the lab tells us. And with that finding we can surmise—that's one thing we detectives do, surmise—we can surmise that the killer had recently been to a stable or corral where horses are kept."

"And you think the killer was here, in my barn."

Finally, the detective cracked a smile. "As a matter of fact, I do."

"And you have the technology to match horseshit from the killer's boots to the horseshit found in some stall? I can't believe that."

"Who said the killer wore boots?"

Deke wagged his head in exasperation. "Boots, shoes, sandals—whatever he wore, I can't believe there's a way to connect Danger's droppings with something you found at a crime scene. There ain't no science like that."

"Mr. Forensic Expert over there," said the evidence tech out the side of his mouth.

"We'll see, won't we," said LaRocca.

Later, as he watched them leave, Deke had a sinking feeling in the pit of his stomach. They were bluffing about that horse manure, they had to be. Even if they had a way to make a match it's circumstantial, and not anything they could use to put him away. Still, it was troubling and he knew damn well that's how they wanted to leave him, worried sick and biting his nails. And their fucked up plan was working only they didn't know the half of it, how their attention would haunt his waking days and possibly his dreams, because now he was a suspect not in Stoney's murder but in the murder Stoney did. What was that called? Irony? Paradox? Something. They had him down for the wrong murder, but did it really matter? Prison is prison.

— 31 —

THE LINE MOVED SLOWLY FORWARD, Francis making his way to the priest holding the chalice. There was a little old woman in front of him and he was focused on her frizzy white hair as he moved step by step toward what could be an embarrassing situation. It was a week after he'd come close to suffocating the elderly priest in his own office, and Francis, though not contrite, had to know if he could still receive communion. If not, he'd have to go to some other parish and that would be a hassle. He could hear the exchange now, the sacred words shared between priest and communicant: "Body of Christ" followed by "Amen." Some of them took the host in their hands, both palms cupped in front of them, but most still took it on their tongue, the old ways dying hard. He watched as the old woman stuck her pink tongue out and waggled it. Fr. Eagan carefully placed the wafer on the quivering lobe, the altar boy next to him holding the brass communion plate beneath the woman's chin in case she fumbled.

Now he stood before Father and the priest regarded him with a mixture of disdain and puzzlement. He did not speak the words he spoke to the others. He did not proffer the Body of Christ. Instead he whispered, "Speak with me after mass." Then he gave him a perfunctory blessing and sent him on his way.

After mass, he entered the sacristy, the changing room behind the altar. Fr. Eagan was hanging up his vestments, and two altar boys, already in street clothes, were talking about some movie they'd seen. Seeing him, Fr. Eagan stood up straight and folded his arms across his chest.

He jumped right into it. "Yes, Francis, thank you for your cooperation. What I wanted to say is before you ask for communion, you must go to confession. You know why, of course. You must be in a state of grace."

Francis just looked at him. "I'll go," he said flatly. "I was going to go anyway."

"It needn't be me, I realize that might be quite awkward. Fr. Moylan will be hearing confessions on Saturday from two to four, before four-thirty mass."

"I've got my own confessor," he said.

"That's right" said Eagan, "I don't recall you ever coming to me. Why is that?"

He felt the blood rush in his veins. The words came out in a torrent. "At the funeral, the words you used. I didn't like it. You said dad was troubled and that he faced life's challenges with difficulty. Where do you get off saying things like that? What did you know about him? You made it seem like he'd taken his life instead of being poisoned by some jealous coworker. Granted, you didn't know that then—you found out later—but you made it seem like he was somehow to blame for his own death."

"As I recall, I was trying to—"

Francis waved it away. "No explanations, please. Just know that

I'll go to confession. When you see me in line, you'll know that it's done."

"And your grievous sin purged? Will you make a sincere act of contrition?"

"Well now, that's between me and my confessor, isn't it?"

The priest was nicely put in his place and it stung him. "Certainly," he said, flushing, "certainly."

Francis left the church wondering if he was a different person now that he had nearly killed a priest and cheated on his girlfriend. This lowlife behavior sure didn't seem like something the nice old Francis would be known for. It was the stuff of degenerates and reprobates. And he would shoulder the burden of his actions, of course he would, and it bugged him that he was walking around with a guilty conscience. Not so much about what he'd done to Eagan but what he'd done to Janie, betrayed her trust. What had happened in that sauna out in the country now produced turmoil in his mind, and to make it go away he would have to tell Janie about it and beg for forgiveness. Or not tell her and hope that the turmoil would dissipate in time. Do I swim in the acid-filled vat? Or do I jump into the rattlesnake pit? Either choice, a bummer.

He drove out to Clayton to see Mary Alice Christman in her law office. Mary Alice had a family law practice and generated a fair amount of paper that had to do with divorce, paternity, child support, guardianship, and the occasional order of protection. There were three women in the small office on the fifth floor of The Sevens Building on Bonhomme, Mary Alice, Harriet, another lawyer, and Rachel, the cute paralegal who doubled as receptionist.

"Well, hello, Francis," said Rachel, looking up from her typing, "so nice to see you. I'll tell Mary Alice you're here." She rose from her station and stretched her shoulders back. She moved her head to one side then the other. "I swear I'll get a permanent crick in my neck from all this typing," she smiled.

"But what're you gonna do?"

"Grin and bear it," she said, "like usual. Okay, I'm going. Her

Highness will be right out."

Francis was peeling the foil from his third Hershey Kiss when Rachel told him to go into Mary Alice's office. He grabbed a handful of Kisses from the bowl on the counter and padded down the carpeted hall to the open door at the end. "Come in, come in," she told him, her voice filled with cheer.

Mary Alice was a slightly plump brunette who parted her straight auburn hair in the middle. She had a beautiful set of teeth which were often caught in a smile. He could imagine both judge and jury being captivated by her—if she was arguing a case, that is.

"So, whatcha got for me today?"

"A bonanza, my friend," patting a stack of papers on her cluttered desk. "Four summonses, all domestic. Divorce or custody or motion to modify. A Show Cause Order out in Eureka, I have a home and a work address. And five depo subpoenas going to financial institutions, banks and brokerages. That should keep you busy for a day or two."

"It's great! I'll need a second satchel to carry it all in."

"I can put it in a box if you like." She saw he was looking off toward the window.

"No, that's okay, I just need to get it to the car, my office on wheels. I'll get started right now."

"Yeah, a couple of those subpoenas are for banks right here in Clayton."

"Perfect, and of course the ones nearby are discounted."

"You've always been fair, I trust you completely."

"That's a nice plant you have, what's it called?" He walked over to the large luxuriant plant which rested on the carpet in a large attractive ceramic planter. It seemed to Francis it was basking in the sunlight offered by the window. The thing had to be three foot tall.

"It's a Fiddle Leaf Fig Tree. I brought it from home because it was turning brown and I thought it'd do better here."

"It's very nice, the leaves are, like, shiny."

"You like my plant?"

"I do."

"Then it's yours."

"No!"

"Really, I've got many more. Houseplants galore. I've got another I'll bring here."

"That is so nice of you. I'll take good care of it."

"I know you will."

With a grunt he picked up the planter, cradling it in his arms, hands firmly grasping the base. He started toward the door. "I won't forget this," he said over his shoulder, "a true act of kindness."

"Try not to overwater it," she cautioned.

He was halfway to the receptionist stand when Mary Alice stepped out and called after him. "Francis, you forgot to take the papers."

He knocked out the depo subpoenas forthwith. Like she'd said, two of them being banks in Clayton, and the rest being more banks and businesses in West County. It was so easy, just walk in and find a banker or financial person sitting in their office, state your business, flourish the subpoena, and they'd automatically sign for it. Three minutes, tops, he even left the car running. Driving off after the last subpoena served, he calculated what he'd made so far: twenty-five a piece for the two in Clayton, and thirty-five a piece for the three out here. A hundred fifty-five for less than two hours' work, not bad.

Francis thought a lot about self employment. He never came close to envying the people with full-time jobs whose lives were based on a set schedule. Folks who had to be at work by 8:30, look busy all day, deal with office politics, then go back home. One day unfolding into another, not much variation, wait for Friday to roll around. You'd never hear him saying "TGIF!" Weekends were work-days, too. In fact, he had better luck on the weekends, people more likely to be home during the day. Try them at eight on a Saturday, coming to the door in their skivvies, yawning. So much for your precious day of leisure; wake up, sleepyhead, you're served! He worked pretty much every day, but not all of every day. He could take off whenever he liked, go to a movie matinee if the mood struck, or head to Fairmount Park on Tuesday afternoons, Horse Hookey, hang out with his track friends. Captain of his own fate, he set the course of his sailing ship. A proven self-starter, each and every day. Once upon a time, there had been a boss standing over him: Do this, do that, don't do that. But that was so long ago that the memory was merely a wisp, reduced to a vague feeling of disdain, a situation he would never return to.

Yes, self-employment was not for everyone but it suited him fine. And he had a decent bankroll to show for it.

It was 1:30. He could quit for the day, run some errands, get to Murphy's around four. But the Tarkington summons was calling. He'd been there four times now, and each time the guy was home, speaking to him through the intercom in various but not very good impersonations of foreigners, always mocking. He'd spoken to the watchman who patrols the exclusive community, and, via professional courtesy, the watchman had told him that Tarkington had no routine that he could tell but it seemed like he went out mid-to-late afternoons, at least he saw his Mercedes pass through on some week days, just him in the car. Francis had always said that so much of this job is luck. Maybe today would be the day.

He pulled up to the mansion on Portland Place at 2:40, having stopped at a gas station for a Snickers and a soda. He didn't walk up to the door. You can bang your head on a wall only so many times. He decided to simply wait and see if anyone would come out. The gate to the driveway in the rear of of the home was partly open and he could see the grill of Tarkington's Mercedes. He reached behind him into the back seat and grabbed a box with magazines. He picked an *Esquire* with Warren Beatty on the cover. He was halfway into an interesting article titled "Things She Can Tell Just By Drinking With You" when a Fed Ex truck pulled up behind him. The Fed Ex guy jumped out with a small package and hustled up the drive to Tarkington's side door. Francis hustled after him.

The Fed Ex guy rang the buzzer as Francis came along and stood a little off to the side. The Fed Ex guy looked askance at Francis and said, "You got a delivery, too?"

Francis showed him the summons, the Fed Ex guy squinted at it. "I guess you do," he said. He rang a few more times and then laid the package down at the doorstep. He went back to his truck. Francis stayed there to see if something might happen.

Then Tarkington came over the intercom, for the side door had an intercom, too. "Yes, what is it?" he said in a normal voice.

"Fed Ex," said Francis, "I've got a delivery for you."

"Oh, just leave it at the door. I'll get it later."

The Fed Ex truck was still parked in the street. "Are you sure you don't want to come get it now?" Francis pressed. "If I leave it unattended, it may get stolen."

"What? On this street? Surely, you jest. Now goodbye."

Francis went back to his car and resumed reading. The piece was written by a woman who knew her way around bars. She had drank with many men in many situations. Some of them she was in love with, and some she fell out of love with because of what they ordered or how they handled their booze. She was pretty judgmental but she wrote with verve and wit and he figured that might have been an act, her judging these guys somewhat harshly just to sell her piece to a top drawer mag. Suddenly, he heard the rev of an engine. He saw the gate at the back of the driveway being opened by Tarkington himself. He grabbed the papers and once again rushed toward the house, this time sprinting.

Tarkington eased the Mercedes out past the gate. He got out to close the gate, leaving the driver door open. As he was getting back in he saw Francis running toward him, paper in hand. He quickly shut the door behind him and hit the pedal, accelerating steadily down the drive toward the street. He went past Francis and waved. Francis could see him laughing. Francis slapped the trunk hard as it went past and he went tumbling onto the lawn. He lie there still, on his back.

Tarkington heard the thump and looked in the mirror to see what had happened. He saw Francis lying motionless in the grass.

He stopped, backed up to get a better look. Abreast, he rolled his window down and leaned his head out.

"Oh shit! Now look what you made me do!"

He left the Mercedes running. First he checked for a dent in his expensive import; there was none. Then, he went over to the lump sprawled on his beautiful lawn. He was standing over him, this miscreant, this nobody, debating whether he should slap Francis into consciousness or simply call 911 and be done with it, when Francis jumped up and thrust the papers at him: "Boo! You're served!"

— 32 —

DEKE TURNED THE KEY AND the padlock clicked open. He slid it off the hasp and eased the door outward with a creaking sound. He stepped in to the steel prefab igloo where he stored his swag, Derrick stepping in after him. Deke flipped a switch on the wall and the place lit up, a row of overhead flood lamps beaming on forlorn merchandise. He set his thermos on a shelf and took out a pair of gloves.

Now he stood in the middle of everything, assessing the task ahead. "Well, let's get to work," he said, rubbing his palms together.

"Get 'er done," parroted Derrick.

In a clockwise direction they went through all the stuff in there, a considerable array, pausing here and there to look at something closely, Deke indicating what should be pulled out and brought to the trailer hitched to his pickup. Derrick followed behind with a wheelbarrow. Whatever Deke pointed at Derrick would remove it from the shelf or pile where it lay and place it in the ample basin of the wheelbarrow. When the wheelbarrow was full they would take it out through the door and up a ramp into the trailer. Once inside the trailer, they would carefully arrange the objects for transportation to the Big Top Flea Market and Antique Mall extravaganza coming up this weekend in Tulsa.

"Should we price the stuff now," asked Derrick, "before it's all covered up by other stuff?"

Deke smiled. Maybe the kid was worth a shit after all. "That's using your brain. I wasn't thinking of that, but you're right. I'll go get the tags and Scotch tape."

Before getting another load they would price for sale what they had already brought out, and Derrick learned what things are worth. "You really think this hedge clipper will bring fifty bucks?" he asked.

"It's a nice round number," Deke shrugged. "It's worth a try, and besides, we can dicker."

"Isn't it the customer who dickers? I think we meet them part way in the price they throw out. Or maybe we hold firm. That how it works?"

Deke punched Derrick playfully on the shoulder. "You gonna go far in this business, boy."

They went back for another load. A tuba, a satellite dish, a mixing bowl went into the wheelbarrow. Derrick took that out and came back for more. "What about this grandfather clock?" he asked, admiringly.

"Yeah, load it up," said Deke. "Too bad I can't get it to work."

"It's nice," commented Derrick. "I wouldn't mind having something like this—when I get my own place, I mean."

"Somebody'll see it and know how to fix it. Come on, we'll lift it on the wheelbarrow."

The base was already removed from the body. They lifted it carefully and as they were moving it, an envelope fell out. The old clock had coughed up something very interesting.

"So what's this?" wondered Derrick, opening the envelope and shaking out the letter inside. He unfolded it and began to read. "Whatever it is, it's pretty old."

Deke sidled up and looked over Derrick's shoulder. "Damn right it's old. Look at the date: June 5th, 1861. Start of the Civil War."

Derrick was moving the letter close then away, squinting and puzzling at the cursive letters like an old man without his spectacles. "I'm having trouble with this handwriting," he said. "How about you read it?"

Deke took the letter, and began. "It's from the War Department, Washington D.C. Says 'To the Father and Mother of Colonel Elmer E. Ellsworth.'" Deke cleared his throat. "*Dear Sir and Madam Ellsworth, In the untimely loss of your noble son, our affliction here is scarcely less than your own. In the hope that it may be no intrusion upon the sacredness of your sorrow, I have ventured to address to you this tribute to the memory of my young friend, and your brave and early fallen child …*"

Deke paused, and riffled through the remaining yellowed pages of the letter, of which there were three. "Well, obviously, it's a condolence letter to the family of a soldier died in the war. Wonder who wrote it." He went to the last page, saw: *Yours, very sincerely and respectfully. A Lincoln.*

"Holy shit!" he whooped. "It's from Abraham Lincoln. We got us a Lincoln letter!"

"Is it worth much?"

"You bet your ass it is!" Deke doing a little jig right there on the dirt floor.

"Aw right, Christmas in November."

"Let me see that envelope," he said. Derrick passed it over. There was a brown canceled stamp in the upper right corner with an image of Jefferson. U.S. Postage Five Cents, it said. On the left, a small but colorful illustration of a Union soldier with pack and musket. Goodbye Dearest the caption. The envelope was addressed to Ephraim and Phoebe Ellsworth of Frederick, Maryland.

"I've seen this name," he said as it came back to him. "It's over here I think," going to a long wooden table with a hundred things laid out haphazardly, taking the letter with him. "Here it is," fingering a newspaper clipping. "I keep track of my exploits when possible," he told Derrick. "Some day I'll put it all in a proper scrapbook." Derrick thought this a bad idea, but said nothing.

"Anyway," he went on, "this here's from the 'Law and Order' section of the *Hillsboro Sceptre*. Listen up. 'The Jefferson County Sheriff Department is investigating the break-in of a home in the 6700-block of Coady Road in Antonia. The home was entered by breaking a window in the rear of the house and is believed to have occurred between the hours of eight a.m. and four p.m. on Tuesday last. Detective Anna Riggs told the *Sceptre* that the burglary appears to be the work of professionals whose m.o. is to surveil certain homes where the occupants are away during the day and then break in when they are certain the home is unoccupied. How they target any one particular home, we don't know, she said, but this is the fourth such break-in we've investigated in the last nine months. In each case, the home was totally ransacked. The homeowner, Gary Ellsworth, president of Charter Bank in Festus, said he would not think of himself as a victim, but warned others to take every precaution possible. Security systems are worth every penny, he said. Unfortunately, I had let my account lapse and the system was turned off. Otherwise thieves wouldn't have been able to carry off my possessions including a grandfather clock, a prized heirloom, that was handed down from my great-great grandfather, Ephraim.' There you have it," said Deke, "proof of authenticity."

Derrick was thinking. "Yeah, but how we gonna cash in on it? Who's gonna buy it from us?"

"You don't worry about that," said Deke. "I know a guy."

"Yeah? Who?"

"I can't say right now, but I'll give him a call and, depending on what comes from it, then maybe I'll tell you."

Derrick put on his bulldog frown. "What if you get five grand from it, it's probably worth that much. You gonna give me some?"

"Did you come along that day when me and Stoney took it?"

"Well, no, you didn't ask me."

"Then why you think you deserve a cut?"

"'Cause Stoney ain't around. I'm your partner now. Plus, I been helping you all along. You wouldn't even have this here hideaway if I didn't arrange it with my boss." He looked Deke square in the eye.

"Well, you got a point. I guess I'd give you something, but don't expect no fifty-fifty." He'd been holding The Letter all this while. He looked at it again. "It was his idea, Stoney, to take the clock. I thought it was too big, too bulky to fit in my truck bed, but he insisted." Deke chuckled. "That damn Stoney, giving me a present from the grave."

"What's that mean?" asked Derrick, suspicion shimmering on the surface. "You kill him?"

Deke folded The Letter, placed it back in its envelope, and put the envelope in his back pocket. "Come on, let's get to the rest of this loot."

— 33 —

"Have you visited our library and museum, sir?"

"Can't say that I have," answered Deke.

"Oh, I think you would find it quite rewarding with your interest in Abraham Lincoln. The museum has a life-sized display of Lincoln's boyhood home. Then we have the actual presidential box from Ford's Theater where, as you know, he was assassinated by the scurrilous John Wilkes Booth ..." Blah, blah, blah, thought Deke, holding the phone to his ear. "And then we have an impressive collection of original artifacts including his glasses and shaving mirror, an axe he once used to split wood, a signed Emancipation Proclamation, and of course the original handwritten Gettysburg Address. We also have several very nice items of Mary Todd Lincoln's. Her music box, for instance—"

"What's that worth?"

"The music box? Well, I couldn't say."

"No, no, the Gettysburg Address."

He heard a light chuckle at the other end. Springfield, Illinois. "Oh, it's priceless. You can't estimate the monetary value of such a thing, one of *the* premier American documents in existence."

"What about just a regular letter, something he wrote to a private citizen. How much would something like that be worth?"

"Why, yes," purred the librarian, "we have many of those in our collection. Personal correspondence, notes on cases he argued before the court. Everything in Mr. Lincoln's own hand. Believe it or not, these letters are still turning up after all these years."

"I asked how much would one of these regular letters be worth. Ballpark."

"Well, sir, I am a librarian, not an antiques dealer."

"Come on," pleaded Deke, "you're around this stuff. You must have some idea."

There was silence and he hoped he didn't piss her off that she'd hung up. "I did hear of a letter to the family of a fallen soldier going for twenty-four thousand. A heartfelt letter of consolation to a grieving mother, an outpouring of sentiment that only Mr. Lincoln could express."

"Hot damn!" muttered Deke.

"I didn't quite hear you," said the librarian. "Have you come across a Lincoln letter? Or perhaps there's one in your family?" her voice taking on excitement. "I could transfer you to Donations. They could better explain the process."

"No, I don't have any letter like that," he told her. "I'm just curious as to how much they're worth."

"Many people have found great satisfaction in donating their cherished Lincoln materials to our museum. It will be archived in perpetuity with your name attached. Plus, it will be safe as safe can be in our fireproof, earthquake proof, bomb proof vaults. Uh, what did you say your name was?"

"I didn't," said Deke, "but it's John Wilkes Booth. The tenth." And he hung up.

Now he had some serious decisions to make. He sat back in his recliner, closed his eyes, and attempted to sort it out, weigh options, evaluate the prudence of seemingly rash decisions. Such as cashing in The Letter and skipping town, his entire life turned topsy-turvy. To disappear for a while or longer, maybe forever, that was the monster question staring him in the face. It was a very tough decision, because to run is to admit guilt. But hell, the cops were already buzzing around him like flies on roadkill. What if he didn't run while he had the chance and they came one day, maybe soon, and took him away? He'd regret not running for the remainder of his incarcerated life. Okay, look at the flip side. What if they arrested him for murder or accomplice to murder of the Schurzinger woman and put him on trial? The evidence would be flimsy at best, entirely circumstantial—horse manure in his barn matching tracked-in mud at the crime scene. Yeah, right. Anyway, he wouldn't be able to afford a proper criminal lawyer so he'd have a public defender appointed. That there would be a real crap shoot, because he'd come across a few public defenders in his day and they definitely left him unimpressed. Unprepared or half-asleep at trial, notes and files disorganized, totally unfamiliar with the phrase "Objection, your Honor!" Let his freedom slip through the fingers of some hack lawyer?

So the option of taking his chances with the prevailing justice system didn't seem very appealing. Back to running—no, that sounded like he was a fugitive and to be a fugitive didn't you need to be arrested first? Call it vanishing. Derrick and Eve would take care of themselves. He would send them money every so often. After he converted the Lincoln letter to cash. But how? He didn't know anyone who might be interested, and he didn't have time to go around to antique dealers or dusty old bookstores which dealt in antiquarian items, making cold calls: Hey, psst! Wanna buy a genuine Lincoln letter?

The only practical solution was to approach a fence, someone with a vast scope of knowledge about the worth of things and more connections to private collectors and legit auction houses than a millipede has legs. That was Al Byington. Big Al. Light-in-the-loafers Al. But Al had banned him from doing business for some undetermined time. How serious had he been with that? Deke considered going against Al's prohibition. If he could only get to him and show him The Letter, let him fondle it, inspect it, then Al would be enticed. He would relent and offer to take on the challenge of finding a home for The Letter. Any hint of reticence in Al's eyes would be replaced by dollar signs.

If Al won't come to me, then I will go to Al. This was Deke's plan and he felt good about it.

He'd been to Al's warehouse just once before, to drop off a Surround Sound speaker system, a special order that Al needed to fill in a hurry. Deke just happened to have one laying around. As he recalled, the warehouse was on one of the roads that twined off Chesterfield Airport Road which paralleled Highway 40 that led westward from St. Louis County to St. Charles County. There were no homes out here, the entire area one sprawling industrial park with scads of big boxy steel and aluminum structures that were put up in about a months' time. All sorts of commercial vehicles coming and going. And Spirit St. Louis Airport was out here, private aircraft flying overhead, taking off and landing, rising above or dipping below the tree line. On the other side of Highway 40 and out of sight, the Missouri River ran eastward toward its confluence with the Mississippi only a few miles north of the St. Louis city limits. Flood plain, that's what this area was called, although the river, known to rise and swell in the spring, hadn't breached the earthen levees for quite some time.

The first week of November. It was cool now, the leaves changing, especially resplendent in areas with lots of oaks and maples. Driving along, he was thinking about where he might go once he had his money. He would stay in the States, of course. Although he'd never tried it, foreign living wouldn't suit him and, anyway, he felt it beyond daunting, the idea of learning another language. He'd been to Cincinnati and he'd liked it. Lots of charming old restaurants and shops, and if you got tired of the Queen City, as they called it, you could cross the Ohio and be in Kentucky, another adventure in itself.

He pulled up to the warehouse as he remembered it, a massive rectangular two story building with drab beige aluminum siding, Appliance Wholesalers Inc. written across the front. There were six vehicles parked near the door, one a shiny red Cadillac Seville, whitewall tires; Al's ride, he figured. Over on a side lot, a parked semi, its rear door open and two guys with hand trucks wheeling washing machines down a ramp where a third guy in a hi-lo waited to take them inside. For the sake of appearances he had placed The Letter in a briefcase. He now took that briefcase and got out of his pickup. A crystal morning, not a cloud, he walked to the entrance, security cameras recording his every move.

There was no reception area, but there was an office just down the hall from the entrance. Deke could see light spilling into the dim hallway and he heard someone talking, sounded like a phone call.

He walked toward the door. He cleared his throat to announce his presence. The talking continued. He heard, "Yeah, yeah, but you know we don't talk about this over the phone. You get over here with the merch, let us inspect it, and then we'll talk. One o' clock give or take a half-hour? That'll be swell. See you then." He heard a click and then the sound of a number being dialed. He rapped on the door and showed his face. A fat man with a slick pompadour in a black satin warmup jacket looked up from his desk and put down the phone.

"Who you?" he said.

"Deke Johnson," came the reply, "here to see Al. Big Al."

Warmup jacket eyed him suspiciously. "You got an appointment?"

"No, I don't, but I'm a vendor. We do business together, and I've got something here with me that he needs to see," holding up the briefcase.

"Al's a very busy guy," asserted the man, "he don't see no one without an appointment."

"Will you just call him, please? Tell him Deke's here with something very special."

He shook his jowls. "I'm not gonna do that."

"Tell him it's Christmas in November."

The man rose from his desk and walked over to Deke standing in the doorway. He wore a gold necklace and stank of Drakkar Noir. "Come on, buddy, turn around, time to leave. I'll walk you to the door."

"Unh uh," said Deke, digging in his heels. "I need to see Al, it's important! He'll agree, call him!"

Warmup was about a foot taller than Deke and had more than seventy pounds on him. He began to push Deke back using only his chest, arms at his side but ready to go. Deke, startled, put up his arms, started to push back. The man said, "You fucking touch me and I'll break your arm. How's that?"

"Okay, okay," flustered, "I'll go. You don't gotta get rough." He backed off and pivoted, shuffling toward the door he'd come in. Halfway there, he turned to look back. Warmup was standing there, arms folded across his barrel chest, watching him.

"Well? Go!" he said.

Deke went out to the parking lot and stood there, briefcase in hand, where the cameras could get a good look at him. He would stand there for as long as it took.

The man in the warmup jacket was Carlo Bustamante, and for many years now he was the right hand man to Big Al. He took care of all incoming merchandise, from assessing it to accepting or rejecting it to writing the checks in payment. Big Al took care of keeping tabs on his cadre of hijackers and housebreakers as well as unloading the more challenging plunder. Sometimes he would make house calls to inspect the merchandise, as he did with Deke over the years. Five minutes later, after Deke had been given the bum's rush, the in-house line blinked on Carlo's desk. "Yeah, boss," he answered.

"Who's the dumbshit standing out there in our parking lot?"

"Just a sec," said Carlo. He was back in a half-minute. "Someone who just showed up looking for you, said his name Deke, uh ..."

"Deke Johnson," completed Al, squinting through designer eyewear at his closed circuit multi-image screen.

"I kicked him out," said Carlo, "but he's still here. You want me to go out there and fuck him up?"

"What did he want?"

"He brought a briefcase, said he had something very special to show. I told him call for an appointment."

Carlo could hear Big Al rasping into the receiver. The man had respiratory problems. "You sure he's alone? I want you to go back out there and look in his truck, make sure he's by himself. I'll wait."

This time Carlo was back in a minute. "Yeah, he's alone," he told Big Al.

"What the hell, send him up."

Deke had felt his hopes swell when Carlo came out to get him, standing on his shadow like a human sundial. Now he was being led through aisles and islands of stuff, nice stuff. High end. Very appealing. Appliances, yes, just like the sign said. Washers, driers, refrigerators, microwaves, dishwashers, stoves, just about every known make from what Deke could see, some of them bound in heavy-duty plastic wrap. Everything arranged neatly. But there were lots of other choice items as well. Electronic devices. Hell, yeah! All the great brands, Nintendo, Sega, Walkman, SONY, Atari. Gaming consoles, synthesizers, camcorders—the new wave of gadgetry that people were only too happy to squander their paychecks on. Deke made a mental note to steal more electronics.

Motor bikes, gas-powered lawnmowers, outboard motors lined the wide aisles. Sportswear—lines of Nike and Adidas apparel, running shoes, top of the line sneakers that read like a who's who of the NBA. A whole fucking closet of Cardinals shirts and caps, price tags still on. He half-expected a salesperson to walk up and with a shiny smile and say, "How May I help you?" Deke marveled at the thought that almost everything he saw here had been stolen. They stepped aside as a guy on a hi-lo came through, the front-loader cradling a seven-foot-long side-by-side General Electric fridge on its forks.

"We just got a shipment in," said Carlo with a wink. "Straight from the factory with a slight detour." Now that Big Al had given his blessing, Carlo was being cordial. They walked along toward the rear of the warehouse, passing the automotive department, shelving three-four tiers high holding tires, batteries, ghetto hubcaps and more.

Deke paused mid-stride to take it all in. He shook his head in amazement. "What you got here, it's Wal-Mart for the black market," he said. "Well done, man, well fucking done."

"Tell that to Al," said Carlo, "he likes compliments."

They came to a wooden stairs leading up to a second floor. Bare bulbs shone on a walkway with railings. "His office is up there," said Carlo. "You go on up, first door on your left. Knock before you enter." Deke didn't move, just looked at Carlo. "I don't do steps," said Carlo, "unless I absolutely have to." He patted his breast. "Bad for the heart." Shooing him off with his hands, "Go on now."

Deke got to the top of the stairs. He looked down, Carlo was gone. He stood at the railing and looked out enviously, covetously over Big Al's domain. A cavern, the place was a magic cavern filled with things that every decent American busted his ass to purchase. For himself or for his family or simply for the prestige it would bring. A hi-lo off somewhere in the maze of aisles made a chugging sound. The door to Big Al's office was partly open. Deke rapped three times and entered.

"Did I say 'Come in'?" asked Big Al, sitting at a desk on the far side of the room. His back to a large window, drapes open, sun shining in, making him a silhouette.

"Uh, no, you didn't."

"Then get back out there and knock again," Deke heard. He went back out.

"Come in," chimed Big Al.

"Hate to get off on the wrong foot," said Deke, approaching.

Big Al gave a harumph. "You did that when you showed up here without calling first. We may give the impression that we're open to the public, but I assure you we are anything but. Besides, I plainly told you we are not doing business for the duration. Did you not hear that?"

Deke nodded agreeably. "I did, but this is—"

"So you heard it, you understood it, but you came anyway."

The lisping, fake reasonable-sounding voice already grating on his nerves. "You would have come, too," he replied, "if you were me. I found something the other day, something you have to see."

Big Al took off his glasses and appraised him. Deke appraised Al as well. For a guy with a nickname like that, he sure didn't look like no big time operator much less a guy to be worried about. Deke took a few steps to the side, going for the oblique view of the large desk and the diminutive man at it. Big Al less of a silhouette now. Chubby, bespectacled, thinning on the top, a black, white, and red checkered sweater vest over a practically luminescent white button-down shirt. Pallid complexion. Probably about five-five if he were to stand up. A fucking twerp, and this was the man whose help he had come to solicit.

There was a stool off to the side of the desk, fronting a built-in library, books on shelves to the ceiling, and Deke thought about pulling it up.

"All right then," said Big Al. "Show and Tell time. Let's see what you've got." Deke walked up, unfastened the briefcase and took out a manila envelope. He passed it to Big Al. He waited somewhat apprehensively, taking in certain objects on the desk in front of him—a miniature bronze replica of the statue of the raising of the flag on Iwo Jima, a framed photo of a smiling young man in swim trunks, a die cast 1/64 scale model of the Batmobile. Big Al took a minute to study it, holding the document delicately, turning pages, the trace of a smile beginning to surface. His eyes crinkled. He nodded slightly, knowingly.

Standing over the man felt awkward so Deke decided to grab the stool and take a seat. Big Al waved The Letter approvingly. "You did right in bringing this to me," he said. "I'm familiar with Lincoln's handwriting and this looks to be authentic." He paused, did a double-take. "You're sitting, did I say you could sit down?"

Deke immediately stood up. Big Al gave a wave of the hand, expostulated, "Simon Says sit back down."

It came out "Thimon Theth." Deke winced and sat back down. "Can I smoke?" he asked.

"Oh heavens, no!" answered Big Al, "I have emphysema. I was a smoker for thirty-three years," he added. "Two packs a day. Winstons, a very satisfying smoke. And it's 'May I smoke?'"

"What?"

"It's *may* I smoke? Not *can* I smoke? Of course you can, it's my permission that you may or may not have."

"Oh … yeah. So what about The Letter?"

"I won't even ask you where you got it, but I assume you're not the rightful owner. No matter. So … I do know a fellow in Arlington who deals in historic documents. A big Lincoln collector, and he's discreet. I could give him a call."

"What do you think it'll bring, a piece of history like that?"

"I honestly don't know, never having handled the sale of such an item before this."

"'Twenty-five grand maybe?" he pursued.

"It's quite possible," commented Big Al. "But whatever it garners you understand that your cut is ten percent of the value."

"What! That's a fucking rip-off!"

Big Al shrugged indifference. "Common rate on the black market," he said.

"When we were doing business in the past you gave me more than ten percent."

"Did I?"

"Goddamnit, I need more than twenty-five hundred. That's chicken feed."

"Got your dander up, did I? Here," said Big Al, unctuously, holding out The Letter, "take it back. There's an antiques mall down the road, they're taking consignments." He coughed weakly and brought up some phlegm, expectorating it into a monogrammed hankie.

"Please," implored Deke, "one old dog to another, I need a certain amount for the thing. Something going on in my life, I need serious cash now. Five grand, that's reasonable, whad'ya say?"

"I say the black market can be quite fickle. In some respects it has fallen off, thanks to the Chinese and their mass production of consumer goods offered at sub-wholesale prices. These days, hell, I hardly even give the time of day to this or that pirate trying to solicit me. The other day, I get a call from from enterprising hijacker:

'Hey pal, I just copped a nice load, hats, all kind of hats, men's hats, stylish. You want a look-see?' The man took me for a haberdasher. I hung up on him. And fencing, dear boy, fencing isn't what it used to be. My god, you end up giving half the stuff away. So, that said, you want a payout today?"

"Yes, sir," said Deke.

"Then go to the devil."

Deke looked for leverage, saw none. "Aw, screw it. I'll go with you. But how long then? Before I get my money?"

"This isn't a sure thing," said Big Al. "I have no idea if I can even sell it or for how much. I'll need to do some checking before I make any calls, put out tendrils. Could take weeks, months."

"Damn! Look, Al, like I said, I don't have that kind of time. A minute ago you said ten percent of twenty-five grand. How about you give me that now, today, and The Letter is yours. You sell it, which you will, and you get all the proceeds. That's very fair, and you know it."

"Advance payment for an item of undetermined worth. Hm. That's not a very sound business practice."

"You'll make out like a bandit," countered Deke.

"Tell you what, let's give it a break. I'll mix us a drink, and we'll talk about it like gentlemen. Oh, by the way, did you tell anyone you were coming here?"

"No."

"Good. Then let's have a drink and discuss this in a civil manner."

"Fine," grumbled Deke, "just so's I get my money today."

"Unh-uh," cautioned Big Al, waggling a finger in Deke's direction. "Drinks first, negotiation later."

Deke couldn't have known this because he was only superficially acquainted with the man, but for several months now Big Al had been living under a death sentence handed down by a qualified medical professional. Because of this, Big Al found himself increasingly envious of those around him who went about their business with a carefree disposition, oblivious to the open grave waiting for them. Yes, envious of ingrates who took life for granted and, at the same time, bitter over his own impending demise. Big Al had no compunction about taking a few of these ingrates with him. In fact, he yearned for it.

He rose from the desk and went to an amply stocked bar in the corner. Besides all manner of spirits, there were shakers, jiggers, tiny plastic spears, glasses on shelves, a sink in the middle. "I'm having a dirty martini," he called. "How about you? I make a wicked cocktail, anything in *Mr. Boston's*."

Deke didn't know Mr. Boston from Mr. Baltimore, but he thought a cocktail might taste pretty good about now. Sure, go for it, he told Big Al. He watched with interest as the man did his thing, measuring and pouring and shaking and straining. He himself had never thought to put that much effort into a drink. Two fingers of Seven in any old glass, and that was good enough. Big Al came to him across the carpet holding two gorgeous-looking drinks in cocktail glasses, one with olives skewered on a pick and one reddish in appearance with an orange peel twist as garnish.

"Here you go, my man, a Harvard Cocktail. Brandy—Remy Martin, the best—Italian vermouth, a dash of demerara syrup, three dashes Angostura bitters, and soda added after the fact. Similar to a Manhattan, but a tad more snobbish. Enjoy."

Deke took the drink, held it at different angles, looked it over and took a sip. "Not bad," he pronounced. "Kinda makes you pucker."

"That's the vermouth," said Big Al, resuming his place at the desk.

"Why are you being so nice to me now?" asked Deke, sipping away.

Big Al wondered if Deke was on to him. He hoped not. Not yet anyway. "We've worked together for several years," Big Al explained, "and we've never socialized. I like to get to know my suppliers."

"Yeah, that's cool. Now about my money."

"Waterford."

"What?"

Big Al held out his martini. "These glasses are Waterford crystal. Only the best, my friend."

"That's fantastic, now how about my money?"

"I'll make a couple preliminary calls later on, after you check out. Leave, I mean. I can get back to you tomorrow or the next day."

Deke leaned forward in his chair, said emphatically, "No, man, that won't work. You see, I'm in a jam and I need—*need*—some funds to, uh, make myself scarce, you know?"

"Oh, why didn't you say so to begin with? I have an associate who specializes in emergency loans. The interest is steep, true, but the money is there when you need it."

"Jesus Christ," sputtered Deke, "I don't need a fucking loan shark! I need an advance on this Lincoln letter. It's worth a lot, you goddamn well know that!" He shook his head disgustedly and took another drink. "What I gotta do to get through to you, huh?"

"May I share a secret with you?" Big Al, speaking in confidence from his chair, sipping at his refreshment. "Thank you. The secret is this: one of my peeves, possibly the biggest peeve, is unexpected visitors. I loathe them. The unmitigated gall they have in thinking that they can simply waltz in to someone else's life and interrupt them at whatever they may be doing at the time. It is the height of inconsideration. And if we do not have consideration for one another then we as a society have nothing. Do you agree?"

"Maybe," allowed Deke, growing suspicious.

"When I saw your lumpish figure in the parking lot and I learned that it was you, well, then and there I decided that you would pay dearly for coming here unannounced."

Deke finished off his cocktail, set it on the carpet and stood. He leaned in, placed his hands on the edge of Big Al's handsome desk, looking down on him now, the man's scalp visible through thinning hair. He was about done with this bullshit. "You talk too much and your voice is annoying," he said. "I come to you with a fair offer, you won't even meet me part way. Well, what can I do? I can't *make* you pay me a portion of what that Letter is worth. But I sure as hell can expose you and your big time operation here. How'd you like that?"

Big Al took this in calmly. He would have killed him anyway even if Deke had played nice and not made threats. Big Al had possibly the blackest heart West of the Mississippi.

He sipped at his dirty martini, licked his lips, and set the drink down. "As I said, perhaps you weren't listening. I used the words 'pay dearly.' Now, what do you think that means?"

"I don't give a ... oh, my gut." With both hands he clutched his belly, looking down at the same time as if there were something to see. "Ahh, feels like a lead weight in there. *Ooo—oooophh. Ug-ahh-ack!*" Bug-eyed, tongue lolling, he fell back in his chair, legs splayed forward on the carpet.

"*Ahhh!*" Breathing unevenly, rocking slightly, he wished he could puke. "What's wrong with me? It's bad whatever it is. Oh, God."

Big Al gave a wolfish grin. "Don't you wish you'd called for an appointment now?"

In addition to the cannonball in his gut, Deke began to feel woozy. He looked at the empty cocktail glass overturned on the carpet and he understood. He looked to Big Al, sitting there calmly. "You fuck!"

"Pathetic," said Big Al, sadly, "you're pathetic and I'll tell you why. Because you are unable to predict danger. You were lulled into my office, my lair, as it were, by a false sense of security. You should have known that danger lurked here, that I am one malicious son of a bitch. You walked into a trap that you could have avoided."

The room was closing in, his vision blurring now. He tried to stand, his legs were rubber. "But you're a queer," he managed to say.

"The better to poison you, my dear!"

Deke retched weakly a few times, but since he'd skipped breakfast nothing of substance came up. He leaned far to one side and fell off his chair. He began to crawl, moaning and gasping. Big Al came over to watch his progress.

"You know, I had my doubts about that solution," he said in a conversational tone. "My private apothecary mixed it, oh, five-six years ago. I wasn't sure about the shelf life, but it sure appears not to have lost its potency."

"*Ahhhh uhh-ooooh ...* you prick, I'll get you ..." Deke was going for the window behind Big Al's desk. He crawled on his belly, fingers gripping the nap of the carpet for traction, feet pushing him forward as best they could. He crawled in small undulating movements, a few inches at a time. Then he began using his elbows and he made better progress. All he wanted at this miserable point was to get to the window. Big Al was right behind him, telling him matter-of-factly that it wouldn't be long now.

He rounded the desk, got to the window, grabbed the sill. With great effort he hoisted himself partway up so that he was on his knees, his head just above the sill. He pushed aside the sheer drapes. He appeared to be kneeling in prayer as he spread his elbows on the sill for support and looked out. A swell of dark clouds met his dimmed vision, scalloped, roiling, a preface to a storm.

"If it's any consolation," he heard Big Al say, "I won't be far behind you. This emphysema is a killer, literally. My physician says two years at best. *C'est la vie.* But I can watch you die, and get a preview. You should be seeing the devil about now."

His sense of self was diminishing, consciousness imploding. Still on his knees, Deke took one last look, hoping to see the sun but it wasn't there. Just before the lights went out, a spark flickered in the dim shrinking reaches of his mind: *I'm dying a free man even if it is under this cocksucker's roof.*

The red light blinked on Carlo's desktop. "Yeah, boss."

"Carlo, I want you to get Rance and come to my office. Bring a roll of plastic and some duct tape."

"Okay, boss." Pause. "You gonna need any cleaning supplies to go with that?"

"No," said Big Al, "but thanks for asking."

— 35 —

THEY WERE SITTING ON THE BACK PATIO at Bruno's, the popular bar restaurant on The Hill where they'd gone for their first date. It was the second Friday in November around six, the sun going down, air turning cool. Art the manager came out and lit two big propane heaters which gave off both heat and light. Though they wore sweaters, Francis and Janie moved to a table closer to the warmth. The two bocce courts were filled with players, four to a team, two teams for each court. Shouts and laughter and the clacking of the clay balls filled the patio. Many streets on The Hill were narrow, and if cars were parked on both sides it meant that, of two cars meeting head-on in the street, one had to find a gap and pull over to let the other pass. Every so often they could see one driver motioning to another: *Come on, come on, go around me!* Catty corner to Bruno's, the church and school of St. Ambrose, the pulse of this Italian neighborhood. More often than not the old church held a wedding at this time on Friday and today was no exception. Looking past the famous statue of the Italian Immigrants out front they could see first the bride and groom and then the whole wedding party being photographed on the church steps, the massive oaken doors as a backdrop. Soon they would be over here, ordering drinks and toasting the lucky couple on into the evening.

"Would you ever get married," she asked.

"Is that a proposal?" he said, perking up. "It's sort of a funny way to put it."

"No, not a proposal. Jeez. I'm just asking if you *would*. In theory."

"Why do I feel like I'm treading on dangerous ground here?"

She frowned a little, shook her head in dismay. "You're not on the hook for anything," she told him, "so just answer the damn question."

He took a big gulp of his Budweiser, burped, and let fly. "The answer is, yes, I would get married to the right woman if she asked me nicely. But it wouldn't last, I know, because I think I'm too selfish to make a good husband."

"You want to do what you want to do when you want to do it."

"That's pretty much it. I'm used to having it that way and it would be really hard to change, even for someone I deeply cared about. I might get bitter."

"I can't imagine you bitter," she said. "Rueful maybe, but bitter, no."

"What about you?" he asked. "Would you?"

"No, definitely not. I feel the same way as you. Life's too short to give up certain things that you love, things that define you, all to make someone else happy. Take something as simple as vacation plans. Let's say I'm married. One year we go to Tuscany because that's where I want to go. And we both have a good time. Everything's cool. The next year it's his turn to choose and he wants to go to Cancun and I balk, because I am not a Cancun girl and I hate being just another tourist to be taken advantage of. Plus, I'll probably come back with some parasite. I won't go to Cancun and that's that, so now he feels cheated. Resentment builds and festers in our relationship and before long—poof, it's over. *Capisce?*"

"Oh, yeah," he said, "I *capisce* all right. It's better to just do what we're doing, spend the night together every so often. But mostly at your place because your refrigerator is better stocked than mine and you have nicer sheets on the bed."

He was having such a good time that he almost forgot that he intended, maybe, to bring up that thing with Rose. It'd ruin the evening, sure, but at least he'd get this hundred-pound anvil off his chest. Selfish, selfish.

The wedding party was filtering outside on the patio with their drinks. They gathered around the propane heaters, in good spirits, toasting the bride and groom and society at large, their merriment just a mite too loud. Francis and Janie moved back a table.

"Did you see the latest episode of *Wiseguy?*" she wondered. They both liked crime shows on TV, and *Wiseguy* was the best they'd ever seen. It unfolded a story in a cycle of five or six episodes like a soap opera. Vinnie Terranova is a handsome undercover agent who infiltrates criminal enterprises, ferrets out the bad guys, and sets them up for destruction. If he gets in trouble he calls Lifeguard, a wheelchair-bound tech wizard occupying a room somewhere that's filled with electronic gadgetry. The show opens with Vinnie being released from prison, eighteen months' time meant to establish his wiseguy credentials. Each week, as Vinnie works his way up the hierarchy of this or that "family," he gets into some very tense situations with the *real* wiseguys and almost gets outed, but somehow his true identity remains safe.

"No, I missed it," Francis said. "What happened?"

"I don't want to spoil it for you."

"I don't care. Tell me."

"Let's just say he ditched that wire he was wearing in the nick of time."

"That's good, 'cause Sonny would've deep fried him and cut out his heart if he knew about it." Sonny was Sonny Steelgrave, *capo* of the Atlantic City mafia. Through a series of ballsy deceptions Vinnie had become Sonny's lieutenant.

"Tracy would stop him from doing that," said Janie. Tracy was Sonny's daughter who was attracted to Vinnie and he to her, complicating his mission to put Sonny behind bars.

"You know," he said, "I never watched the Soaps, but now I see how people could get addicted. You're biting your nails at the end, and you've got to wait a week to find out what happens next."

She took a drink of her vodka tonic. "Well, I have watched the Soaps and they're all right, but, trust me, *Wiseguy* is to *Days of Our Lives* or *General Hospital* as espresso is to decaf."

He chuckled. "That's what I like to hear." He gazed at her meaningfully and she felt it.

"What's up?" she asked.

"I've got something to tell you," he said, a trace of dread in his tone.

"And I've got something to tell you," she countered, "something big. But could we order first? I'm famished."

* * *

They found themselves staring at the same two-story wood-frame they had entered three weeks before, the one with the gruff mechanic and the dead parakeet. Lenihan hadn't been home then and maybe he wasn't home now but they had to go look. This time there was a third person in the car, a friend of Brunt's named Jumbo who took up much of the backseat. It was now around 5:30, still light, but Derrick didn't feel it necessary to wait for dark to barge in. There was no one around, no one watching, and the last time the front door had been unlocked. They could walk right in. It would look as though they were paying a visit to the occupant within. Which in fact they were.

Earlier that day Derrick had called Brunt and told him how Deke hadn't come home for three days now, no phone call, no note, no nothing. And the trailer loaded with goods still parked out at the hideaway with nowhere to go. This was to be their weekend in Tulsa, the promise of flea market lucre. "Something bad's happened," he told Brunt over the line, "and I've got to find out what it is. I want to start with this Francis Lenihan, he seems to be at the bottom of all this shit going down."

"I'm with you, bro. You want to pay him another visit?"

"Fuckin-A I do. Later on. We could use one more guy, though. Can you round up Hutch?"

"Hutch is laid up from an accident, decided to run his hog off the road at seventy-five miles an hour. He's lucky to be alive. But I got someone better. Jumbo."

"Jumbo? I thought he was in EMCC, for huffing glue or some shit."

"He was, he did his bit. He's out now."

"Well shit, bring him along."

Like the handle implied, Jumbo Winkler was a big lug, a bloated torso with arms and legs, head like a pumpkin, face like a Jack-O-Lantern with a constant and somewhat annoying happy expression. For seven years now he was gainfully employed by Big River Chrome Plating, a job so unhealthy, low-paying, and downright demeaning that most folks quit after two weeks. Being around Jumbo, the phrase half a bubble off came to mind. Right now he was picking his nose and eating the boogers.

"You about done there, Jumbo?" asked Derrick from the front seat. Jumbo had his pinkie finger deep in the recess of one nostril, mining for something solid.

"Huh?" said Jumbo.

"Never mind," said Derrick. "Let's hit it." They got out of the car and walked up to the porch, three locals coming home after a hard day at work. Zero attention paid. Like before, the outside door was unlocked. They entered and up the steps they went. They tried the door to Francis' apartment. Locked. They keened to hear any sounds from within. Quiet. Shh. The door jamb, already weakened from the previous forced entry, easily gave way when Brunt threw his bulk against it.

The place looked like any typical bachelor's digs, ratty sofa in the main room, coffee table in front of it with beer cans and magazines, a half-full bowl of trail mix, and a porcelain mallard duck that served as an ashtray. They walked through the apartment, commenting on what they saw, the way his T shirts were hung in the closet by color, the colorful posters on the walls commemorating various concerts. "I was at that one," said Jumbo, standing before an Asylum Tour 1985 poster. "You shoulda seen Paul Stanley, that guy can really smash a guitar," pantomiming Paul Stanley doing just that.

On the kitchen counter, a phone hooked up to an answering machine, the little red light blinking. Derrick reached over and hit Play. The first message was from some cohort. "Francis, this is Quinn. I wanted you to know there's a wake for Mike Flannery at Murphy's later today, from three o' clock on. The booze'll be flowing. The old boy's about to pass and we're gonna say our last goodbyes. I know he liked you, he always said hearing 'The Minstrel Boy' tugged at his heartstrings like nothing else. See you, there, man." Next in queue, a feminine voice, kind of husky. "Francis, this is Rose. I'm in St. Louis getting provisions for the farm. Soulard Market is a trip and a half! Anyway, I was hoping to reach you before I head back, maybe have a drink and we can catch up on things. See ya if the Fates allow. Thinking of you, bye."

Derrick snapped his fingers. "Murphy's is that place where we saw Lenihan with that cop, just down the street."

"We'll have to blend in," said Brunt, "might be a problem. They all know each other."

"I never met this Flannery guy," said Jumbo, "but I'll drink his beer."

* * *

Their food came and it looked good enough to devour. One order of Buffalo wings grilled and one deluxe pizza, jalapenos on the side. Night coming on, they ate with gusto. More Bud for him, but she had switched from vodka tonic to wine coolers. The wedding party was still hogging the propane heaters, blocking all those BTUs from effusing their way.

Francis was busy chowing down but even so he was secretly composing the opening lines of his confession. "Have you ever found yourself in a situation that you weren't quite ready for, a situation where a temptation arose that just turned your willpower into mush?" Um, no, too flip. Maybe this: "Janie, there are times in a man's life where he is called upon to do the impossible, like resist the wiles of a beautiful, sexy woman. I recently had one of those times ..." That's better, play up one of your many character flaws that she already knows you have. Or maybe, put the shoe on her foot. Like, "What would you have done with a set of perfect knockers star-ing you in the face?" Thing was, he had to sound contrite, which he really was, and he had to lower the boom softly, inflict the least amount of mental anguish on poor Janie. And sadly, he knew that was beyond his powers.

He placed another thoroughly-gnawed bone atop a pile of gnawed chicken bones already on a Styrofoam plate. He waited for her to look his way. "Janie, there's something I've got to—"

"San Francisco!" she interjected.

"San Francisco?"

"Yeah, San Francisco, I'm being transferred! Can you believe it? I'm just so excited, I've known it since two o' clock this afternoon and I'm just walking on air. I've been bursting to tell you, but I didn't want to just blurt it out. I wanted to wait until the time was right.

Like now."

She was positively beaming, this was her moment, and he saw that now was not the best time to come clean. "Wow, that's great news … I guess. I'm happy for you, but what about us?"

"I've thought about that," she went on, excitedly. "And I suppose it's out of the question that you follow me out there. I know how much you like St. Louis and you're all established here with your practice, but think about it: We could get a nice apartment near the wharf, go to the quaint little markets on the pier, eat seafood every day if we wanted." She looked for a positive reaction but he was just listening, mulling it over. "Oh, I know it's expensive to live there," she continued, "but it's not just a transfer, Francis, it's a promotion too!"

"I don't know," said Francis, "it's almost too much to think about."

She took his hand, squeezed it affectionately. "I know it is, lover, I know. You just think about it, and let me know. Either way, I'll live."

Francis called to a passing server for another beer. "They don't have seasons in California," he ventured, "I like seasons, hot or cold. I like greenery, too. They don't have a lot of greenery there, it's pretty much brown. And there's always the fear of earthquakes. But I do like you. Hm. I don't know, I just don't know."

"If you have to analyze it, weigh the pros and cons, then you're not on board. It's all right, like I said, I'll live. In fact, it'll be a fun new chapter in my life."

"I didn't say no."

She gave him a sweet sad look. "Yes, you did. But look, I'll come back from time to time. My family's still here. And you can come out anytime you want."

"Right, and you'll have a boyfriend within a month."

"I'll tell him to get lost while you're there."

"When do you leave?"

"A week from today."

"Then let's make each day count."

She held up her glass, winked enticingly. "Salute!"

He held up his beer bottle. "Salute!" he returned.

"I can't believe you just did that!" someone shouted over on the bocce court.

— 36 —

SOME OLDTIMERS WERE OFF IN A CORNER talking about Juggie Banton's wake. Juggie was a city license collector who, back in 1968, had the good fortune to die an Irishman. It had been Juggie's lifelong ambition to be waked decently and so he was laid out in Kinealy's Funeral Home on St. Louis Avenue. It was a proper Irish wake, they recalled, brimming glasses of whiskey taken neat at one go, tearful recollections of Juggie told in reverence with knowing nods from certain mourners who, unacquainted with the deceased, had dropped by just because an Irishman died. Between the funeral home and the toddle house next door, the wake lasted a good three days and there were missing persons reports still being filed a week later.

Now another Irish wake was in progress at Murphy's Bar. To be accurate it was billed as a barbecue though everyone in attendance knew it was a wake and a macabre one at that. The wake was unique even by Dogtown standards in that the object of attention, one Mike Flannery, fifty-five, former barge operator, saloonkeeper, and devoted family man, was present and enjoying himself as much as a dying man can enjoy himself.

It was only fitting that the living tribute was held in a bar, for Mike had long been associated with drinking establishments—as a bartender at The Bay Horse, and later as manager and eventual owner of The Confluence, a downtown nightclub popular with sports figures and entertainers. There were other bars and taverns as well. Mike was fond of quoting a line from Winston Churchill: I have taken more out of alcohol than alcohol has taken out of me.

Wearing a shamrock necklace and tri-color cap, Mike was holding court at a long table, pals around him talking old times, good times, joshing him and throwing back the suds. They called him Riverboat, a moniker from his fifteen years on the river, culminating as chief engineer on the Inland Oil & Transport Barge Lines. When his last bar folded, Mike was able to get on with Local 513 Hoisting Engineers, which includes operators of tower cranes, bulldozers, and other heavy equipment. He was working on the new federal building when a coworker noticed he was jaundiced. Mike went to the doctor and the news was dire: Liver and pancreatic cancer. The doc gave him four to six weeks to live. And now two weeks after the news, Mike Flannery, red around the eyes, a bit green around the gills and puffed out—a combination of effects from the cancer and the heavy painkillers he was on—was being feted and glad handed like there was no tomorrow.

And they were all there to see him off , Mike's friends and family, packed in the little bar, trying to hold it together, although at least one sensitive fellow had to bow out. "I've gotta get outta here before I start bawling like a tyke," he told the sot next to him.

"Oh, go on witcha," said the sot, "just cry in yer beer. Everyone's doing it."

The sentiment fairly oozed as friends painted a picture of Mike in the big St. Paddy's Day Parade—not the Hibernian one in Dogtown, but the big one downtown with all the union-sponsored fanfare—decked out in his green tuxedo and black derby, waving, walking down Market Street, pushing a wheelbarrow filled with potatoes. The wheelbarrow was sometimes helped along by Rosebud, a goat dyed green for the occasion.

Red Rush, Mike's fellow carouser, recalled the night Mike got creamed trying to cross the street. They were coming out of Kelly's Korner when a woman driver smacked into Mike, flipped him on the hood and took him a good sixty yards down South Broadway as far as White Castle. "She turned her windshield wipers on and she couldn't get him off," said Red, his arm around Mike. "Mike was the biggest junebug she ever saw."

Mike had a full life. He even had a shot at stardom, being cast in a 1975 made-for-TV movie, *The Runaway Barge*, starring Nick Nolte. "Typical TV action movie," wrote Leonard Maltin in his *TV & Video Guide*, "including a trio of two-fisted scalawags."

Mike was one of the scalawags.

The wake, barbecue, whatever it was, was ending. Mike rose and moved toward the door. This was the longest he'd been awake in weeks. People were hanging on him, kissing him on the cheeks, the lips. He was helped into a car, which vanished down Clayton Avenue.

No sooner had Mike left the bar when Derrick, Brunt, and Jumbo walked in. They were immediately pegged by several drunken patrons as outsiders, not even Irish and certainly not here to pay respects to Mike Flannery. It was the worst possible time for these goons to come calling, thinking to start something.

They went to the crowded bar and tried to get a drink. "You with the party?" asked Tommy, knowing they weren't. "If you're with the party, drinks are on the Local. Until seven, anyway. If not, it's cash on the line. What's your quaff?"

They stood there with their Busch longnecks in hand, scanning the crowd for a sign of Francis, hoping, as Brunt had cautioned earlier, to blend in. It wasn't working. Within minutes a scrawny fellow with a flat cap sauntered up and said, "Fellow down at the end of the bar wants to see you." They looked in that direction and saw a beefy middle-aged redhead with a ruddy complexion smiling at them. Thinking here might be a connection to finding Lenihan, they went down there.

Jumbo was the tallest and the biggest in bulk, and Brunt wasn't far behind him. Derrick was a squirt compared to both of them, but Derrick was by far the most vile of the bunch, cruel and unbending. Between them they had a cumulative IQ of about two-hundred ten.

As they approached, Red Rush turned on his stool and regarded them. "Good to see you boys," chipper, effusive, "come for the hooley, did you? Well, sorry to say, but Our Man just departed—and I don't mean died, although that's not far off." He chuckled at his own dark joke.

Derrick gave him the once-over. The W.C. Fields nose, the flushed and bloated face—the sign of an alcoholic. The guy sporting a red, white, and blue jersey, TEAMSTERS LOCAL 688 written on the front, looked like something he'd bought when he was forty pounds lighter. Derrick took him for a harmless drunk.

"We're on a tour," Derrick told him. "The bars of St. Louie. Taking it all in, the lively atmosphere, the friendly faces."

"And the drinks," offered Jumbo, displaying his Busch longneck.

"I see," said Red, "but if you're really looking for a genuine taste of Dogtown and its shanty Irish traditions, then plain old Busch just won't do. You can get that anywhere. You come to this joint, you drink something special." Red gave a wink. "Tommy," he called, "get these fine fellows each a car bomb."

"Ah, you ain't gotta do that," said Brunt. "What's a car bomb?"

"Something that'll start your engine and get you going," answered Red. He appeared to be looking out into the crowd, then said, "Come on now, boys, why're you here? You can tell me, it's all right."

Brunt was gazing at a poster behind the bar. It was a cartoon of a constable chasing a seal with a pint of stout balanced on its nose. MY GOODNESS MY GUINNESS, it read. "Heard there were strippers gonna come," he said.

"You go to the East Side for poontang," said Red, dubious. "Where'd you hear that?"

"Guy named Lenihan," said Derrick, "Francis, maybe Frank Lenihan. Know him?"

Red slapped his knee in delight. "Hell yes, I know him. We all know him, he's one of us."

"Could you point him out to us?" asked Jumbo. "Ow!" he cried as Derrick elbowed him in the ribs.

"Do you take me for a Judas?" asked Red, leaning in. "Will I point out my friend so you louts can lay hands on him? No, boys, I would never do such a thing. You know, Francis has had some bad luck lately—"

"Here's your car bombs," said Tommy, setting three glasses on the bar in front of Red.

"Here you go, boys," Red, handing out, "nectar of the Gods, a shot of Jamie and Bailey's, lovingly sunk into a pint of stout." They examined their drinks with curiosity, and yes, there was something in there, a shot glass, a friggin' bonus.

"All together now," said Red, holding up his glass of Four Roses, leading them into a toast. "One-two-three … down the hatch."

"Wow!" said Brunt, wiping his mouth. "That's some boilermaker."

"That's for certain," agreed Red. "Now, as I was saying, Francis has had his share of misfortune lately. First, he was woefully assaulted by unknown cowards out in the countryside somewhere, and then, more recently, he had his apartment broken into and ransacked, his beloved pet killed." Red looked to Derrick inquisitively. "Can you imagine the grief he felt?"

"Sounds like a personal problem," said Derrick, "and none of our business. But hey, thanks for the drinks, we gotta move on to another bar."

Red gave a slight nod to the scrawny fellow with the flat cap standing off to the side, who, in turn, gave the high sign to certain compatriots nearby. Within seconds the three were surrounded by a seven or eight lackeys, standing at loose attention, waiting for the word.

"Do I detect a country accent in your voices?" asked Red.

"Country, an' proud of it," said Jumbo.

"I made you the second you walked in," said Red, tone ominous now.

"What, you think we messed with your boy out in some pigshit town?" Derrick retorted, indignant. "That wasn't us, you old fool."

Red gave a sneering laugh. "So fucking what? You'll do."

What happened next happened fast. From his barstool Red jabbed a right into Derrick's astonished face. Derrick stumbled back, dropped his drink. Jumbo took a roundhouse at Red, but Red easily ducked and the punch connected with Barney McVey standing beside Red. Before the fracas could turn into a balls out donnybrook, out came the hardware—switchblades, a set of brass knucks, a sap, a prison shiv, a busted beer bottle with a wicked jagged neck. The owners of these tools quickly, efficiently encircled Derrick, Brunt, and Jumbo, pressing them with sharp points and menacing looks.

Still, the trio struggled to break free, pushing back, grunting and elbowing, gnashing their teeth, not believing that they could be taken in such a way.

"Stick one of 'em," said Red under his breath. Angelo McConkie, standing at Jumbo's heels, gladly complied, thrusting the point of his switchblade into Jumbo's thigh.

"Yow!" howled Jumbo. "Why'd you do that?"

"To get your attention," said Red. "Now boys," he told them, softly, in confidence, "we're going to move into the back room and you're going to come along without a fuss. If you make a fuss we'll just have to cut something off, something you may be fond of. Tommy," he called down the bar, "we're going to use the back room for a bit." Tommy nodded assent and continued the pour he was working on.

The back room was where the Ancient Order of Hibernians kept their gear and regalia for the various parades and festivals in which they paraded about. It was the size of a bedroom; in fact, once upon a time it had been a bedroom. There were chairs lining the walls and a kitchenette over in one corner with a wooden table that held a box of saltines and some coffee cups and today's newspaper opened to the sports section.

They stood around their captives, Red's boys—most with beer bellies and bloodshot eyes, only a few of them actual tough guys, the rest just, well, along for the ride—throwing their best hard looks. "C'mon, try something," dared one emboldened henchman to Jumbo, "we'll stick you again."

The three interlopers had their backs to each other. Red paced around them, slowly, deliberately, eyeing them with scorn. None of those regulars present could recall Red ever being this far from his barstool. He came up on Derrick, sniffed him theatrically. "Did you step in something, boy? You smell like a sewer." Derrick spit out a heartfelt fuck you. "Oh, but you're a bold one," Red went on. "Ugly, too. Plug ugly, I think that's the phrase, but I like *pug* ugly. Like the dog. Tell me, are you a bad doggie?"

"Bad enough," answered Derrick with a curled lip.

"You know what we do to bad dogs around here? We swat them

on the nose with a rolled up newspaper. Let me show you." Red turned to a hatchet-faced character standing nearby. "Sean, good man, hand me that *Post*." The newspaper was fetched and Red rolled it tightly. "Hold him," he said, and two strapping fellows put a bear hug around Derrick's thick torso. Red began to swat him on the face, at first almost gently, playfully, then harder and harder, getting into it. *Thwack Thwack.*

Derrick could only move his head this way or that to try to avoid the blows. So mad dog enraged was he, all he could manage was to spout unintelligible gibberish through gritted teeth, those teeth practically turning to dust from the pressure. Finally, his words came. "C'mon, you assholes, help me out here!"

This cry, both plaintive and chiding, was what it took to spur Brunt and Jumbo into action. Looking certain injury in the face, the two lashed out at their captors, swinging, kicking, gouging, grabbing at limbs, clothing, whatever. Derrick lurched forward into a standing tuck and flipped one of them forward, off his back and onto the floor. Red was shouting. Suddenly it was a free-for-all, one moment looking like a rugby scrum and the next moment like a prison riot. Jumbo knew that if he could just get hold of an arm or leg he could break it, and that's just what happened with Blinky O' Meara. A sickening snap of Blinky's forearm followed by piercing yelps of anguish put them all on notice that they had better get control of the situation and quick. The fact they they were half-to-mostly wrecked from drinking steadily since noon both helped and hindered them. Helped in the sense that they were fearless in taking on these country boys, built like bulls or oxen, take your pick, and hindered in the fact that their fuel was over in the bar and without access to glorious libation their fighting prowess was sorely diminished.

Derrick snatched a switchblade from the hand of Finn Talbott and stuck him in the ribs, once, twice. Derrick backed off with just the shank protruding from Finn's side, Finn reaching behind him trying to pull it out.

Just before he was cold-cocked by a brass-knuckled fist belonging to Evan McNew, Brunt cracked two skulls together hard enough to roll their eyes up and switch off their circuits. Both men fell to the floor, as did Brunt.

Jumbo soldiered on, punching and grabbing, trying for another limb. He held three of them at bay, knives outstretched, feigning attack but holding back, waiting for Red to do something. Suddenly, a hard blow to the back of Jumbo's head. The big man went down on his knees, bluebirds and asterisks orbiting around his skull. He looked up to see Red standing over him, holding a gnarled cudgel. Down came the shillelagh hard on Jumbo's ear. He grunted and fell over with a thud.

Derrick saw his two pals on the floor and some of the fight went out of him.

After that they were quickly subdued. Red had his men stand them at attention. He stood before them, again, in the demeanor of a school principal addressing some truants.

"You boys come to Dogtown looking for a fight. Well, you got one, didn't you? And who came out on top?" Red waited for an answer. Nothing. He got up in Derrick's face, Derrick glaring. "Did you think that was a rhetorical question? I said who the fuck came out on top?"

"You guys," mouthed Jumbo, "you guys won."

Derrick looked over at Jumbo, wiping his eyes, snot coming out his nose. "Shut your piehole," he said. "Don't give them any satisfaction."

"Oh, we're not satisfied," said Red. "We're not satisfied until we leave ya's with a final parting blow." The three of them, bleeding and sore, were leaning on each for support, Derrick on one end, his hand on his hip. With the thick end of the shillelagh Red took a whack at his elbow. Derrick gave a startled cry then rubbed his elbow, flicking off the pain like you'd flick water off your hands at the sink. He smiled.

"That had to hurt," said Red.

Derrick spit on the floor in contempt. "You prick, you fucking Irish prick. You need all this cutlery to get it up. You outnumber us, okay, we'll fight even harder. But you hit a man when he's down, do you?"

Red seemed amused by this. "Did you and your shitheel pals fight fair when you ganged up on Our Man Francis, smacking him around with a pipe of some kind? Of course you didn't. Why should you? I learned long ago, sonny, that those who fight fair, if there is such a thing, well, they don't always do so well. No, lad, if I fought by Queensbury Rules, you might somehow take advantage of that and land me a low blow. Like this—"

Derrick gave a low, visceral *oooomphh!* as Red kicked him in the nuts. Derrick doubled over and stayed that way for a minute. Then he stood back up, a defiant sneer on his mug.

"Well, I'll be damned," said Red, somewhat impressed. "Are you Irish? You sure can take a blow like one."

"Here, let me try." Dennis "Hognose" Hearn stepped forward. Dennis was the 1982 city-wide Golden Gloves light welterweight champion. He had gone to pot in recent years, but he could still throw a mean punch.

"Hold him," said Red. And several obeyed, separating Derrick from his pals, who were immediately surrounded by knifepoint in case they decided to come to aid, as before. Derrick steeled himself just as the first blow landed square on his gut. He tightened his stomach muscles, tried to withstand the punishment as Hognose worked his torso like a punching bag. Unlike Red, Hognose did have a sense a fair play, relatively speaking, and the line he would not cross stopped at punching a bound man in the face. After a long two minutes of this, Hognose changed his stance from pugilist to bystander. He opened his fists and dropped his arms. Wiping the sweat from his brow, he looked to Red and Red snarled, reluctantly, "All right, enough." Derrick had slumped into the arms of the men holding him. They were bent over, straining, trying to keep him on his feet.

"Give me his wallet," said Red. He opened Derrick's wallet and took out a ten and a five. "That's for the car bombs," he said, "plus a three dollar tip. You didn't think the drinks were on us, did ya?"

"*Ooof,*" said Derrick.

"Get them the fuck outta here," said Red with a wave of his hand.

"Kick their asses out the door." They hauled Brunt and Jumbo to the back door which led into the alley. Derrick had to be helped, two men holding him by the armpits, his feet half-dragging, barely shuffling along. At the door, about to be given the boot, he turned and called out. "No matter what you say, old man, yer a fuckin' asshole, an' you know it!"

Red gave his most indifferent shrug. "Takes one to know one," he said.

Again, they began to shove him toward the door, but Derrick held fast. "Yer mother drinks from the toilet and licks dogs' asses," he called to Red.

"You gonna take that from him?" asked Evan McNew.

Red shrugged. "You don't boil your cabbage twice."

Derrick hawked up a bolus of blood and bile, spit it on the linoleum floor. Red looked to Derrick, beaten, though still spirited, said with a lilt, "My mother was a fuckin' saint. She nursed me on piss and vinegar, that's why I have such a sweet temperament."

Derrick gave a snort of contempt, and then he was gone.

Red put the shillelagh back among the Hibernian trove where he'd found it. He stood there gazing out at the upturned room, the men gathering their wits, inspecting each others' boo boos. "I've got to compliment Brother McDonald on his excellent choice of walking stick," said Red with a wink.

"I NEED TO GET TO THE DRUGSTORE for some bandages and ointment," said Jumbo from the backseat. "My leg is swelling, starting to throb. My head, shit, I could have a concussion. *Oooo-oh.* You got any aspirin?"

"We'll get there soon enough," said Derrick, turning to Jumbo in the backseat. "We're all hurting, but we need to sit tight for a bit, watch that house."

"What kinda ointment?" asked Brunt, in the front passenger seat.

"First aid cream," said Jumbo, "Mom used to use Unguentine. That stuff really helps a cut."

"You got stuck with a blade," said Derrick. "No topical cream is gonna help that. You gotta get *inside* the wound, clean it out, then put in the antibiotic ointment. If it's throbbing, it's probably infected. You'll need some penicillin."

"How you know this stuff?" wondered Brunt.

"I just do," said Derrick.

Jumbo shifted his great bulk, trying yet another position but it wasn't any more comfortable. "I got to be at work in the morning, how'm I gonna do that with this leg?"

"You work on Saturday now?" asked Brunt.

"Yeah, just a half-day and I get time and a half."

"Reckon you either call in sick or you tough it out," said Brunt. "Can I bum another smoke?"

Jumbo took out a crumpled pack of Chesterfields, shook out a cigarette. "What time you got?"

"I musta lost my matches," said Brunt. "Gimme a light, will ya?"

"You want me to smoke it for you, too? I asked for the time."

"Quarter to eight," said Brunt, lighting up.

Derrick fanned the space between him and Brunt. "Y'all gonna smoke in my car, open the windows, will ya."

Brunt cracked the window.

"More," said Derrick.

"This ain't working," said Brunt. "I mean, look where we're at. Three big dumb sons a bitches, just got their asses kicked in a local bar, and now we're sitting in this tin can all fucked up, just wanting to get back home, least me and Jumbo here, and you've got us waiting on some dude to come home. How long we gonna wait? I don't think we can do this for much longer."

"I've got to get up in nine hours," whined Jumbo, gingerly touching the goose egg on the back of his head.

Derrick turned and gave them both a look. "I'm disappointed in you guys, I thought you had more spirit. Here we drive all the way into the city to do a job and because of a little setback you wanna leave before the job is done. It's shameful, that's what it is, shameful, you all pussyin' out like this."

"Nobody's pussyin' out," said Jumbo, "we wanna grab this Lenihan and beat the snot outta him, make him tell what happened to your old man. But now that we're under the weather, you might say, we'd like to do it another day."

"Yeah," said Brunt, "we could go recuperate and come back another day. How's that?"

"That's a great plan," encouraged Jumbo, "even get some more guys and go after those assholes from the bar. Even the score."

"Hold up," said Derrick, "what's this?"

They looked to the house across the street and saw a figure on the porch. A large woman standing under a single sixty watt bulb, wearing a blue denim duster and a gray Aran jacket with a fleece collar. Long honey-brown hair fell from the dome of an Outback leather stetson. She began to knock at the outer door.

"Who is it?" wondered Brunt.

"Someone for Lenihan," answered Derrick. "Let's go."

They all three got out, and walked briskly across the street, Jumbo limping painfully. She stopped in mid-knock and turned as they came up the steps.

"Hey," she said.

"Hey, yourself," said Derrick, looking up at her six-foot frame. Then, a flicker of recognition. "Damn, I know you. You're the one came out to our place that Saturday morning, you and Lenihan, trying to talk up my sister."

Derrick was on the porch, while the other two were holding back on the steps, watching, waiting. Rose had a canvas satchel slung at her side and the strap, as straps worn by women will do, fell diagonally across her chest, between her breasts, attracting their attention. Brunt licked his lips.

Rose fixed on the ape in front of her, she silent, no expression. Then, she nodded. "That's right, I remember. You and your dad didn't give us the kindest of receptions. Fact, you were downright hostile. And me, being a former neighbor. I used to live right down the way from you, remember? Elizabeth Schurzinger was my mom."

"Shame about that," said Derrick. "They ever catch the killer?"

She frowned. "What're you guys doing here?"

"Same as you, looking for Lenihan. Gonna ask him some questions just like you and him came out to our place to do. Ask questions, get to the bottom of things. But he ain't come home yet."

"Oh. Well, in that case, I'll just come back later." She started to walk past them off the porch. Derrick grabbed her by the arm, spun her around. "You'll be coming with us."

"No fucking way," she said, and raised her free arm to swat him. He put one leg behind her and pushed her down, her hat rolling away. He leapt on her and cupped her mouth with his palm.

"Come on, let's get her in the car.," he commanded. Jumbo and Brunt looked at each other, shrugged, then complied.

Francis rolled up about twenty minutes later. He parked behind Rose's Toyota, thought it looked familiar but couldn't quite place it. He and Janie had called it an early evening, she heading home and he the same, feeling spent from the heady conversation back at Bruno's. Janie leaving, he was still mulling this new turn of events. He would miss her for sure, but how long would it be before someone else came tripping along into his life? He was a free agent once again. The hat caught his eye as he turned the knob to go upstairs. He picked it up, examined it. A stetson with a braid on the brim, all leather, soft and brushed. Feminine in style. He put it to his face and smelled it. Some exotic fragrance. Who could have dropped it? Its owner would be missing it.

The door to the left opened and Phelim came out, Pall Mall hanging from his lips. "Evening," he said.

"Evening, Phelim," said Francis. "You know who might've left this nice hat here?"

"Has to be that girl they kidnapped off the porch here."

"What're you talking?"

"Just a little while ago, I heard some knocking and was looking out the window. What I saw, three guys carrying off a woman. She was kicking something fierce and they dropped her once, but they picked her up again and threw her in the back of a Buick Regal, early eighties. Then they drove off. You think I should call the cops?"

Francis sniffed at the hat again. The scent of Patchouli oil, that was it, Rose's balm. "Three of them, huh. And this happened when?"

Phelim exhaled a plume of smoke which drifted toward the naked light bulb overhead. "No more'n a half-hour ago. And one of 'em, Francis, one of 'em for sure, maybe even two of 'em, were the very same assholes who came in my shop and broke my fingers."

"Don't bother calling the police," said Francis, "I'll take care of it, all right?"

— 38 —

FRANCIS LAID ON THE HORN for the second time, and Joe came trotting out, a small backpack in his hand. "Sorry, brother," taking up the shotgun, "I had to find my wallet." In the overhead light, he saw Francis behind the wheel, decked in boots, jeans, and a bulky gray hoodie that read WASH. U. LADY BEARS. Joe wore a flannel shirt over a long-sleeved T shirt. "Think I'll be warm enough? I better go back in and get a jacket."

"It's all right," said Francis, pulling away. "You'll be fine. I'm just glad I caught you."

Joe glanced at his wristwatch. "Yeah, nine-thirty on a Friday, I'm normally out testing my luck with the ladies, you know? But I had a big night last night and thought I'd take it easy tonight, charge up my batteries for tomorrow."

"What's tomorrow?" wondered Francis.

"Sammy Hagar playing at Mississippi Nights. I'm taking Carol Leonard."

"The Red Rocker, you'll have a blast. Bring your ear plugs."

"Okay, dad. So, where we going?"

"Jefferson County, a subdivision outside Cedar Hill."

"Okay, what's up there?"

"Uh, some halfwits abducted a friend of mine off my porch and I think that's where they took her. This was tonight, just a while ago." Francis filled him in on the details, who Rose was, her circumstances, his relationship with her, leaving out their hot play in the sauna. He then segued into Derrick, the probable abductor, although he couldn't fathom a motive for her abduction, divulging Derrick's connection with Deke and Deke's likely connection to Stoney, the missing murderer. By the time he finished the briefing they were already on I-270 and heading for Gravois Road.

"Well," said Joe, "I've gotta say, this sounds like some serious shit. Kidnapping, a murdered woman, country boys who like to play rough. Hell, Francis. I asked you for some PI experience, but I didn't know that we'd be heading into Tombstone Territory."

Francis' face illuminated as he struck a match and put it to a Marlboro. "I know it's a lot to ask and there may be trouble—I can't see how there *won't* be trouble, but you're the only one I could think to call." He looked to Joe, "And I wouldn't want anyone else for a backup."

"Backup? Excuse me, we get there we're as one. Equal footing. The dynamic duo."

"Yeah, I like that. You bring a weapon?"

"Right here," said Joe, lifting the backpack. "Throwing stars. I've been practicing, watching Kung Fu movies."

Francis nodded. "I don't know what kind of weapons they'll have, if any at all. But it's their turf, they'll have the advantage."

"We'll get her back," said Joe. "Rose, that her name?"

"Yeah, Rose Schurzinger."

"She pretty?"

"Yeah, very pretty. Young and on her own, into the hippie life. Free spirited. Lives in a yurt on a commune with a bunch of animals, human and otherwise. She's got her own unique style ... I'd hate to think of anything happening to her."

"It's already taken care of. I'm glad you called me, brother."

* * *

"You best start talking before I get *really* pissed." Derrick, standing before her, was near the end of his patience, in short supply to begin with. He had no tolerance for people who failed to do his bidding, and this woman was dangerously close to having her nose broken. He had already slapped her up, her cheeks nice and red. Derrick and Brunt had Rose in the barn, in a corner, up against some cobwebs and dirty siding. Jumbo had been allowed to go home and lick his wounds, catch a few winks before the 5:30 alarm went off.

She looked down at him, said with great scorn, "You little monkey, I fucking told you I don't know what happened to your dad. But if he had anything to do with my mom's murder, I hope he's in hell right now."

Derrick punched her in the gut, hard, and she doubled over. Brunt stood beside Rose, a bulwark against any notion of her trying to make a break for it. He was not put off by this violence, although in the back of his mind he understood that he could go to prison for being a part of it. In the here and now, however, it was exciting to see and he was getting aroused.

After a minute, she straightened up and shook her head in disbelief, waiting for the next blow.

Derrick reached for the half pint of Beam in his back pocket. He took a good hit, and handed it to Brunt. "I know you know something," he told her. "You won't say, fine." Brunt passed back the bottle as Derrick chin-pointed to a fixture over near a wall. "Get her over to that sorting table and strip her down."

Brunt looked to Derrick all caught up in this thing, a thing now about to get pretty fucking serious. And him standing there, brow furrowed, mouth all scrunched up, bottom lip out like he's some big cheese calling all the shots—almost comical. He had thought it before, and he was thinking it again right now, that Derrick looked like Curly from the Stooges. Just in appearance, though, not the behavior.

So Brunt went ahead and wrapped his arms around Rose's torso, arms included, and lifted her like she was a piece of furniture. He carried her kicking and squirming over to a rectangular wooden platform, waist high, about six feet long and four feet wide, one side running along a wall and the remaining sides open, supported by wooden legs, four-by-fours resting on the dirt floor. Back when this place had a produce stand down the road, the table was used for sorting various grades of tomatoes, cucumbers, zucchini, and peppers. Brunt laid her on the table. She sat up, he pushed her back down. Derrick came along with a rope and some leather strips from the tack room around the corner. Rose clawed at them as they began to tug at her denim duster, buttons popping. They had already yanked off the nice wool jacket that she wore.

She wasn't going to go gentle into that good night.

"I'll hold her," said Derrick, his breath visible in the cool night air. Standing over her at one end of the table he held her arms down by the wrists, but her arms were in the way of her outfit coming off. "Hell with it," he said. "You got your Buck knife? Cut the dang thing off."

Derrick bound her wrists and tied them to some slats in the siding behind her. Brunt leaned on her legs to hold them down, but still she kept bucking. Now, laying on her legs, he lifted the fabric of her garment and began to cut away. He stopped at her throat, and she gulped. He got down close so she could smell the whiskey on his breath. He whispered in her ear, "One little slip of this here knife, it won't be my fault, you keep fightin' like that."

These dire circumstances prompted a flashback to a time not so long ago when another numbskull decided to force himself on her. Now, as she was being trussed and manhandled, it played out in the theater of her mind. She was an undergrad at William Jewell College in Liberty, Missouri. There was a party off-campus, things got a bit out of hand, she ended up in this boy's bedroom. The same scenario seen in so many movies. Plied with liquor, the girl loses inhibitions, loses her pants. He looked like one of those beautiful boys in a Calvin Klein ad, so the prelude of French kissing was easy, enticing. Then he goes for second base, she doesn't stop him. Encouraged, he heads for third, she puts him off. What, is he really heading for home plate?—"No, stop! I'm not ready and we don't have protection!" And Calvin Klein here, a senior, bullheaded, ruled by his cock, ignores her pleas and has his way with her, she fighting him all the way. But in this case, she doesn't just go back to her dorm room and sulk, doesn't go to the police. There's no self-pity, only anger at herself and the man who took advantage of her. Calvin is on the school golf team, captain. There's an intercollegiate tournament each spring. She goes to the golf course and walks out on the green when he's trying to sink a crucial putt. She has it out with him in front of everyone. He is livid. "See here," he sputters, "you can't just walk up to me while I'm playing, you can't *interfere* with my game." The links police are on their way, but meanwhile she has taken a nine iron out of his bag and is beating him about the upper body with it. He tries to get away and she chases him around the green like some comedy routine, the spectators all laughing. The upshot? He is ejected from the tournament, his scholarship is in peril, his prestige at the school diminished, and Rose is the new champion of women who won't take it lying down.

She looked up at the brute standing over her. This was going to take all the fortitude she had. She imagined that Elizabeth may have thought the same thing as that animal brutalized her, only mom didn't come out of her ordeal. And it was hard to think of her life ending as it did. Her own life would go on, she knew with certainty, but she must be brave in the face of this outrage. They might have her body, use her to their own unspeakable ends, but it was only her corporeal being; her mind was her own. She would not allow them to debase her.

Brunt made the final cut and with both hands he tore the denim garment apart. She wore no brassiere and her breasts quivered and spilled off to the sides. Derrick nodded toward Rose's panties featuring a depiction of wild strawberries on leafy green stems. "Off with that pretty thing, too," he said to Brunt. Brunt lifted the garment by its elastic band and with one deft stroke of the blade the panties fell away, exposing tufts of fine blonde hair. Brunt looked to Derrick, and Derrick looked to Brunt, a noticeable lump in the front of his jeans.

"I ain't seen one of them for a while," said Derrick.

"I swear, I just saw it twitch."

"Go for it, big boy," he grinned. "Climb aboard. Get your dick wet, have one on me."

Brunt quickly kicked off his shoes. He unbuckled and dropped trou. Her legs freed for the moment, Rose kicked at him, her boots still on, and succeeded in pushing him back but he was on her almost immediately, his hard on ready to go. But she rocked her hips from one side to the other so that he couldn't get it in, and then she brought her leg up and kicked him upside the head.

"Damn!" said Brunt, holding an ear, "she's a hellcat." Derrick, watching with interest, offered to tie her legs. Brunt climbed down off the table and, bare-assed, took one leg as Derrick took the other and tied them by the ankles to nearby objects that would hold. Now she was spreadeagled on the table, vulnerable as a fledgling in a field of tomcats. During that task, Brunt had gone flaccid. Now he climbed back on the table and knelt over her spread legs, taking in her luscious form, his hard on resurgent.

Derrick, too, felt the blood rushing, getting some wood now, but it had far less to do with the nubile feminine body before him than it did with Brunt's stiffy, so close he could reach out and touch it.

Rose, supine, lifted her head, took in Brunt's erection, poised to penetrate, and gave a caustic laugh. "Such a little dick, a pee shooter. Oh, please, give me a magnifier! Your girlfriend must be embarrassed when you pull that little weezer out. What are you gonna do with that thing, huh? Tickle me?"

"You bitch," Brunt seethed, "I'll show you what I'm a do with it."

* * *

"You think we should call for help?" asked Joe.

"The police, you mean?"

"Yeah, I mean, kidnapping, hell, that's right up their alley. They could meet us out there, probably bring some weapons, too."

Francis looked at him, leaning back in the seat, smoking, one leg up on the dash. "I don't know, let me think about it."

They rode on for a while, no lights on this country road, headlights guiding them around curves and bends, eyes out for any sudden surprises. Francis driving cautiously, anxiously. The night was cool, bordering on cold, but he had the window half down.

"Will you roll that back up," asked Joe, "you're gonna freeze me out here."

"Keeps me alert. I was out earlier, eating and drinking with a friend, and my body's telling me it wants to lay down." He stuck his arm out the window to channel more outside air on his face.

"How much further?"

"Fourteen-fifteen miles maybe. A half-hour. You ready? You want to ask me anything?"

"Why do you go to mass?"

Again, Francis looked at Joe. "No, I mean ask me anything about the situation at hand."

"I don't have any questions about that," he said. "But I see you at mass, I just wondered why you attend like you do."

"I guess it's because it's something I've always done. Ever since I can remember I've been in that church, either with my parents or my classmates and teachers. I was an altar boy, same as you. Made a few bucks serving at funerals and weddings. It's just a part of my life, something I do partly out of habit, partly because it feels right, and I don't see any reason to give it up. How about you?"

Joe's answer took long enough that Francis thought he hadn't heard him right. "To glorify God, Jesus, and the Blessed Virgin," he recited. "To pay respect to the saints. To partake of the body and blood of Our Savior, to cleanse my soul anew each day. That, and the chance of hooking up with Claire Delaney."

Francis chuckled at the answer. "Well, yeah, those are good reasons, too."

"I'm a big sinner," said Joe, "mass and confession helps me deal with that."

"I doubt you're a bigger sinner than I am," countered Francis. "My sins would fill a million-gallon swimming pool."

"My sins would stretch from the Earth to Jupiter—and that's not just the venials."

"My sins would turn a sunny day gloomy."

They both laughed, Francis longer than Joe. A minute later, he asked, "How come I never see you at Murphy's?"

"I don't go in much for all that Irish shit," he said. "The Hibernian Parade, yeah, wouldn't miss it, but drinking toasts to the terrorist IRA with a bunch of sad drunks and listening to Tommy Makem sing "The Unicorn"—you can have that nonsense. I like the clubs downtown, lots of chicks to dance with." He gave a merry chuckle. "That's where I do a lot of my sinning."

Joe wondered about something. "Why are you sucking your thumb?" he asked.

"I'm not, I'm chewing on it."

"There's a difference? It's still in your dang mouth. What's up with that?"

"Nervous habit," said Francis, "I've been at it all my life."

"So you're nervous?"

"Well, yeah, of course, and with each passing mile it gets worse."

There was a glow up ahead, and they came to a service station. Four pumps, a quickie mart with big propane tanks off to one side. Francis pulled up in front of the glass doors. He got out, Joe following. There was a pay phone inside, but you didn't need a quarter to call 911. Joe saw what was happening and immediately he felt better.

The call was answered on the second ring. "Dispatch," came the male voice.

"Detective LaRocca, please."

"Not on duty at the moment," he heard, "what is your emergency?"

"Well, I guess it could be an emergency," he spoke, "you decide. There's reason to believe a woman has been abducted from St. Louis and she was brought out here, you know, in Jeff County, and she's being held at a house in the Avonhurst subdivision but we won't know for sure until we get there, which'll be in about fifteen minutes. You want to send someone out?"

"What is the address?" Francis said the address, slowly, distinctly.

Some clacking in the background, he could see the dispatcher keystroking the address into a console glowing with buttons and knobs. "The address should already be on your radar," Francis told him, "LaRocca's already been out there."

"I'll send an officer," declared Dispatch, all business. "Do not, I repeat, *do not* act on your own, wait for the officer. And what is your name?"

At that, Francis hung up.

* * *

Eve was dropped off by her friend Alicia who had a black Chevy Impala that really guzzled gas. In fact, on the way back from the Dairy Queen in Hillsboro, Eve had sunk her last four dollars into the tank, otherwise they'd have hoofed it back. Alicia, not one to plan ahead, had spent the last of her funds on cheese fries and Blizzards.

"See ya," called Alicia as Eve clambered out the car.

"Wouldn't wanna be ya," Eve shot back.

She was walking up he path to the front door when she heard some sounds from the back of the house. She did a detour around and saw the lights on in the barn. Derrick. His car here, another one as well, an old Plymouth. Something going on, she decided to check it out.

—39—

BRUNT WISHED SHE WOULD JUST LIE THERE and take it without a fight. Twice now she had bucked so hard, and rocked her body so vigorously that his dick had slipped out. Each time he had to plunge it back in and start all over. The table's legs weren't built for such weight, nor was it stable enough to withstand the piston-like downward force of Brunt's thrusts, so it creaked and wobbled, threatening to fall apart. This was another distraction for Brunt, thinking that this rough bed might break any moment, and it was keeping him from getting off. He held his torso over her with palms flat on the table, doing push-ups, grinding his member into her, thinking only in the moment, feeling like a real stud, ravishing this wench like he was Conan the fucking Barbarian. At first she called him hateful names and spat at him and tried to bite him, all she could do in her circumstances, but now, maybe five minutes into it, the bucking and rocking had subsided and she was just scrunching her eyes and gritting her teeth in resignation.

Brunt had lifted himself over her in the push-up position so he could get a good look at her prodigious breasts, jouncing with each thrust he gave. This visual combined with the sensation of his dick immersed in a warm, sticky swamp sent a strong signal to his reproductive system. He felt an army of sperm marshaling in his epididymis, rendezvousing with a nearby regiment of semen, on the move now, passing through a maze of tiny passages, up, up, up his urethra. Ejaculation was nigh. He looked to Derrick, about four feet away, jacking off furiously. "I'm coming!" he cried.

"So'm I," said Derrick through clenched teeth, his face a grim mask of concentration as he shot his load onto the floor of the barn.

Brunt gave one final, mighty thrust and the table collapsed. One side, the length of it, was still attached to the wall by some ten penny nails, but the legs were shattered. Brunt lost his perch and tumbled off onto the floor. Rose, still bound with rope and leather strips, was now at a precarious angle, having rolled on one side, her head lower than the rest of her. She realized several things at once: that she had been raped by this clod and his semen was now dripping out of her; that they might choose to kill her rather than let her go and worry about her going to the cops; that the table had broke and now was a good time to escape.

She was on her left side, half-facing the dirt floor. She began to struggle against her binding, feeling for a weakness. There, at one wrist, the rope had play. She jerked her arm hard, rotated her wrist one way then the other, trying to get free. The knot was only getting tighter. She tried the other wrist, but it was no use. A length of rope still held that wrist to the siding, her arm outstretched, her weight pulling at the taut binding, cutting off her circulation. In her peripheral vision she saw her rapist get up. His thing was limp now, drained of vigor. It looked like a baby bird, all shriveled up. He was brushing the hay and dirt from his belly and cock, slick with her juices, and dust was in the air. He stood over her, not saying a word, just looking. She saw the imperfection in his upper lip and it was clear why it was called harelip. She almost said something cutting, but then she held back. It just didn't seem right. She could mock his dick, but not this other. It wasn't a weapon.

She heard him say, "You see that tat she's got?"

"Yeah, I saw. Some kinda Chinese symbol. What's it mean," the other one asked her, "you fuck chinks?"

"Maybe," she said. "Maybe I'd pull a train with two dozen well-hung Asians and it'd be better than having to deal with you pathetic losers."

"You're nothin' but a piece of meat on a table," said Derrick. "That's all you are, so shut the fuck up with your bad language."

"I like a woman with tats," said Brunt, who had several of his own, including one on his bicep that said FUCK THE SISTEM. "Okay, what's next?"

"My turn," said Derrick, a wicked gleam in his eye. "Only I won't be putting it to her like you, I've got something else in mind, something hard core." He leaned over her, and took a nipple between thumb and forefinger. He played with it, kneading it with almost scientific curiosity, and it became hard, erect.

"Fucker! Get your filthy pig hands offa me!"

He pinched her nipple harder, and she grimaced. He got in her face. "One more time: What happened to Deke? What did you and your boyfriend do to him?"

"Fuck off!"

Derrick said to Brunt, "Hand me them snips over there." There were some small tools laying on a workbench nearby, among them tinner's snips looking like heavy-duty scissors. Brunt, still pantsless, passed them to Derrick. "Fuck off, huh?" He lifted her breast by the nipple, gripping it firmly at the roseate tip. He put the snips at the base of the nipple, poised to cut.

Back in close, his face inches from her's, almost with intimacy, "You wanna say that again?"

She hawked up some phlegm from the back of her throat, and spat in his face. "Your breath stinks like shit!" she ragged in that husky voice. "That what you had for dinner? Shit?"

Derrick made the cut and Rose screamed bloody hell. He jumped back and watched her closely, crimson blooming on her chest. She gasped and went into a series of deep respirations, heaving and perspiring heavily. Her blood pressure had shot up forty points, yet, even so, the practical part of her brain telling herself to keep it together. Brunt, too, stood watching, mouth agape, not prepared for this level of barbarism—never mind that he had just violated her in his own sick and twisted way. Suddenly, there was movement, someone else in the barn.

"What the fuck are you doing, you fucking psychos!" Eve screamed at them, the force of the exclamation practically blowing their hair back.

— 40 —

"LET ME OUT, DICKHEAD!" pounding the door from the inside.

"I can't," Derrick told her, "you'll mess everything up." He was talking to his sister through a door leading to a small room under the stairs, down the hall from the kitchen. After she'd burst in on them, he had summarily frog-marched her back to the house and locked her in this room. "I'm trying to find out what happened to Deke," he added. "She knows something."

"Looked to me like you were torturing her."

"That's how you get information from stubborn agents," he said. "You've seen the James Bond movies."

"Let her go, Derrick. She's my friend."

"Since when?"

"Just let her go, do it for me. Please?"

"When's the last time you did me a favor, huh? I'm walking away now. I'll be back later, let you out."

"You unlock this door right now!" No response. Did he really leave? She pounded the thick wooden door with both hands balled into fists, mighty blows landing with dull thuds. She placed a few karate kicks, well, what she'd seen on TV, near the edge of the door just below the doorknob. Door barely budged. "I'll get out of here," she yelled, "I'll fucking escape, you'll see, and then I'll fix your wagon, you cocksucking prick!"

At thirteen, Eve could swear like a trooper.

Francis cut the headlights as he turned onto Bolingbroke. He parked fifty yards down from Deke's place. They sat for a minute, going over the plan, loose as it was. Francis reached in the glove compartment and took out a handgun, a revolver. He nudged a catch on the side and the cylinder popped out, six chambers. He spun it and checked to make sure it was fully loaded. Joe watched with amazement.

"You told me you don't carry a piece, so what's this?"

He held the gun out, its finish glinting in the glow of a distant streetlamp. "I said I don't carry a gun, I didn't say I don't own one. Actually, this is my dad's service revolver. He was a guard at The Workhouse on Hall Street."

"Yeah? Lemme see it."

Francis passed it over. Joe hefted it, drew a bead at some imaginary target down the way. "Sweet," he pronounced.

"Thirty-eight caliber, six-shot, Smith and Wesson," said Francis.

"Good to know we've got those dudes on our side," said Joe.

They approached the house in a crouch, keeping a low profile. At the side, they hugged the stucco walls, keening for any sound, eyes peeled for any movement. Moving along, getting snagged on shrubs, they peeked through the windows. Lights on inside, but nothing stirring. Stealthily, they made their way to the rear of the house. Then they heard some commotion. Angry words, multiple persons and someone very pissed. It was coming from a large structure about seventy yards away, down a gradual slope, a barn maybe, light coming from a door partway open.

"This is it," whispered Francis.

"Bring it on," said Joe, gamely.

They looked to one another, simultaneously made the sign of the cross, and strode down the hill toward the unknown, a cone of light from Francis' flashlight leading the way.

Derrick, coming out of the house and heading back to the barn, stopped in his tracks. Off in the distance, near the door of the barn, he saw two figures, hunched, looking inside. They were no more than silhouettes, but whoever they were, they were uninvited. This wasn't good, not at all. "Damn," he muttered, and turning, he went back in the house to get one of Deke's guns.

Lights on the ceiling, the interior lit up pretty good. From outside, looking through the door, they scanned the scene as best they could. It was a barn all right, a hayloft, tools hung on pegs, sawhorses, a riding lawn mower. Ah, the smell of horse manure and fresh hay, and the reason for that was standing in a nearby stall, looking at them. The reddish-brown horse with a black mane whinnied a greeting. Then they heard voices, a male voice, agitated, and a female voice moaning balefully. They opened the door some more and stuck their heads in, looking this way and that. Again, moaning, repetitive, sounding like a chant or a dirge. Whoever it was they were just out of sight on the other side of a partition or wall. They moved in that direction, Francis with his gun drawn.

"I've had it," they heard as they got closer, a male voice sounding agitated. "You don't cut that shit out right now, I'm gonna gag you with your own underpants."

They looked to each other, nodded, and moved around the wall blocking their view. They saw Rose stretched out naked atop a slab or platform, one end on the floor, the other end affixed to a wooden siding about three feet higher. She lay cantilevered, her shredded clothing around her, one breast bloodied. Eyes fixed on something distant, she uttered, "Oooom ... oooom," really emphasizing that one syllable. "Oooom ... oooom."

There was a guy standing over her, wearing socks and T-shirt, but no pants, his bare ass in plain view. Built like a bull, head shaved on the sides but full on top and tied in a sort of bun. It wasn't Deke's son. Francis had never seen this guy. He had his fingers in his ears as Rose mouthed her spooky note.

"Okay, you asked for it." He had something in his hand, the panties he'd threatened to gag her with. He leaned over her, dick dangling, reached for her mouth. "Oooom," she intoned.

Francis stepped forward. "It's over," he announced with crisp authority. "Step away from her and put your hands up."

Brunt twirled around, a stunned look on his mug. "Who the fuck're—"

"Just do it," said Francis, an edge to his voice. He cocked the hammer on the .38.

"All right, all right," Brunt scowled, following orders. "There ain't no call for violence, we just havin' us a party here."

"Sure you are," said Joe. "Thing is, you didn't invite us and now we have to crash it."

"Oooom!" said Rose, apparently oblivious to the rescue in progress.

Francis looked to Joe. "Untie her, will you, and truss Nature Boy here with those ropes."

"Love to," said Joe.

Brunt still had his hands up. "You just hold that position until we get to you," Francis told him. "Guy like you can hold out for a long time, I'll bet. But this won't take long."

"Can I put my pants back on?" he asked.

"As much as I don't want to look at your wiener—no, you cannot. Where's the other ones?"

"Who's that?"

"The ones who lives here," clarified Francis. "Deke and his son."

"Oh, they're around," said Brunt, coyly. "I 'spect they'll be back any time now."

But his arm was tiring of holding the handgun outstretched, the weapon starting to shake a bit. "How you doin' over there?" he asked.

The very first thing Joe had done before extricating Rose, was to take a moment to etch in his mind her lovely and highly erotic nude form, the chest wound notwithstanding. Only then he started to untie her. "Coming along, just about done," he answered. "She's gonna need medical attention," he added.

Unbound, he stood her up on wobbly legs, her teeth chattering. She was shivering something awful. "*Oooooom*," she said, seeming to be looking right through him. "*Oooooom*." Joe took off his flannel shirt and put it on Rose, the tails reaching down just below her crotch. He buttoned it for her, ran his palms briskly up and down her arms, trying to generate some warmth. She flinched like he was hurting her, but he saw that she did seem to come out of her trance, the glazed look gone.

He tapped on her forehead, looked her in the eyes. "Hello in there," he said.

"I'll be okay," she murmured.

He turned to Brunt. "Okay, big man, your turn." Joe got behind him with the ropes in one hand. "Bring the one arm down, slowly."

Francis waved the revolver at Brunt. "Don't even think of trying something. One false move, I'll blow you away."

"*Starsky and Hutch?*" wondered Brunt. "No—*Spenser For Hire*. I heard that line on a TV show."

"Never mind," said Francis, "just do as my partner says."

"I think it was *Magnum P.I.*," said a voice behind them. "Only it was the bad guy talking to Magnum."

There stood Derrick with a Remington double barrel 12-gauge pump action leveled at them, a shit-eating grin on his face. He racked the shotgun dramatically and Joe about shit his pants. Looking to Francis, motioning to his weapon. "Drop it, fool." Francis dropped it. "And you," he called to Joe, visibly shaking, "step back from my boy." Joe stepped back, stuffing a length of rope in his back pocket.

"Yes sir," said Derrick, quite happy with himself, "the shoe's on the other foot, ain't it. So what happens now?" He moved the shotgun to the other arm, cradling it, but still pointing it in their direction. The four men had paired up, Brunt and Derrick side by side, Francis and Joe standing opposite, about eight feet away, the space between them crackling with tension. Rose hung back just watching the drama unfold.

"Let's see, we could kill the three of yous and bury y'all in an unmarked grave that only the worms know about. Or, better yet, there's a hog farm down the road. We could take you there, conscious or unconscious—your choice—and we could feed you to the hogs. Them animals is something, seems they like the taste of us as much as we like the taste of them. Y'all ever see a passel of hogs eat a man? I haven't either, but it's got to be entertaining. And we may do just that, but not just yet. First I need to hear something from you—yeah, you," eyes on Francis. "I'm gonna lay it out, so listen up. You and Missy here come to us one Saturday morning, y'all asking questions, tryin' to get my sister to talk. Dad and I rolled up and we nipped that shit in the bud. Then, to return the favor, me and Brunt here paid y'all a visit in the city. We didn't find you at home so we partied with your downstairs neighbor—"

"Grouchy bastard," put in Brunt.

"Oh, an' I nearly forgot," Derrick went on, "we fucked up your bird just for fun."

Brunt raised his hand. "Can I keep her for a while? You know, before we kill 'em? I ain't done with her yet."

"Where you gone put her?" asked Derrick.

"I dunno, here maybe. I could keep her here, just for a week or so, check on her after work."

At that, Rose started in with "*nam-myoho-renge-kyo, nam-myoho-renge-kyo, nam-myoho-renge-kyo*," building, "*nam-myoho-renge-kyo, nam-myoho-renge-kyo*," rising to a crescendo, "*nam-myoho-renge-kyo, nam-myoho-renge-kyo ...*"

"I told you cut that shit out," scowled Brunt. Looking to Derrick, "She's on some kinda trip. I don't know how to get her back."

"Gone bonkers, huh? Whatever, but she ain't no pet and you ain't keepin' her here."

"*nam-myoho-renge-kyo, nam-myoho-renge-kyo, nam-myoho-renge-kyo—*"

"Speak American, bitch," Derrick commanded, but Rose kept right at it.

"Damn your ass," he told Brunt. "If you don't do something, I will!" Brunt reached around Rose's head and went to cup her mouth. Bad idea. She bit him good on the web of the palm and he immediately withdrew, cursing. On a shelf behind her, a can of wasp and hornet killer. Quickly, she took it up and sprayed Brunt in the face. He shrieked. Rose turned the can, glanced at the label: KILLS THE ENTIRE NEST. She held it out and sprayed him again, Brunt, hands on his throat, retching, gagging something terrible.

Joe saw his chance and grabbed Brunt from behind, looping a rope around his thick neck. They were both about the same height. Joe put the squeeze on, tightening the rope-garrotte with all his strength, thinking to choke the man until he blacked out. Within killing distance Derrick pointed the shotgun at the tussling couple, yelling something, but he couldn't fire without hitting Brunt. Brunt, even though disabled, bent down at the waist, flipping Joe forward. Joe landed hard on his shoulder blades, and, in a whiplash motion, bonked the back of his head on the hardpack floor.

With Derrick distracted by the fracas, Francis reached in the back pocket of his jeans and brought out a lime green plastic squirt gun, made to look like a Flash Gordon raygun. He took three paces toward Derrick and shot him in the face with a stream of ammonia. Derrick went for his eyes, clawing at them, while Francis moved in and placed a kick to Derrick's knee. Derrick buckled and fell but didn't drop the shotgun. Sprawled on the floor was not the best position to fire away, but Derrick fumbled the shotgun to working order. No time to rise, for Francis was now charging in. Half-blinded, Derrick raised the shotgun. Seeing twin barrels pointed at him, Francis skidded to a halt like some cartoon character, reversed direction and dove for cover. Derrick tracked him in a sloppy arc and let loose with both barrels, peppering Francis on the lower body. Francis lay there some ten feet from Derrick, wondering how bad was it, for the one leg was on fire with what felt like a thousand bee stings. He looked to see his jeans scored with buckshot, blood oozing out the holes, the denim turning from faded blue to bright red.

Raging like a bull, Brunt charged Joe still sprawled on the floor and kicked him repeatedly about the back and ribs. Leaning over, his weight bearing down, Brunt got his hands around Joe's throat and began to choke off his air. Joe was on his back and Brunt was on top of him, one knee pressing on Joe's forearm. But Joe's other arm was free, and it was desperately reaching out, looking to grab something. He found Brunt's cock and he pulled, but Brunt head-butted him hard and he lost his grip. Just as Joe was seeing his life pass before him, Rose came from behind and with all her might brought down the back of a shovel on Brunt's spine. Brunt growled, released his hold on Joe, and rose to his feet. Joe sucked air ravenously.

Brunt's eyes were still tearing profusely from the bug spray attack, but he could make out the figure of Rose, holding something linear. He saw the thing coming toward him and he reached out and grabbed it. Huh, a shovel of some kind. Brunt jerked the thing out of Rose's hands, turned it, and swung it back at her. A wild swipe, and she dodged it. She ran to the wall where she'd found the shovel, one of several implements resting on the floor or hanging from hooks, looking for a replacement. Brunt, wiping at his streaming eyes, started after her with the shovel, but he felt resistance. He

looked down at the problem. The guy he'd nearly strangled, clutching at his ankles. The shovel he held was actually a spade and it had
a sharpened square-tipped blade but Brunt, vision swimming, didn't
know that. Brunt took the spade and brought it straight down, hard,
like he was breaking half-frozen ground, and chopped off Joe's hand
at the wrist.

As Francis lay there bleeding, Derrick began to reload the
12-gauge. He dropped the shells a couple times, had to wipe them
off, and almost had the first one in when Francis tackled him, the
shotgun skittering out of reach. They wrestled, both men punching,
gouging, vying for superiority, first Francis on top, then Derrick,
rolling over each other like Greco-Roman wrestlers. It was very
close quarters. For a moment they were cheek to cheek; Francis saw
a finger near his face and he chomped it—*yow!*—it was his own.
Brunt came over and went to pound Francis with the spade, but the
grapplers suddenly switched position and he hit Derrick instead.

"*Unhhh!*" Derrick looked up, surprised to see Brunt standing
over him with a shovel. Francis squirmed out of Derrick's hold and
went for the .38 laying in the dirt about ten feet away. Brunt had one
thing in mind, to make quick work of these intruders. He went over
to Francis, head down, fooling with something in his hands—a pistol—thinking to behead him with this nifty garden tool. Standing
over him, Brunt brought the spade up and behind him, a woodsman
about to swing his ax, and, as he swung, a shot rang out. Brunt fell
back and hit the floor, writhing, holding his side.

Derrick was right behind Brunt, same idea, kill these fuck-
ers right now. He paused to look at Brunt, flopping like a salmon.
Worse, Lenihan stood tall, had the pistol pointed at him. Just as
bad, the shotgun behind him, on the floor, still not loaded. Derrick
decided the situation was no longer manageable. The two men faced
each other, staring, waiting for the other to make a move. In the
background they heard Joe dolefully asking for his hand. They heard
Rose offer soothing words. They heard Danger in her stall, whinny-
ing, being skittish over the events taking place just out sight.

Derrick broke the silence. "What happened to my dad?" he implored.

"I really don't know," answered Francis, his tone so genuine that Derrick believed him.

Derrick shuffled a bit and Francis saw that he was about to make a move. He had the barrel of the .38 pointed at Derrick's chest, holding the piece with both arms outstretched. "So, what'll it be?" said Francis.

"Well," said Derrick, shrugging his shoulders, "as they say in the movies, you've got the drop on me so I reckon we'll just have to finish it another day." He turned and walked off, Francis feeling like a fool holding the weapon that would stop him.

— 41 —

DET. ANNA RIGGS STEPPED OUT of the cruiser and came around to the other side where Patrolman Jason Kilo already waited. It was 11:30, the night very dark, only a distant street lamp illuminating the scene. They had spotlighted the street numbers and they were at the right house, the purported hold of kidnappers and their victim. Rather than knock at the front door they choose to make their way around the domicile, going for the element of surprise. They hadn't gotten twenty feet into their canvass, flashlights out, when they heard the gunshot. Riggs quickly returned to the cruiser, got on the horn and called for backup and EMT assistance. Then, cautiously, they hastened in the direction of the trouble.

A puzzle waiting to be put together. That was the challenge for the two officers entering the barn, weapons drawn. Here were four people, three men and one woman, all of them young, two of them scantily clad, all showing injuries, some worse than others. Riggs quickly took control of the scene, first announcing their presence, then telling them to surrender any firearms they might have. Francis handed over his pistol and squirt gun. Kilo, six-one, muscular, handsome, serious as a storm front, saw the shotgun on the floor and seized it. "Anything else?" he asked, looking from face to face. In turn, they shook their heads no.

Rose, cross-legged on the floor beside Joe, had wrapped his stump of an arm in a strip of her denim and was putting pressure on it. Francis was inspecting the damage to his right hip and leg. Brunt, bare-assed and self-focused, was staring in disbelief at the hole in his side, the .38 slug having pierced a roll of flab. Riggs surveyed this motley group, not knowing at this point who the bad actors were. "You won't mind if we frisk you," she said. "I can see you're injured, and we'll be careful, but we have to take every precaution. I've already called 911 and the paramedics are on their way. Until they get here, we're going to talk to each of you individually, try to get some idea of what happened here."

"I'll tell you what happened," spouted Rose, "these assholes kidnapped me and raped me."

"We'll get to that in a minute, after we frisk you for weapons," said Kilo.

"Which assholes?" wondered Riggs.

"This one," she pointed to Brunt, "and his idiot partner, guy who lives here but took off just before you walked in."

Riggs shot a glance at Kilo. "We've got one at large. You want to check the premises, just this building, inside and out."

"Roger that," answered Kilo, who was a second lieutenant in the Missouri Air National Guard.

"There's a horse in a stall as you walk in," said Francis, "at least there was. I thought I heard it riding off."

"Check for the horse," said Riggs over her shoulder.

"Roger that," said Kilo, taking up the mission, walking off somewhere.

Riggs still had her service revolver pointed at the foursome. One by one she patted them down and, satisfied, she stood before them but not close enough that one of them could pull a surprise attack. She holstered her weapon. She took out a small notebook and a ball point. "Okay, listen up. I'm going to take your names, your addresses. You first," she gestured to Francis. Francis gave her what she asked for, no asides.

"Now you," she motioned to Joe, sitting up now, raising his

wounded arm for her to see.

"I need help," he said, raggedly. "My hand, maybe reattach it ... if we get to the ER ... but gotta hurry ..." He was breathing fast, too fast; his eyelids fluttered and his eyes rolled up into his head.

"He's gone into shock," said Francis.

"I see that," said Riggs, watching the stricken man intently. She had always been fascinated by medical conditions.

Facing Riggs, Francis explained. "His name is Joe Lennon, and he's my neighbor in Dogtown. He's a security guard at the community college. I asked him to come with me tonight because I thought there'd be trouble and—"

"Dogtown?"

"Yeah, it's a neighborhood in St. Louis, where me and Joe live. These other two, they live out here."

"That right?" she asked Brunt. "You a local?"

Brunt nodded. "I need help, too," he said. "I've been shot."

Riggs looked at her watch. "It's been thirty minutes, should be any time now." Riggs jotted some notes on her pad. She looked at Brunt again. "And your name is?"

"Randy Bruntraeger."

"Where are your pants, Randy?"

"Over there," sheepishly.

Riggs walked over to where Brunt pointed, came back with his grungy trousers. "Put these on right now." She dropped them beside Brunt. "And this friend of yours, the one who's missing. His name?"

"Aw, he can tell you that when he shows up."

"It's Derrick," offered Rose, "I heard pencil dick here call him by name."

Riggs nodded. "Seeing that this is the home of Richard Johnson—we were briefed en route—may I assume that Derrick is the son of this Richard Johnson and that his surname is also Johnson?"

No one answered. Riggs made an entry in her notebook. She looked over to the busted sorting table, saw the torn and ripped clothing on the floor. "Your clothes?" she asked Rose.

Rose affirmed. "They cut my clothes off, this one raped me while the other one watched. I've got his filthy jizz inside me. I want to be examined at the hospital, tested. I want him to pay."

Riggs turned thoughtful, pursed her lips. "That right, Mr. Bruntraeger, you and Mr. Derrick Johnson violate this woman?"

"Hell no," he spat indignantly. "We was at the bar over in Festus and this girl, she come on to us, saying if we give her some weed she'll do some tricks. She didn't have no car, so we brung her out here to party, see what kinda tricks she was talkin' about."

"That's total bullshit!" Rose's eyes flashing.

Francis' eyebrows went up. "You can't believe that."

Just then Kilo came back. "Nothing on the premises, no sign of any person or a horse."

The EMS unit showed up the same time as the backup from the sheriff department, three more officers in two patrol cars. Blue and red lights strobing the house, the street. The officers entered the barn first, weapons drawn, making sure it was safe, and then motioned the two male paramedics in. Now it was a full house, a constabulary of seven including the paramedics, and four suspects and/or victims. The paramedics did a quick triage and attended to Joe first, placing him on a stretcher, wrapping his stump, starting an IV. Rose pointed out the severed hand, and they placed it in a sealed bag with single-use cold packs Then they dressed Brunt's wound, which they considered superficial.

One EMT, hearing Rose's complaint, found an enclosure to give some privacy while he discreetly examined her wound. His name was Patrick Delgado and he had wanted to be an EMT ever since he'd seen *Mother, Jugs & Speed* at the movie theater when he was sixteen. Kindly, he gave Rose a sheet which she draped around her like a toga.

She doffed the flannel shirt, and stood there bare-chested like some Roman goddess. He saw what they'd done to her. He cringed. "That must really hurt," he said.

"It does," she said, "and I'll miss it. Lucky I've got another one."

Delgado went into his bag and brought out a container of saline solution and a packet of four-by-four gauze pads. He wet the gauze with the saline solution and began cleansing the breast, dabbing here and there at the blood as Rose watched, hands at her sides. In a minute he would apply antibiotic creme to the area of the ravaged nipple, now starting to scab over. But her breast was heavy and wobbly, it wouldn't stay still. He wondered if he should hold it with the one hand as he tended to it with the other. It wouldn't be like he was copping a feel. After all, he was a medical professional. Besides, he had latex gloves on. In the end he said, "Would you hold your breast, please, so it doesn't move while I'm doing this?"

"I was about to offer," she told him.

The three arriving officers were gathered around Riggs, who was filling them in on the situation. From Francis she had already gotten a full description of Derrick, including the clothes he wore. We have a fugitive, she told them. He's probably ridden off on his horse, but he may still be around. He may be hiding. Two of them were to re-traverse the area around the barn, while Kilo and the third deputy were to check out the house up the hill. "But don't go in," she cautioned, "unless you have probable cause."

This was more like it, thought Riggs. In charge of a crime scene, making sound decisions, dispatching underlings to potentially dangerous missions. She was trained for this, she was more than capable, and best of all, there were no other ranking male officers around to steal her thunder. It was her show, her shot at glory.

If they didn't turn up this Derrick character soon, she would issue an APB, throw a big net around this rabbit on the run, draw him out. It shouldn't be too difficult, where can you hide with a horse? She imagined it, every available cop in Jefferson County and maybe adjoining counties, too, on the road at daylight, and all her doing. But meantime, these four perps, whatever they were—the one, a process server supposedly, claimed that he knew LaRocca—would need to be questioned extensively. It would be an all-nighter, probably at Jefferson Memorial in Hillsboro, where the EMT's would likely take them. By dawn they will have gotten to the truth of this muddle.

It wasn't long before Kilo and the other returned escorting a teenage girl. Kilo presented her to Riggs, saying, "This is Eve Johnson. She lives here with her father and brother. We heard some cries coming from within the home and so we went in. Rear door was not locked. We followed the calls for help and found her locked in a room under some stairs. We did break down that door."

Riggs looked to Eve, mascara running down her cheek, hair looking like a rat's nest, eyes fiery, shooting bolts of indignation. Riggs put on her nice, sympathetic voice, asked, "Who was it locked you in there, honey?"

Eve didn't trust cops, feeling like anything they asked and anything you gave them, they might use it against you. "Some guy," she scowled, "I don't know."

"Some guy, huh? Just some random stranger, you never got a look at him?"

She just stared at Riggs, mulish, incompliant. "Well," said Riggs, "I'm glad you're okay. You'll be coming with us to Hillsboro for questioning along with these other characters. Officer Kilo, you want to escort Eve here back up to her house so she can get some things for the night? We'll meet you up at the car."

Then they exited the barn, Joe on a stretcher carried by two EMTs. Joe had regained consciousness, and he could be heard saying, "Damn, I never got to use my throwing stars." Brunt ambulatory, was being helped along by a deputy. Rose had given the flannel shirt back to Joe and was quite the sight now in her white sheet toga and hiking boots, Francis limping at her side. Riggs and two deputies brought up the rear.

Francis said to Rose, "That was a nice play with that bug spray."

"Yeah, thanks. Not only was it handy, it was perfect for the job. I mean, the guy was being a pest." They walked on, expectantly. She slipped her arm inside his. She said, loud enough that Brunt up ahead would hear, "And that was some nice shooting on your part. Too bad it didn't get him a foot higher, through the heart. Oh, I forgot, he doesn't have one."

Once at the street they were consigned to vehicles. The three guys in the back of the forty-one foot tricked-out EMS unit, where Joe and Brunt were laid on gurneys. Francis was shown a seat, a deputy across from him with a loaded Glock, unholstered, at the ready. Once settled, Francis tapped Joe on his outstretched leg. Joe raised his head. "Now we're blood brothers," Francis told him. Joe smiled, gave a thumbs up, and put his head back down.

Riggs cut loose the two late-arriving patrol cars, one deputy to each vehicle, and invited Rose and Eve into the back of the remaining patrol car, she and Kilo up front. First stop, Jefferson Memorial Hospital.

Riggs liked being driven by Kilo, whom she secretly fantasized about though he was at least twelve years her junior. It was like being chauffeured. Not having to be vigilant against deer and other creatures on the road, it gave her time to think. And what she was thinking was that she hadn't been laid for a hell of a long time, and she missed it, the presence of a warm body in her bed. A strong man, willful, sure of himself, someone who would take her in his arms and screw her so masterfully that her puss would be sore for a week. He would have black wavy hair, a mustache, and a hairy chest. He would smoke a cigar after sex. She'd bet her next paycheck that Kilo had a hairy chest, and on occasion she had seen him smoke a cigar.

Rose and Eve were talking low in the backseat. Riggs guessed that they knew each other before now. Riggs turned to look. Rose had her arm draped around Eve and Eve was snuggled up against Rose's body. Riggs pondered this development. She said something to Kilo about it being a long night and how it was going to get longer. Kilo retorted with some quip about sleep being overrated. Riggs looked back at the two and now they were even more glued together. Fact, they were nuzzling. For a moment, Riggs thought to tell them to stop. After all, it was probably some sort of crime—indecent behavior with a minor—but then she held her tongue. Let them have their moment, she only wished that she and Jason Kilo were doing the same thing.

— 42 —

FINALLY, THE MOON HAD COME OUT, its light casting shadows on
the ground as he rode. It was a half moon and so the shadows were
not entirely formed and certainly not sharp. Danger with Derrick
astride her cantered along into a cheerless shadow world, a place
of great uncertainty. He had ridden through pastures and along
fences, skirting woods with no trails, keeping away from the lights
of houses, avoiding roads. At first he knew the land, having hunted
here as a kid, but then, as the trek went on, the environment became
more and more strange. Now he followed a trail, tall conifers on
both sides of him, leading to where he did not know. He came to
a clearing, paused. No watch, but he guessed it was around two. A
new day, Saturday, the beginning of—what? Running for the rest of
his life. He was fucked, and he knew it.

He dismounted, and, holding the reins, began to pace the perim-
eter of the clearing. Here and there trees had been cut low to the
ground and hauled away, so it wasn't a natural clearing but made
by man for some purpose. No sense in going on if he didn't know
where he was heading. Sunrise would offer some sense of direction.
Here was a decent spot to rest, do some thinking. One problem,
though, he didn't have anything to tether Danger with. No rope, and
his belt wasn't long enough. He would have to tie the reins to a limb,
but then she couldn't get her nose to the ground and munch some
foliage. He felt bad about it and he told her so. Having secured her
to a pine, he removed the saddle and laid it on the ground. He put
the pad next to it. He would sleep like a cowboy for a few hours,
then move out at dawn.

He lay there on the ground, staring up at the night sky. He was
cold. No blanket and him with only a sweatshirt. He wished he still
had that half-pint, but it had fallen out of his pocket during the tus-
sle. He panned the wash of his mind for some encouraging thought,
but all that would come to him was the notion that he was now an
outlaw. He tried to see if he could feel good about that. The movies always made outlaws look cool. *Butch Cassidy and the Sundance*

Kid, cool as cool can be. *The Outlaw Josey Wales*, pretty fucking cool, but Derrick had to admit that Josey Wales was an outlaw on principle and not because he had kidnapped some bitch and snipped off her nipple. Still, it was all about how you looked at it. Being an outlaw might not be that romantic right now, hungry, shivering on the ground, a horse farting in his direction, but with any luck it would get better as the days went on. Maybe he would find other outlaws and join their outfit, like the Hole In The Wall Gang. But that was long ago. Did outlaws still have hideouts? He would find out somehow. Maybe he would continue solo, a lone wolf, but one thing for sure: he would not turn himself in. Deke had scared him with all those lurid tales of prison life. But to be a righteous outlaw, he would need a gun. He cursed himself for leaving that shotgun behind.

Derrick nodded off a daring outlaw, and he awoke a pitiable wretch. Cold and stiff and feeling very sorry for himself. First light coming through the trees, he pushed himself up on unsteady legs. Slowly, he began stamping his feet, rubbing his sides with opposite hands, up and down, briskly, finally starting to warm up. He started doing calisthenics, jumping jacks, touch your toes, reach for the sky, whatever came to him. He went to Danger, untied the reins, and began leading her around the clearing, getting her limbered up, too. He stroked the animal's long neck and said soothing words to her. He told her it wouldn't be long, they would get to a place where there were burgers and beer for him and oats and water for her. She pricked up her ears and snorted. He got the pad and the saddle. He was tightening the cinch when a sharp crack sounded and Danger went down. Derrick stood there not believing, the horse on its side, kicking at nothing, the one large brown eye visible, wild with terror. At that moment, an incredibly astonishing moment for him, a 165 grain round from a 30-06 ripped through his chest just below the heart.

Sixty yards away in a tree stand, a man named Clinton Wilcox began to climb down to the ground. He took it slow, Springfield rifle with scope strapped to his back, taking the steps, short sections of two-by-fours nailed to the trunk, taking the makeshift steps one by one, mindful of falling. No thermos with hot coffee for him, he had a flask of Old Overholt in one pocket of his woolen hunting coat and various snacks in another. Clinton felt lucky, here it was, six a.m., only minutes into the first day of hunting season and he had bagged himself a deer. A buck, he was pretty sure, and a big one at that. He was hoping for a twelve pointer at least. Once mounted, he would bring it in to the VFW Hall. Happy hour, all the guys sitting around—boy, would they be jealous. Give him new standing among his peers, drunks just like him.

The very life was oozing out of him when Clinton Wilcox came crashing into the clearing. He saw immediately what he'd done. "Oh, shit!" he exclaimed. "Oh, shit, shit, shit!" He went over to Derrick, flat on his back, and knelt beside him. Derrick turned his head, saw some middle-aged guy with an Elmer Fudd hunting cap, holding a rifle. "I'm sorry, I'm really sorry," the guy was saying. "I thought you was a deer."

"Call for help," Derrick gasped, voice strained, blood foaming at his mouth.

"I will," said Clinton Wilcox, "I'll go right now and get help."

Now Derrick decided he didn't like the sound of that. Help meant not just medical attention but the law, too. "No, never mind," he whispered, breathing labored, "just stay here. Stay with me."

But Clinton Wilcox was already standing up, looking around. "No, you were right. I'm gonna go for help, that's a good plan. Again, I'm really sorry." He reached in his pocket. "Look, here's a Snickers. You can have it. I gotta get to my car, drive to a phone. It won't be long."

Derrick held the candy bar that had landed on his chest. The guy just tossed it, he didn't even open it for him. He heard footsteps. "Wait!" But the sound of the footsteps grew faint as did the crunching of brush and leaves. He turned his head slightly to see the clearing empty again, just he and his horse, and Danger had gone to verdant pastures. He turned again so his head was straight up. He coughed weakly and it felt like his insides were coming apart. Soon, a calm settled over him, and he knew it wasn't long. It was a clear dawn, daylight streaming into the clearing, illuminating some trees but silhouetting others. He thought for a second, glanced again at the silhouetted stand of trees. Oh, so that was east.

— 43 —

They cut him loose just after five. Still dark, the streets in Hillsboro deserted. The buses didn't start running for another hour. At least there was a diner, he could see a counterman through a plate glass window. Francis began to walk toward it. The brisk morning air bracing, therapeutic, replacing that stale, germ-ridden, piped-in air that he'd been breathing in the hospital for the last five hours. Upon arrival, they had all been together in the ER, fairly bustling on Friday night going into Saturday. He had waved to Rose and Joe in different treatment stations, giving the okay sign with thumb and curled index finger. Brunt was there too, but he could go to hell. Within minutes, Joe was wheeled into surgery. Brunt, under surgical lights, had his wound cleaned and packed. A nurse asked if he wanted some morphine. Brunt told her that would make him happy as a pig in shit. He and Rose and Brunt were outpatients, but there would be no discharge until they were questioned separately and exhaustively throughout the night.

After they were patched up, Riggs and Kilo and some other officers took each of them into different rooms. He never saw the others after that. As for him, he was the ideal interrogee, completely forthcoming, at times going into tangential asides that verged into shaggy dog stories. Even so, it was the same questions, same demands over and over. How did he know that Rose had been taken to that particular residence? Describe the scene once he and Joe got there. Did he witness the sexual assault firsthand? What was his relationship with the suspects, the one in custody as well as the fugitive? First, it was Riggs questioning him. Then, it was another detective. Grilling him as well as the others, in different rooms, zealously questioning and comparing notes like it was the Crime of the Century. LaRocca showed up after a couple hours along with a man he introduced as chief of detectives, and they had their turn with him. Francis was glad to see LaRocca, and he told him so. LaRocca, on the other hand, did not bestow any favors or gratuities or show any signs of deference. When Francis asked to smoke, they said no. He asked for a sandwich, they gave him a bag of chips. He asked for a soda, they gave him a glass of water. He wasn't too worried, he knew they had nothing on him. Rose would back up his assertion that he shot Brunt in self-defense. Look at what he'd just done to Joe. And that weapon? Well, it wasn't registered, but as a process server he had an automatic permit to carry.

The counterman had a boil behind his ear and looked like one of the hillbillies in *Deliverance*, but that didn't stop Francis from ordering coffee and eggs over easy. One smoke left, he shook it out and crumpled the pack. He sat there smoking and drinking coffee, thinking how things were not going to be the same. He was changed. For better or worse, too soon to tell. But one thing for sure, the harrowing events of last night had left him unnerved, and this was a new, unwelcome feeling. There was a dread inside him now, a trepidation of … what? Interacting with strangers? Inserting oneself into strange situations? Fear of violence breaking out? You can't have that and be a process server. He only hoped this unease would fade, otherwise he'd find himself selling batteries at Auto Zone or taking up some other sheltered work.

An older guy four stools down the counter asked if he could bum a cigarette. All out, sorry, said Francis. The guy took it personal, muttering something about "the new breed" not having any respect.

The counterman slid a plate of eggs and toast in front of him, refilled his coffee without a word. The eggs were greasy, unpalatable. What did he fry them in, lard? Francis asked for A-1; he got Country Bob's All Purpose Sauce. The door opened, and Rose walked in, wearing light green hospital scrubs. She plopped down next to him.

"Good morning, Sunshine. Did you sleep well last night?"

"No," he replied, "I had a nightmare that people were trying to kill me. Coffee?"

"I'll have a soda. Mine was a bad dream, too, only there were stubby erections poking and prodding me. And I was the damsel in distress until my heroes showed up, took care of the villains."

"Yeah, and with no time to lose either." He gave her a squeeze on the arm. "Good we got there when we did." The counterman came over. Rose didn't have her belongings. Francis offered to buy.

"A bowl of oatmeal with crushed walnuts, raisins and honey, if you please."

Counterman gave her a look. "We got brown sugar to go with it, take it or leave it," he told her.

"So what happened with the others?" Francis asked.

"Eve is on her way to some shelter run by the DFS. A caseworker came and picked her up. She's a minor and apparently has no rights. It sucks big time. I wish she could come home with me. And Joe, he's being kept on as a patient, probably a day or so."

"I'll come see him later today," said Francis, looking down at his coffee, frowning. "Poor guy, it's all my fault, too."

"You needed him. He knew that. He's a trooper, he'll be all right."

"It'll be hard at first. He'll get a prosthetic."

"They've got some amazing devices these days, even better than what they gave the *Six Million Dollar Man*."

"Oh, I was thinking he'd get a sharp, pointy hook for a hand like what's-his-name."

"Captain Hook?"

"Yeah. It'd play well on Halloween."

"You can stop now."

"And Joe's assailant, the hand-chopper. Any word on him?"

"They had him cuffed and were taking him to the Jeff County jail when last seen," she said.

"Well, at least he's got a ride. We don't. I'm trying to figure how I can get to my car. Any ideas?"

"I can call the farm for a lift, but it's hit or miss. There's one phone in the main house and they'll be in and out throughout the morning. And only Rainbow has a car."

"Glad to hear the modern world hasn't caught up with you guys down there." He studied her for signs of stress, saw only Rose. "And you, how're you doing?"

She spun on her stool, doing a three-sixty. She did it again. "Hey, this is fun," she said. "You should try it."

At that moment LaRocca came in. He took the stool next to Francis. "Greetings from one tired son of a bitch," he said. "Why couldn't you kids have had your little drama at more decent hour? I've been up half the night and I've still got a full shift ahead of me." He looked at them both, shrugged. "Oh well, it is what it is, right? The coffee here decent?"

"Not as strong as it could be," said Francis, "and I don't think this guy does espresso."

The counterman came over, stood in front of LaRocca. "Coffee, black," said the cop, "make it a double." The counterman walked off, LaRocca whispered to Francis, "I just hope that oozing sore on his neck doesn't drip into my coffee."

"I heard that," said the counterman down the line. Moments later he was back with a porcelain mug of steaming joe. He set it in front of LaRocca hard enough that it splashed on the counter. The man walked off without wiping it up.

"One of these days I'll learn to keep my thoughts to myself," said LaRocca.

"It was a long night," offered Rose, "that's for certain."

"Actually, it was somewhat abbreviated. Usually when we come upon a crime scene with multiple persons it takes a lot longer to sort it out. But this situation, well, it seems pretty clear who the culprits are, and one of them is in custody, the other on the run."

"On a horse," said Francis. "All the open country down here, he can probably travel unseen for a while."

LaRocca sipped at his coffee, made a face. "Funny, it just so happens that we have an equestrian unit for this very type of pursuit. I wish I was part of it, it'd be like in the movies. 'Round up the posse, boys, we're heading out at dawn.' But we'll get him, don't you worry. And when we do, he'll be charged, arraigned. Bail will be set but he won't make it, and he'll sit in jail awaiting trial." He leaned forward and looked past Francis to Rose. "At which time you will be called to the stand to testify against both him and his partner and they will be put away like the criminals they are."

The old man four stools down got up and came over to where they were. He stood behind them, agitating for something. LaRocca turned on his stool, saw a drunk who'd probably been out carousing all night. "You know this guy?" he asked, indicating Francis.

"What's it to you?" said the cop.

"He's a liar," said the old man, "a liar and a stingy bastard. I ask him for a cigarette, ask politely, and what does he say? 'I ain't got none.' But I seen him smoking, he lit one up right in front a me. That ain't right, not at all. Someone asks you for a smoke, you oblige, it's a, uh, uh, common courtesy, brotherhood of smokers kinda thing. Am I right?"

LaRocca let this shitbum finish then opened his sport coat and badged him. "You see that?" he said with venom. "You don't get the hell out of here right this second, I'll cuff you here and now. And I don't mean go back to your stool there. I mean pay the bill and walk out the door. Now!"

The old man shuffled back to his coffee and half-finished plate of eggs. He made a big show of slapping down a five and walked past them, grousing about the state of the world and how he just wanted a simple favor, that's all.

"You guys got a ride?" asked LaRocca.

"We were just wondering about that when you walked in," said Rose. "I guess the buses don't run way out there, huh?"

"No, they don't, but I don't mind running you out."

"Better than being run in," said Francis with a wink.

"Aw, I got nothing to do for the next while. A drive might be just the thing."

"That's very kind of you," said Rose.

"Taxi's out front," said LaRocca, "any time you're ready."

* * *

Jumbo sat on a chair in his skivvies. Q-tip in hand, he dabbed some Unguentine on his wound, carefully covered it with a large Band-Aid, and put on his trousers. It was 5:50 and he was getting ready for work at the chrome plating plant. He put on his work shirt, the one that said Arliss on the patch above the breast pocket. His real name. Scooping Cheerios into his mouth and watching the clock, he wondered what had become of his pals, Derrick and Brunt. That sure was nice of those guys to ask him along. And he didn't mind all that much, getting stabbed in the leg and clubbed in the head. Some roughhousing, that's all it was. He thought of the guy whose arm he'd broke, that sound of a bone cracking, his doing, no other sound like it. Yeah, just a little roughhousing. Heck, he'd been in mosh pits worse than that. Those guys were okay. He'd phone them later on, see how it went after he'd left.

CITY OF ST. LOUIS
DECEMBER 1989

"I TOLD YOU, I DON'T KNOW WHERE HE LIVES except I've seen him in Soulard. On the street, going in or coming out of bars there."

"What time of day?"

"Afternoons, he's an afternoon drinker."

"Which bars do you think he's in?" Francis was on the phone with the petitioner, a woman named Teri Friedhoff. She had hired a lawyer to draw up paternity papers, and now she was hoping to have her ex served even though he was a bum and had no money for anything except drink. She had been told by her lawyer that Francis was some kind of miracle worker.

"I don't know their names," she answered. "Just the regular old dive bars down in that neighborhood."

Francis asked for a description once again, thinking maybe she'd left something out, like the guy wore an eye patch or was missing an arm. He said he'd put his detective hat on and head down there.

"Have fun," she said.

He walked to the front of the office where Barry Condon sat typing at an IBM Selectric, doing the hunt and peck with a middle finger on each hand. A legal pad beside the typewriter; he was transcribing his own scribble into proper legalese, crafting a petition. Francis stood before him. Barry kept typing. Francis cleared his throat. "Hey, Bare, that Friedhoff case? I just got off the phone with your client. It's an investigation from the get-go. The guy's a barfly, hangs in Soulard. She'll have me canvassing the dive bars in the afternoon. I'm telling you because it's going to be more than my standard thirty-five bucks. You don't just walk in these bars, look around and leave. I need to spend some time in them, win some confidence, then I can ask around or maybe he'll walk in."

"You want drink money."

Francis guffawed. "I've *got* drink money, it's the time involved. Like I said, it's an investigation. From the moment I get there I'm on the clock at twenty-five an hour, that's in addition to the thirty-five base fee."

"Not a problem," said Barry, "I'm happy to subsidize your pub crawl. Just don't get so tanked that you forget to serve the guy when you do encounter him. You'll know him when you see him, yeah?"

"Sure, long brown hair, wears a ball cap backwards, jeans and a sweatshirt. Maybe a jacket that says South Broadway Radiator Shop on it, missing teeth, long arms, walks like an ape."

Barry cracked a half smile. "The same as every other Southside Hoosier." Hoosier was a St. Louis term, obscure in origin, that meant a low-bred person, a sort of urban hillbilly.

"You got it."

"Go for it, Francis. Get your man, you always do."

Barry went back to typing and Francis began to walk off. Barry called after him. "Oh, by the way, I got a call from a friend of yours, Rose Schurzinger. Wants to initiate an adoption."

Francis turned. "Yeah? I told her to call. So you talked with her. Good. You think she has a chance? It's not your normal situation, I know. Not the established married couple in their thirties, childless despite screwing three times a week for ten years, having the means to support several kids but can't produce even one on their own."

"No, nothing like that," said Barry, "and it's going to take some doing to convince the juvenile court judge that this is a good match. That she's a single woman is not the obstacle, not so much, but the fact that she's only ten years the senior of the adoptee, more like a big sister than a parent, well, that gets into some potentially awkward areas."

"Plus, she lives on a commune," said Francis.

"Oh, really? I guess she forgot to mention that item. But again, that shouldn't matter. You can't dismiss a petition to adopt because of lifestyle and imagined connotations surrounding that lifestyle. If so, bikers and gay couples and pagans would never be able to adopt."

"Pagans adopt kids?"

"They do," said Barry.

"Oh." Francis seemed genuinely aghast. "Then does anyone ever check on the kid later on? I mean, what if they used that kid as a human sacrifice?"

"You're not serious."

"I am! Didn't you see *The Wicker Man* with Edward Woodward and Christopher Lee? That was pagans today, not a thousand years ago, needing someone to sacrifice as a blessing on their crops to grow. They put the constable in a giant man made of wicker, an effigy. They lit this effigy with him in it and sent him up in flames to their spirit in the sky while they all danced around and sang their pagan songs. Horrible!"

"Just a story, Francis, not real. But back to your friend and what she wants. The prognosis, if you will. We have to make a diligent attempt to find the mom and dad, and you may play a role in that. If they cannot be found and no immediate relative steps forward—the older brother is deceased, we know that—then the adoption has a chance. Meanwhile, with the girl, Eve by name, in a foster home and not happy from what I hear, it may just succeed."

"I hope so because Rose is a good person. She deserves something good to come her way."

Soulard was an old working class neighborhood just south of Busch Stadium. It had a locally famous open air farmer's market which had been going, if you believed the sign, since 1779, and some of the vendors looked that old. It also had more bars per capita than any other neighborhood in the city. Whether they were so-called dive bars was open to interpretation, but they all offered great drink deals and some of them boasted happy hour all day long. Not a one was upscale; in a staunch blue collar neighborhood like Soulard upscale was anathema. Francis knew the territory, had partied down here with his pals on certain weekends in summer and of course during Mardi Gras, St. Louis having a walloping big parade second only to New Orleans. In fact, Soulard was often referred to as the French Quarter of St. Louis. It had that feel to it. So Francis knew that the greatest concentration of sleazy bars, where a guy like Chuck Friedhoff might frequent, started on the south side of the market and stretched off further to the south toward the brewery. In a rectangular grid about six blocks long and three blocks wide there were maybe eight little bars which would be open for business on a cloudy Thursday afternoon, the temperature down around freezing.

Francis had just walked out of the Paddy Wagon, a joint not exactly rife with patrons or good cheer. The place more like a mausoleum. Still, he had two schooners and made inquiries of the barkeep about his man, his target. It was just past two. In the next hour he hit three more watering holes: Mitzi's Rendezvous, the Tip-A-Few, and the Cock and Bull, a gay bar. At this last place he was joined at the bar by two guys in leathers and chains, patently channeling Brando in *The Wild One*. He knew they were only posers because he'd seen no hogs parked on the street, but still they had a great time talking about fist fucking and cockrings and the proper use of the butt plug. When they asked him to join them in the bathroom for "a quickie," he decided to split.

He was striking out left and right, no Chuck in sight. No one who even knew the guy or where he might be found. Despite the cold he had chosen to walk, and now he was heading back toward his car parked by the market, the unserved papers still in his back pocket. He rounded Ninth Street onto Geyer, two sheets to the wind, looking at three, and saw a sign for the Gold Mine. Wasn't that the place that Fr. John had mentioned?

Yes, it was, for that had to be the barmaid the priest had spoken of, wearing that loose fitting, cut-off sweatshirt, plunging V-line, bending down to rummage in the cooler below the bar and showing her ta-tas to the guys on the other side, leaning over to see. He was reminded of a ditty from his army boot camp days, and it made him smile:

> *Well, she looked so fair in the midnight air*
> *and the wind blew up her nightie*
> *that her tits hung loose like the balls on a moose ...*

Her name, Francis learned, was Misty, and she was the muse of myriad masturbatory fantasies enacted by the bar's male patrons, either here in the dreary confines of a lavatory stall, or later, at home, in the lonesome privacy of their bedrooms. So Francis settled in at the bar and had a Guinness for a change, and then asked Misty for the use of the bar's phone. She handed him the cordless, but try as he might the phone number was not there.

"You got a phone book?" he asked.

"Do I look like Ma Bell?" she said. He felt like answering, No, you look like an over the hill divorced mother of two who likes to get guys off by flashing your striated boobs and hoping that'll bring you a few extra bucks at the end of your shift. But he didn't.

She brought over a crummy phone book, all dog-eared and stained with whatever. He turned to the Saints, and there were several pages worth. He found the right saint and dialed. Fr. John Benda himself answered.

"Hey, Father, it's me, Francis. I'm in that bar you talked about, the Gold Mine. You want to join me for a cold one?"

"Is Our Lady of the Cooler there?"

"Right in front of me."

"I'll be there in fifteen," he said, and hung up.

The priest walked in and joined him at the bar. He wore a full-length winter coat, tweed with a leather collar, a gray scarf, and a woolen flat cap. He took off his gloves and put them in his pocket.

"I wanted to order for you," said Francis, "but I just didn't know if you'd want something cold or hot."

"A Budweiser sounds about right," he said.

Misty came over, "What'll you have?" Couple Buds came the answer, and she hunkered down to dig them out from the ice-filled cooler. They leaned over to see the show. It seemed that Misty was taking her time with the order, hands probing beneath the ice, coming up with Bud Light then Busch then Miller Lite, all the while muttering choice imprecations. "She stood up, holding a single can. "I'm out of Bud except for this one," she told them. "There may be more down there somewhere but I'm gonna get frostbite if I keep searching."

"Bud Light's fine with me," said Fr. John.

"Same here," said Francis.

"Now we're talking," said Misty, and she popped the tabs, setting the beers in front of them. She leaned over the bar, rested on her elbows. Cleavage galore. "You's want a glass with that?"

"Nah, we're fine," said Francis. "Just come back in a bit and we'll do it again."

"Now we're talking," said Misty with a wink.

"You enjoy the view?" asked Fr. John.

"Yeah, sure, it's all right. Kind of a low rent version of PT's." Among the dozen or so strip clubs on the East Side where they take it all off, PT's Show Club was the best known and most attended.

"So how's it going? I've been wanting to talk with you ever since I read about your exploits in the paper last month."

"Yeah, that was some night," said Francis. "Serious mayhem in that barn, lasted probably all of about ten minutes but it was settled then and there and that's why I went."

"Your friend lost his hand, I read."

"Yeah, but he's doing okay. Now he has a prosthetic hand—you can't hardly tell from a distance if he's wearing a long sleeve shirt, and he was able to keep his job as a security guard at the community college. But bowling, he has to use the other hand."

"I can't imagine what that's like," said Fr. John, "walking into a dangerous situation like that, knowing you might get seriously hurt or killed. You have to be either very brave or very reckless."

"Probably a little of both," said Francis. "The young woman, the one I told you about who hired me to find her mother's killer? She was taken from *my* porch, she had come to see *me*, so I felt that I had to act and I couldn't dwell on what might happen, only that I had to get her back."

"Very noble of you," said the priest, "very noble." They drank in silence for a while.

"I wonder if they have peanuts or chips here," said Fr. John at length. "It's been a long time since lunch."

"There's some pickled eggs in a jar over there."

"I don't think I could keep such a delicacy down," he answered dryly.

"We could order pizza, I'm pretty sure they won't mind. Look there." Francis pointed to a place on the wall near the cordless where numbers for two pizza places were posted.

"No, no," said Fr. John, "let's just drink."

Francis took a healthy swig of his beer, burped, said excuse me, and patted his belly. "You know, John ... Father—"

"You can call me John, it's all right."

"You know, John, a lot happened that night, some stuff I've been wanting to, uh, kind of, I don't know ..."

"Talk about?"

"Yeah. Might be time for a confession. Can I make an appointment?"

"No need, we can do it right here."

"Here?"

"Well, not *right* here where others can hear, but over there at that table in the corner. People will think we're just having a private conversation, which we will be. Okay by you?"

"Sure, but let's get some beers."

They got two more from Misty and this time, as she was digging through the ice in the cooler, one of her breasts popped out of her top. She stood up, and made a show of putting it back in place but not before letting every panting hound at the bar get a good look. She looked down the front of her shirt, made a cute little frown, said, "Silly thing, you stay put now."

They brought their drinks to the table and found their places. Francis asked if he should start. Go ahead, said the priest, leaning into Francis, elbow on the table, hand on his chin, head slightly cocked to listen. Francis got through the preamble and began reeling off the times he'd sinned through pride, through duplicity, through omission, through arrogance. He came to a lull and said, "And I have cursed, something terrible."

"Talk about it," whispered Fr. John.

"That night, in the barn out there, I swore like a sailor. Normally, I am not one to curse and I want to confess that."

"From what I read you shot a man." Francis nodded affirmatively. "In the heat of the fight you shot a man, and you're concerned with a little swearing?"

"Yeah, because it was uncalled for. The way I see it, the guy attacked my bullet with his body. That's on him. But I lost control and used both obscenity *and* profanity. That's on me."

"You took the name of the Lord in vain?"

"I did, several times. A whole string of, you know, goddamns and f-words."

"All right, I'll add cursing to the list. What else?"

"I took my friend Joe out there, knowing that there could be serious trouble and that he might be hurt. I shouldn't have done that. I involved him unnecessarily, and look what happened."

Fr. John looked at him, raised one brow. "If that's a sin, I'd like to know which category it belongs to."

"Pride? Maybe I wanted someone along to see how cool I was, how I could handle myself."

"You asked him to come because you needed him, because you going alone wasn't going to do the trick. Cops usually work in pairs, it's only practical, one has the other one's back."

"Maybe so, but I still feel terrible about it."

"All right, if it will ease your soul, I'll add that as well. What else?"

During the course of this confession Francis had gone back and forth as to whether he would bring up the attack on Fr. Eagan. Now it was time to fish or cut bait. If he confessed like a good Catholic, he risked the censure of his friend and new-found drinking buddy. Even though confessors were supposed to be strictly non-judgmental, he couldn't imagine Fr. John assessing the onslaught as just another sin to be forgiven. No, this would be viewed as an *uber* mortal sin, his deliberate intent to harm, intimidate, and possibly kill a priest, albeit a deceitful, two-faced priest. Fr. Benda did not know Fr. Eagan, but there had to be a bond between men of the white collar, Francis supposed, a strong sense of fellowship like *Semper Fi* Marines. On the other hand, if he did not confess that which was on his mind then he would be walking around with guilt on his conscience. His linen would still be soiled, and it would grate on him. Or would it? In actuality, he really did not feel guilty about it.

"That's it," he told Fr. John.

Fr. John gave him absolution, and Francis said the Act of Contrition, said it a bit too loud so that some of the barflies heard. They turned their heads toward the sound and saw the two men making the sign of the cross. "Hey, no praying in here!" called one.

Afterward, they continued talking at the table, two friends enjoying each other's company.

"Hey," said Francis, "I have a joke for you. It's about confession."

"Yeah, let's hear it."

So Francis told the one about Paddy, the prototypical chucklehead of many Irish jokes. The Otto of German jokes, the Guido of Italian jokes, the Ivan of Russian jokes.

Francis cleared his throat, summoned his best affected brogue, and launched into it. "Paddy was going to confession for the first time in ten years and he asked Sean to come along for support.

'Now, Paddy,' says Sean, 'what you do is you start out with the soft sins and you work your way up to the vile ones.' So Paddy heads into church, waits his turn, and goes into the confessional. He starts with the venial sins, adding a few mortals here and there. He's wrapping it up, and then says, 'Oh, and one more thing, I've had relations with a married woman.'

'Ah,' says the priest, his ears pricking up. 'And tell me, lad, 'twas it Missus Murphy?'

'I canna tell ye, Father, I give her me word.'

''Twas Missus McGowan then?'

'I canna tell ye, Father.'

'I'll make it easy for ye,' says the priest. ''Twas that trollop Brigid Flanagan down the lane, was it not?'

'I'm sorry, Father, I really canna tell ye.'

'Well,' says the priest, 'if ye canna tell, I canna give ye absolution.'

Sean sees Paddy coming out of the church. 'So, how'd it go?' he asks.

'Not bad,' says Paddy, 'I didn't get absolution, but I got three good leads.'"

They both laughed heartily at this, Fr. John slapping the table, tears running down his cheek. "Oh, that's funny," he said, "and what's even funnier is that I heard a variation of that one back in Czechoslovakia when I was a boy, only instead of Paddy and Sean it was Petr and Jaroslav. And the one got three good leads to sex with married women, yes, but also a good lead on a particular hunting ground for truffles."

At that moment the door opened and daylight flooded the dim bar but for a moment. A figure walked in, looked around, made his way toward the bar, slouching as he went.

"Hey, it's Chuck," someone called. "Ol' Chuckles. Chuck Roast. Sit yourself down, man, have a brewski or two."

Francis got up from his chair, felt his back pocket for the papers.

"'Scuse me a minute," he said to Fr. John, and headed toward the bar.

—45—

"How's that soda taste, Detective? You through belching? In case you didn't notice, I've got the floor."

"Sorry, Chief," said Pilchow, and he put the can down.

There were four of them in the briefing room. Chief of Detectives Vincent Stockman, Detectives Pilchow, Riggs, and LaRocca. Kostedt was on vacation, and Berlinger was on temporary assignment, loaned out to the Major Case Squad, a multi-jurisdictional super-investigative unit presently throwing themselves into yesterday's double homicide over in High Ridge. There were only three days left in the year. It was three p.m., the one shift coming off and the other coming on. Outside big fluffy snowflakes were falling, the landscape two stories below shrouded in stark white.

"As I was saying," continued Stockman, "these numbers are preliminary. They'll be updated in the coming year as some of the open cases close. Not that I have scads of free time to be tabulating numbers, it's just that I had this crazy idea that you'd like to see the stats as they stand right now. And I've got to tell you, they're not looking that great. So, listen up, this is your work in a nutshell. First category: armed robberies. Banks, people at ATMs, stores and shops, your random opportunistic encounters. The tally? Ninety-six with sixty-four arrests."

"My favorite was the guy who robbed the liquor store with a tomahawk," said Pilchow.

"Yeah," said Stockman, "he was gonna get all drunked up on firewater, but now he's cooling his heels in EMCC. Next, burglaries, two hundred twenty-three, some of it penny-ante stuff, true, but an increase of twenty-five over last year. Seventy-four arrests. Not your best result."

"Burglars, sneak thieves, are hard to apprehend," said Riggs. "They're in, they're out, and they cover their tracks well … of course I don't need to tell you that."

Stockman nodded in acknowledgment. "Just like I don't need to tell you that it's bad form to make excuses for ineptitude."

Riggs folded her arms and looked to the floor.

"Just wondering," said Pilchow, "are you going to share these numbers with the deputies? I mean, in almost every situation they're first on the scene."

"They're the foot soldiers, you guys are the command. I'm sharing this with you. Be happy about it. Next, domestic violence. Three hundred forty-eight calls, two hundred eighty-one arrests. In some cases the antagonist fled the scene before we got there." He licked his thumb and flipped over a page in the sheaf of papers. "Kidnappings, including child abductions by a non-custodial parent, only five with five collars. Well done, well done. What else? Counterfeit activity, passing funny money, fourteen instances, thirteen arrests. That's a percentage I like to see."

"Counterfeit's old school," put in LaRocca. "It's on the way out. Used to be cash is king, real or fake, but now plastic is king."

"Noted," said Stockman. "Now we come to the biggest category by volume, drug busts. The amount of time and resource put into this dwarfs all other categories. If it weren't for the pervasiveness of methamphetamine and heroin in this county, we might have time to sit around and twiddle our thumbs. From January to now, there have been five hundred twenty-seven arrests, many of them resulting from raids in which multiple suspects were taken into custody."

"And it never ends," said Riggs. "You take down five crackheads and ten more take their place."

"The priority for the coming year," said Stockman, is to concentrate on the manufacturers and distributors. We have at least six CIs out there feeding us information. Hopefully, that'll make a dent in the problem."

"I could grow my hair out, put on my best grungy clothes, and be your Serpico," said Pilchow.

"How about you try for Employee of the Month first?" said Stockman. "Okay, next. Homicides, here we go. You guys know these numbers by heart, you've worked every one of them. Nineteen homicides in our county last year. We're getting to look more and more like that Wild West Show, St. Louis. How many arrests? Thirteen.

What is that? Something like seventy percent. This is where we're falling short and we need to do better."

"Schurzinger still really gets to me, said Pilchow.

"It gets to us all," said LaRocca. "What a head-scratcher that was. Two suspects disappearing like that, one after the other."

"Presumed dead," said Riggs.

"Officially missing," said Stockman, "until we find the bodies."

"Vince," said Riggs, "you think there's any chance they've absconded and are living it up in Mexico or somewhere?"

"Highly doubtful," answered Stockman, "they're born and bred Jeff County. These folks don't stray too far from home, they get xenophobia."

"Nice word, chief," said Pilchow. "Could you spell it? I'm gonna write that down."

"That mess in the barn out there," said Riggs. "The Johnson boy found dead eight miles away, his horse, too. But not a homicide."

"Some careless hunter," said LaRocca. "It happens."

"Well, anyway," said Stockman, "there's been no new leads and therefore no further investigation. If nothing develops before long, it's going to the Cold Case file."

"We tried, we really tried," said Riggs.

"Trying is diligence and diligence is what is expected of us," said Stockman. "And you may try and try until your eyes become crossed, but what you really need is a lucky break. With Schurzinger, we didn't get a break or maybe we caught a break and failed to see it. Either way, there's no warm body to pin the crime on, and that's a crying shame."

Peace Haven Farm
March 1990

"I can't decide if this looks like gerbil food or the stems and seeds you see at the bottom of a nickel bag."

"It's muesli," said Rose, sitting across from her. "We make it here. It's got all sorts of healthy stuff. Oats, nuts, seeds, fruit. It's really good for you."

"See? Seeds, what did I say?"

"Try it with some honey."

But Eve was pushing around the mixture with her utensil, peering into the bowl. She brought something up, a black speck floating in the milk-laden spoon. She held it out for Rose to see. "An ant," she said, "a dead ant."

Rose frowned, squinted at it. "That's just a burnt oat."

"Ant," insisted Eve.

"Burnt oat."

"Whatever, but this is not for me, okay? I'm used to eggs and bacon, maybe some leftovers from the night before like pork roast or mashed potatoes and gravy."

"Clogs your arteries," said Rose.

"I don't care," said Eve, pushing the bowl away, "at least it tastes good."

"You don't want to do that to your body, especially not the first thing in the morning. Your body is a temple. It needs high octane fuel, not sludge."

"My body wants regular food, the same good things everyone else eats." She looked at Rose, shook her head in dismay. "Nothing wrong with bacon and eggs. Jeez."

"All right, I'll make you a poached egg with toast. We'll talk about this later. There's a magazine you need to read, it's called the *Whole Earth Catalog*. It'll really open your eyes to healthy alternatives and not just food but—"

"You're not gonna convince me to eat a bunch of Nature crap."

Rose sighed. She looked at her headstrong, if not obstinate daughter. And she was still not comfortable with that appellation, daughter. But what else could she be. Her charge? Ward? To call her "my adoptive daughter" seemed too formal. She thought of all the trouble and expense it took to officially adopt her and she wondered if she'd made a mistake. Only two weeks here at Peace Haven and already the rosy glow of togetherness had worn thin and now she found they were at odds half the time. Over food, chores, pastimes. She'd witnessed Eve's reaction when she learned the farm did without a TV—bummed to say the least—Rose and the others trying to tell her that today's programming leads to brain rot. But then Rose had watched the tube when she was thirteen and it didn't rot her brain. And so Rose was having second thoughts about TV, like maybe she could get Eve a portable for her room just to make her happy, although she doubted that they could get reception way out here. That was one concession, maybe there would be more. But Eve would have to bend, too, and Eve wasn't exactly a sapling to bend with the wind.

Anyway, it was done, she'd succeeded in bringing this amazing young woman into the fold, having laid out her own crazy life for the family court to pick through and evaluate. It had helped quite a bit that Eve was amenable to the idea of coming to live with her. And it had helped immensely, in fact, it couldn't have happened at all, that she had finally come into the money that was her due, some one hundred eighty-thousand dollars that her mother had the good sense to will directly to her, insuring that the inheritance would not be tied up for months and maybe years in probate court. Three thousand to the lawyer, Condon, and twenty-thousand to Francis, for all he did. That left one hundred fifty-seven thousand to her and Eve. They should be living like queens, organic whole grain queens, instead of bickering.

"It's March seventeenth," said Rose, "St. Patrick's Day. They have that big parade in St. Louis, starts at noon. I'm thinking of going up—"

"Why don't you throw the I Ching or lay out the Tarot cards, let that decide for you?"

"'That's not funny, Eve. Like I'm saying, see Francis, take in the parade. You want to come? You could skip this once. It'll be fun."

"Naw. There's a pep rally after school, I'll be going to that."

"Since when did you like to go to pep rallies?"

"Since I started liking this kid on the basketball team."

"Oh, really? That's great, Eve. Does he like you back?"

"I think so. He threw a dirt ball at me."

"Yeah, that's a sure sign." She walked over to where Eve sat and put a hand on her shoulder. Eve shrank ever so slightly. The days of social experimentation, brief as they were, had ended with bittersweet misgivings. "Well," she said, "better get a move on or you'll miss the bus."

"Okay, mom." That last word deliberately facetious.

* * *

Murphy's was close to overflowing and the regulars weren't happy about it. Everyone's an Irishman on St. Paddy's Day, got to find an Irish bar with Guinness and Jameson. Rub elbows with colorful old Irish sots who might say "begorrah" or "eejit" in conversation or talk of leprechauns and banshees. Oh yeah, get your drunk on here, go watch the parade, but puke somewhere else. Most of these new faces no more Irish than the Pope. Erin Go Fucking Bragh.

The other thing that pissed them off was not being able to get a drink as quickly as they would like. Some of them stood at the bar, arms locked, blocking anyone from walking up and ordering. You want a drink? Get one from the roving waitress.

Tommy the bartender was hustling, double-timing with the pours, which were never-ending. Earlier this day, he had hung a framed document on the wall just off to one end of the bar. The document was on Deaconess Hospital stationery and it was the diagnosis of one Terrance "Packy" Gillespie, who, it seems, had developed cirrhosis of the liver after drinking here faithfully for thirty-some years. Packy couldn't be here to admire his own proclamation, for he could no longer walk due to extreme edema of the lower extremities which made his legs look like tree trunks. Packy's diagnosis, posted by the thoughtful bartender was, however, a hit with the other regulars.

One odd duck, mischief in his eyes, leaned over the bar and got Tommy's attention. "What is it?" asked Tommy, glancing over in mid-pour.

"I hear it's a good day for the race," said the fellow.

"You mean the parade?"

"No," insisted the fellow. "I mean the race."

Furrows formed on Tommy's brow, you could see him pondering. "And what race is that?"

"The Human Race," said the fellow, holding a hand over his mouth as he snickered.

Tommy didn't find the quip quite as funny. "Okay, buster, now you're cut off."

"All right, then, give me another black n' tan."

"You want the regular size or the Big Gulp?"

Tommy had a helper today, young Eamon McFadden, an exchange student from Cork. The barbacks were practically blurs in their shuttling back and forth, keeping everything in stock. There was talk they might run out of glasses.

The jukebox was playing Celtic rock and people were dancing jigs on the floor, spilling their drinks to the Pogues and Dropkick Murphy's, getting all whipped up if they weren't already. In the back on a folding table, a couple crockpots held Irish stew, bowls, spoons, and napkins to the side, compliments of the house.

Some four blocks away, folks were gathering at Tamm Avenue, lining the curb in wait for the parade, which would start at noon across the highway in Forest Park. Bagpipers would lead as the massive production snaked its way across the highway bridge and into the streets of Dogtown. The Parade Marshall would be second in line, chauffeured in a limousine or some other ostentatious conveyance, waving majestically at the throng, his subjects. No one could say who the Marshall was this year; they were mostly muckety-mucks from St. Louis' Sister City, Galway, a mayor or councilman which no one had ever heard of. Following up were the family floats, probably more than a hundred, some professional-looking, some barely slapped together, folks dressed in green with funny hats proclaiming this or that clan's proud heritage. Some riding, some walking behind, each and every float eliciting rousing applause, hamming it up, getting into the spirit of the event, tossing beads into the roaring crowd, stepping curbside, handing candies and little flags to the children. Antique fire trucks with horns blasting, decorated pickups with Irish shanties built on the beds, trucks pulling flatbed trailers with a score of prancing lassies from this or that School of Irish Dance, a wonder that no one falls off. Forever, that was how long the parade seemed to go on. In reality, it lasted about two hours with a giant street party afterward.

In Murphy's things were ratcheting up, rounds here, rounds there, Tommy and Eamon pouring at superhuman speed, downing several themselves along the way. The floor wet with spilled beer, shouting, loud laughter, jostling. Lines forming to the johns—"Lads" and "Lassies"—the women's line twice as long and some of them taking cuts into the men's line. Somewhere on the floor a cry went up, "Listen up everyone, Jimmy's gonna make a toast."

Then, some guy none of the regulars had ever seen climbed up on a chair. Shouting over the clamor, holding out his fresh pint with the foam collar, "Okay, now, this was my granddad's toast, fellow by the name of—"

"Get on with it!"

"Yeah, yeah, okay," hoisting his glass even higher, "so, it goes: Here's to a long life and a merry one. A quick death and an easy one. A pretty girl and an honest one. A cold beer and another one." Whoops and hollers. One and all they drank up, slapping each other on the back, the crowd now fully primed for the great Hibernian Parade and all it might bring.

Just before noon the bar let out, about half the patrons making their way down to the parade route, the others staying behind so as to be able to drink in relative peace. Francis was among the stay-behinds, although he would venture down there after a bit. Red was on his customary stool down at the elbow of the bar, holding court with a frothy pint in his age-spotted hand. Francis went to Red and they talked of the annual arm wrestling tournament coming up next month. Red had won the last two years, besting the same runner-up both times with an overpowering final push, summoning superhuman strength and an indomitable will. The runner-up was Francis.

"How's your arm doing this year?" asked Francis.

Red pretended the pint in his hand was a small barbell, and he pantomimed a strenuous hoisting of the vessel to his lips. "Just fine, my boy, just fine, getting a good workout here."

"I had a dream that you were feeling poorly on the day of the tournament and I walked off with the trophy."

Red guffawed. "That's all it was, boy, a dream."

"A bee flew on your nose, you went to scratch it, and I seized the moment."

"In your dreams. I'll be taking home that prize. Never count me out, never."

A stout woman came over and asked Red if he'd dance with her. The jukebox was playing "The Maid of Ballydoo" by Tommy Makem, her favorite tune. Red declined politely, said he didn't feel quite up to dancing. The woman, crestfallen, said maybe another time, and she walked off to find another candidate. Red watched her go, said to Francis out the side of his mouth, "You know, boy, I can drink 'em pretty, but I can't drink 'em thin."

Then they were listening as some guy tried his best to convince Tommy that he needed to put in a Golden Tee arcade game. "It's golf," he was saying, "actual golf right here in the comfort of this bar. It's really the rage right now, people get hooked, trying to beat the best scores from other players around the country."

"Too much trouble," said Tommy, wagging his head. "Just another machine to break down and have to get repaired."

"It won't break down," said the salesman, "but it will make you a bundle for only a modest initial investment."

"Oh, and how much is that?"

The fellow took a pull of his schooner, and said, "Twenty-four hundred new, but I can get you a good used for, say, sixteen."

Tommy started laughing and he kept it up until he turned and went back to his pouring, the salesman's pitch deflated.

Francis looked out over the remaining patrons, saw easily a dozen familiar faces, everyone in good spirits. St. Patrick's Day will do that to a person, but you have to be receptive to it. Then he spied one more familiar face, standing by the door, scanning the crowd. Looking for him.

He waved vigorously, she saw it and came over. "Glad I found you," she said, giving him a warm hug. "There's a jillion people out there. I had to park about a mile away."

"Glad to be found," remarked Francis, big smile. "What'll you drink?"

"Oh, some tonic and lime sounds good."

"Throw a little vodka in there, too?"

"No, I'm going alcohol-free these days, but thanks anyway."

Francis called Tommy down, and got one for Rose, for himself, and for Red. He saw that Red was interested in this large, captivating woman at his side. "Red, this is Rose. Rose, Red."

Red took her hand with both his own. Such was her charm that he even got off his barstool and stood to greet her. "Ah, Rose of the vine, won't you be mine?"

"Only for a day," she answered liltingly.

"Then make it today."

"Sorry, Red, but I'm with Francis for today."

"The story of my life," Red giving them both a wink and climbing back on his barstool.

They went on talking, Francis and Rose, catching up. Francis telling her he was spending his windfall wisely, trying to drink all the local bars dry. "No, really, I still can't believe your generosity. I've put a good portion of it away for my old age fund, something to retire on."

She chuckled. "Retire? As long as you can drive a car and pass off a summons, you'll have a job. And what would you retire to?"

"I'm thinking of becoming a spelunker—it's a secret ambition, but now I've told you."

"Plenty of caves down my way."

"A-spelunking we will go, a-spelunking we will go, hi-ho the merrio ..." He handed her the untouched tonic and lime. "Here, the ice is melting, your Shirley Temple is getting watered down."

"There's a reason for that," she said. "You want to know what it is?"

"Sure."

She took his hand and pressed it to the fabric of her tent-like dress, the area endearingly known as the tummy. On his quizzical mug, a look of great surprise as she stood there grinning. His palm lightly massaged the area, rubbing her belly like a genie's lamp. One word came out of his mouth: "Wow."

"That's why I'm not drinking any alcohol," she said, "but I'm making it up by eating for two."

"Yeah," he said, trying to grasp the import of this sudden new development. Did it mean they would live together and raise a kid. Did she want that? Could he suddenly change horses at this point in his life and do the parent thing? Was that even possible? Would she nag him about his drinking? And Janie, thinking how she'd come to him after he was tenderized with shot from a 12- gauge, tending to him like before. Their lusty farewell between the sheets. He was thinking about going to see her in San Francisco, guess that would be on the back burner now. "Amazing," he went on, "I mean, I hope you're good with this. A bun in the oven. This makes you happy, right?"

"I am happy," she said, "but don't assume it's yours."

"Okay," he said, patently puzzled, "thanks for telling me. But if not mine ..."

"Take a good hit of that drink and brace yourself." She put her arms on his shoulders, leaned in, held him so close their noses practically touched. "Okay. We did it on October twenty-ninth," she whispered, "I was raped on November seventh. It's just too close to call, it could be either one of you."

"Me versus Prison Boy? There's no contest. I've got the better genes."

"You do, you definitely do, and I hope it's yours. But either way I'm going to keep him and raise him. You can be in the picture if you like. No pressure, I wouldn't want you to feel coerced."

"How do you know it's a him?" he wondered.

"I just know," she said.

Just then there was a row at a nearby table, some guy holding a paperback in his outstretched arm, playing keep-away with a young man who apparently had been reading it. "You ain't reading no book on St. Paddy's Day," the aggressor was saying. "What're you, some kinda queer?"

"Just give it back!" the young man countered, his cheeks flush with anger or embarrassment.

"Fag. I'm gonna rip it up!"

Red's voice bellowed out. "Here now, stop that." There was a lull in the action, everyone looked to Red. "Come here," he said, "the both of ya's." They came over, the bully sauntering, the one bullied with head hung low, holding his book. They stopped about four feet from Red. "Come here to me," Red commanded. They moved in closer. "Now," he said, looking them both over, "I will adjudicate this little spat. Give me that book." Red was handed the book. He held it out like a preacher holds a bible. "You see the title? *Borstal Boy*. You see the author? Brendan Behan. Tell me, do you know who Brendan Behan was?"

"I don't know and I don't care," said the bully, truthfully.

"Well, let me give you the briefest of explanation," said Red. "He was one of Ireland's greatest characters, a poet, a novelist, and a playwright. He was also a great champion of the cause for a free Ireland. Everything he did, wrote, and said went to furthering that cause. He joined the Irish Republican Army at age sixteen and was caught tossing a bomb in Trafalgar Square, for which he was sent to Borstal youth prison. And *Borstal Boy*, that's his story, and a very inspiring story it is. I speak from personal experience, I've read this book. It is the *only* book I've ever read cover to cover. Now, I loaned this book to Harry here, and you—I don't know your name—you try to stop him from reading it."

The fellow shuffling his feet, needing to get to the john. "Yeah, yeah, I didn't know it was such a big deal to you. Let him read, what's it matter?" He started to walk.

"I'm not done with you yet," Red's erstwhile reasonable-sounding tone turning menacing. One of Red's henchmen, always nearby, turned the fellow and shoved him back at Red. "Tell us, lad, what name do you go by?"

"Ed, Ed Wilkes. My friends call me Eddie."

Red nodded affirmatively. "Now, Ed, because you have humiliated Harry here in a public setting, this otherwise friendly and gracious pub, you must pay the piper, and I am the piper. Step up to me."

"Screw you, man." The aforementioned henchman, a great lumbering fellow, came behind Ed Wilkes and put him in a full nelson. He simply lifted him off the floor and set him before Red, the henchman holding tight, otherwise Ed Wilkes would have fled. Red's fist jabbed into Ed Wilkes' snout, the nose bleed instantaneous. The man now blinking back the tears, spluttering expletives.

That was for bothering Harry," said Red. "And this one's for Brendan Behan."

"Oh," said Rose, turning away. "Is he always like this this?"

"Yeah," pretty much," said Francis. "You don't want to get on the wrong side of him."

"Could we go, please?"

They paid up, said their goodbyes, and walked down to the parade. Tamm and Clayton, ground zero, the crowd twelve deep from the curb back. Floats rolling past, beads and candy in the air, thunderous cheering, music blasting from balconies of apartments up over the action. They didn't try to get up close, but there was an elevated feature in the middle of Clayton Avenue, about three feet tall, concrete, filled with soil; it served as a flower planter and a median. Francis scaled it, set his beer down, and helped Rose up. It gave a great view of the parade, the shenanigans, the people—his people. He was in love and he knew it. Not with a person but with an idea, a grand and crazy idea with a name attached: Dogtown. Forever in his heart. He put his arm around Rose and she leaned into him. Across Tamm the crowd was just as big, two massive contingents facing each other with a lively green procession between. He saw Sgt. Brian Scanlan at the fore of the crowd, at the curb, out of uniform, conducting the parade with a fifth of Jameson for a baton. Scanlan saw Francis waving. He waved back. Together, they lifted their drinks in a boozy heartfelt toast to Ireland and all it means. Sláinte, Scanlan mouthed. Francis grinned big, gave it back to the cop. The raucous parade moved on.

About The Author

IN A CHECKERED LIFE, Wm. Stage has been an ambulance driver, groundskeeper, public health officer, and newspaper columnist. In 1972, after a three-year tour with the U.S. Army Medical Corps in Germany, he began natural history studies at Thomas Jefferson College, the now-defunct "hippie college," in Allendale, Michigan; he graduated four years later with a Bachelor of Philosophy degree, the same degree awarded every student attending TJC. In 1978, he was recruited by The Center For Disease Control, Atlanta, and assigned to the St. Louis City Health Department as a public health officer and STD epidemiologist. Soon after arriving in St. Louis, he began to moonlight as a feature writer for local newspapers and magazines. In 1982, he left his position with CDC to devote himself to journalism and photography. His popular columns and features appeared in *The Riverfront Times* from 1982 to 2004. Adopted at three months, he found his natural family at the age of 50 and has since enjoyed a warm relationship with his "new family," seven half-siblings; this dramatic and unfolding series of reunions was chronicled in the comic memoir, *Fool For Life* [2009], and in an episode of the Canadian television series *Past Lives* [2004].

Wm. has taught feature writing at the Defense Information School, Fort Benjamin Harrison, Indiana; and photojournalism at Saint Louis University School for Professional Studies. He has been a commentator on KWMU-FM, the NPR affiliate in St. Louis. In 1998, he became a Special Process Server and continues to this day, on call with a score of law firms and independent lawyers. He enjoys playing bocce, shooting pool, meat shoots in the autumn countryside, and bicycling in the cornfields across the river in Illinois. Wm. Stage lives in St. Louis with his wife, Mary, and their five daughters.

For more information, please go to wmstage.com.

Wm. is also one of the foremost learned persons on the topic of of vintage brick wall signs. To learn more about this topic, please visit paintedad.com.

St. Francis of Dogtown

Also By Wm. Stage

Creatures On Display

Saint Louis, 1981. Epidemiologist Shaun Malloy is overworked and under-appreciated. Chasing STD cases day in and day out, Malloy and his fellow investigators in the clinic are not prepared when a fatal wasting disease appears that seems to hone in on the city's gay community. As they strive to understand this new threat, matters are made worse by Trey Vonderhaar, a talented entrepreneur who runs a lucrative private men's club that caters to the appetites of a privileged class. Despite warnings from health officials, Vonderhaar is determined to benefit from his enterprise without regard to the dangers the luxury sex hotel presents. Perhaps too dedicated to his job, Malloy is just as intent on shutting down Vonderhaar, and, along with best friend and bondsman Teri Kincaid, isn't above resorting to extreme measures to do it.

"*Creatures On Display* is not for the faint of heart; it is quick-moving, irreverent, often explicit in the situations and attitudes it describes. But it also displays the author's ability to combine history and memory, bold acts and flawed heroes, the devilish and the noble." — Aarik Danielsen, *The Columbia* [MO] *Tribune*

"Stage's novels excel at capturing the grit and weirdness of life on the streets of St. Louis ... [*Creatures*] envisions a fascinating historical moment as the tab came due for the Dionysian revels of the 60s and 70s ... a fun time-travel back to St. Louis in its more feral days."
— Stef Russell, *St. Louis Magazine*

"The story reads as a crime novel without the dead bodies, gun battles, barroom brawls or frequent fisticuffs. But none of these elements seem to be required for a thought-provoking novel that is unique in both subject and insight."
— Stuart Shiffman, *The Illinois Times*

Fiction / Literature / ISBN 978-0-692-87027-3

Fool For Life

Wm. Stage Gets Paid to be a Nuisance, and he is good at it. A process server in St. Louis, bearing bad news to strangers—no wonder people shun him. Apart from this peculiar work, he has his own secret mission: To find his unknown biological family and have cocktails with them. His neurotic mother aids in the search, hoping to bolster her theory that the child she and her husband adopted has indeed become a sociopath. Meanwhile, Stage desperately seeks a woman with a "friendly womb". Why is he trying to reproduce like some rutting animal? It takes a series of painful and awakening life-lessons for him to find out.

Troubles abound yet Stage takes it all in stride, stumbling through life like a hod carrier at a tea party. Whether trying to weasel out of a shoplifting charge, chasing after troublesome factory workers, or being held prisoner at Lambert International Airport, he manages to land buttered-side up. But where will it take him?

"Stage weaves a journey filled with hilarious situations, tightly written with sharp one-liners."

— Jim Orso, *The St. Louis Beacon*

"Stage's vignettes and life stories are all over the map, some heartbreaking, some satirically funny, but all of them telling of the human condition. And humor, some of it dark, pervades the book."

— Lynn Israel, *The Columbia* [MO] *Daily Tribune*

"... a poignant and illuminating work that walks a fine balance between side-splitting humour and philosophical seriousness."

— John Gillis, *The Inverness* [Nova Scotia] *Oran*

Memoir / Literature / ISBN 978-0-962291247-4

St. Francis of Dogtown

Not Waving Drowning [Stories]

A Panhandler Has a Plum Situation in the city, until she takes in a stray dog. A process server is caught relieving himself in an alley, a seemingly mundane event that sets off a cascade of ever-worsening misfortunes. During their getaway, two bank robbers make a wrong turn and accidentally end up in St. Louis' Hibernian Parade—a serious problem since Black Irish are not welcome. These are some of the hapless characters in *Not Waving, Drowning*, Wm. Stage's new work containing eight short stories, all set in the St. Louis area. Drawn from people he has either known or observed, the characters in these stories ring true, evoking drollery, pathos, and wonder.

"For what it's worth, reviewing serious literature from 'Midwestern' writers always seems to be an afterthought versus the treatment given to newest, hottest writer emerging from New York with her trendy version of life in the Big City, a story that frankly makes you want to gag. Stage's stories are about real people who face up to life like the rest of us.

No bullshit, no pretense, just the guts of what makes life work for the fringe players in this old river town."

— Steve Means, *St. Louis Journalism Review*

"Stage has developed a prose style that is quite his own, and really can carry a story convincingly."

— Chris King, *St. Louis Magazine*

Fiction / Literature / ISBN 978-0-9629124-9-8